The Inner Voice

A Study of the Fiction of Alice Munro

Mala Sharma

ATLANTIC

PUBLISHERS & DISTRIBUTORS (P) LTD

Published by
ATLANTIC
PUBLISHERS & DISTRIBUTORS (P) LTD

7/22, Ansari Road, Darya Ganj, New Delhi-110002
Phones : +91-11-40775252, 23273880, 23275880, 23280451
Fax : +91-11-23285873
Web : www.atlanticbooks.com
E-mail : orders@atlanticbooks.com

Branch Office
5, Nallathambi Street, Wallajah Road, Chennai-600002
Phones : +91-44-64611085, 32413319
E-mail : chennai@atlanticbooks.com

ISBN: 978-81-269-1876-8

Printed in India at Nice Printing Press, A-33/3A, Site-IV,
Industrial Area, Sahibabad, Ghaziabad, U.P.

Preface

Alice Munro has been awarded the Nobel Prize in Literature (2013) for her short-story collections. The greatest short-story writer of Canada, she has been hailed as "master of contemporary short story". Munro, by her innovative ideas and concepts, has expanded the parameters of the genre of short story to new heights. She entered the literary world while she was a student of Western Ontario University. Her first story "The Dimensions of a Shadow" (1950), was published when she was only 18. Since then, she has gone a long way, with numerous publications, all of which have won her accolades, both within the country and outside. Ranging across the breadth of Canada, from Ontario to British Columbia, her fictional world has a strong regional focus, delving into the lives of common people. The stories are mainly women-centric, with an in-depth study of their living conditions under the traditional social conventions. Munro's fiction has drawn the attention of readers and critics of literature, and her work has been translated into a number of languages.

Although researches have been carried out on Munro's works, much still remains to be assessed and studied. This project has been undertaken with the purpose of studying her works anew. It also attempts to seek out the message that Munro wants to put forward to her readers. What makes this work challenging and stimulating is that, although Munro is constantly drawing attention to the universal problems of women, she does not seem to put up strong resistance against male domination, as Atwood and Laurence do. Rather, she unfurls the miseries and sufferings in the lives of women, and their social victimization. Thus, she seems to open up new ways of looking at women's problems in society.

In this book, I have restricted my area of study to three decades of Munro's works, beginning from 1968, to 1998 though Munro has been publishing till date. Her later works have been cited at appropriate places. A list of abbreviations and a comprehensive bibliography have also been provided.

The subject matter has been divided into six chapters, including Introduction. In all the chapters, an attempt has been made to search the 'inner voice', underlying the fiction of Munro.

In Introduction, an analysis of the socio-cultural transitions of Canada, from the early forties to present times, has been made. Corresponding to this, Munro's life and works, and her subsequent achievement of national and international recognition have been overviewed. The Introduction also reviews the criticism that Munro's work has been subjected to.

In chapter 2, "The Short Story: Patterns and Paradigms", patterns and paradigms of the genre have been discussed. Besides, the development of the short story in Canada from its early settlement to twentieth century has been studied.

In "The Maze of Munro's Narrative Discourse", the third chapter of the book, Munro's narrative art has been examined, keeping in mind the modern theories of narratology. The second part of this chapter is concerned with photography, which features as an analogue in Munro's narratives. The title of the section is "Snapshots: The Still Moments of Life." It attempts to present life as a series of momentary events, where the past becomes responsible for the present, and the cultural history rooted in the past becomes a determiner of the present.

The next chapter, "Reality or Fiction: Munro's Autobiographical Quest", explores the autobiographical elements present in the author's works. Questions such as whether Munro's art can be considered as autobiographical narrative, or is it a fictionalization of reality, have been taken up for discussion.

The fifth chapter, "The Inner Voice: A Women Speaks Out", describes the women's cry of protest against oppression and social injustice that Canadian women have had to endure for decades. Fear, subjugation, servility and defiance of set rules of social conduct—all find a voice in the fiction of Munro, and this has been looked into, in details, in this chapter.

Chapter 6 sums up the findings and arrives at the conclusion that women have always been rendered inferior by patriarchal constructs. Their voices have remained unheard in literary history for long. Because of social constraints women have always suppressed their inner selves, maintained a double life—one of surface appearance—and an inner hidden reality within them. Being concerned about women, Munro in her fiction has recreated the world of women, with its psychological and physical transition. Here lies her distinction from her contemporaries, and her achievement as a Canadian short-story writer. Indeed, she is a woman, speaking for women, revealing their inner voices and thereby unveiling the hidden mysteries of their lives. A rich bibliography has been provided for enhanced reading on the subject.

The book will be useful for students and teachers of English Literature and researchers in this field.

Mala Sharma

Acknowledgements

In order to complete the task of writing this book, I have visited Shastri Indo-Canadian Institute, New Delhi and Canadian Study Centre, Delhi University. I hereby acknowledge with gratitude their kind help. I am also thankful to the Canadian Embassy, New Delhi, for supplying me information and relevant study materials. I am especially thankful to Shastri Indo-Canadian Institute for sending me a huge collection on Munro from Canada. Ms. Nita Ramaiya, in charge, Canadian Study Centre, SNDT University, Mumbai helped me by providing some rare materials and valued information on my work. I am thankful to her. I would like to acknowledge my indebtedness to American Resource Center, Kolkata for providing books on several occasions. I am thankful to Gauhati University and Assam University, Silchar for allowing me to use their libraries.

I am especially grateful to the management of Ramkrishna Nagar College, where I am in service. I would like to record my deep sense of gratitude to the then principal of the college, Dr. K.R. Paul for his constant support and encouragement. I am beholden to him.

Dr. Aparna Bhattacharyya, Reader, Department of English, Gauhati University, my supervisor and guide gave me valuable suggestions, advised me from time to time.

Finally, I remember at this moment my late father Subhas Chandra Sharma, who always encouraged me in this project. I also express my strong feelings for my mother Mrs. Juthika Devi, without whose support, this work would not have been possible. I also acknowledge the love and support of all my family members.

Mala Sharma

Contents

Contents

Abbreviations

BG	:	Boys and Girls.
Dance	:	Dance of the Happy Shades.
DSV	:	Dreams of Speech and Violence.
“Everything”	:	Everything Here Is Touchable and Mysterious.
Friend	:	Friend of My Youth.
Lives	:	Lives of Girls and Women.
Love	:	The Love of a Good Woman.
Moons	:	The Moons of Jupiter.
OS	:	Open Secrets.
OUP	:	Oxford University Press.
Progress	:	Progress of Love.
Shades	:	The Dance of the Happy Shades.
Something	:	Something I’ve been Meaning to Tell You.
Who	:	Who Do You Think You Are?

1
Introduction

Alice Munro, the great living short story writer of Canada today, has by her enormous contributions to the genre, drawn international attention to Canadian literature. Her gift of story telling has equated her to all time great master of the form, Anton Chekov. The American writer Cynthia Qzick has also referred to her as "our Chekov" (Qzick: Website citation: par. 5). Munro's acclamation has been worldwide. She has garnered a host of accolades both national and international,[1] including a 1978 Booker Prize nomination[2] and winning of 2009 Man Booker International Prize for her lifetime body of work.

The range of Munro's works includes collections of short stories and two interconnected short stories (*Lives of Girls And Women & Who Do You Think You Are?*) where she explores the lives of women of her own generation bound up by its traditional social milieu and setup. Through her art, she expresses her deep concern at the conditioned lives of women in its every phase, and presents their inner quest under patriarchal domination. Set in the small rural town of Ontario, the stories are autobiographical in nature, and looks into human relationships through ordinary and everyday events. However, Munro is a little ambiguous about her subject matter. She once said: "The stories are not autobiographical, but they're in that way. I seem to know only the things that I've learned. Probably through observation, but what I feel I know surely is persona" (Wikiquote: Website citation: par. 11).

I

Born in the small rural town of Wingham Ontario, on 10 July 1931, Alice Ann Laidlaw was the daughter of Robert Eric, a fox farmer, and Anne Clarke Laidlaw, a schoolteacher. Both her parents grew up on farms—her father near Blyth, Ontario in Huron County, while her mother on a poor farm near Carleton place in the Ottawa valley. Defining themselves as "the privileged poor" (*The Literary Encyclopedia:* Website citation: par. 2). Munro has told Alan Twigg: "We lived outside the whole social, structure...kind of little ghetto where all the bootleggers and prostitutes and hangers-on lived.... It was a community of outcasts" (Twigg: 14).

Munro grew up in this environment, and later on this formed the base of her fiction. She says—"I thought life was interesting. There was always a great sense of adventure" (Tausky, Website citation: par. 3). Munro's family history shows her lineage to Scottish and Irish descent, and her family can be traced to the eighteenth century writer James Hogg. Munro's father too had literary qualities. He wrote towards the end of his life a novel *Mac Gregors: A Novel of an Ontario Pioneer Family*, that was published posthumously in 1979. The family had to tide over great crisis when in 1929, the stock market crashed, bringing in a ten year economic depression. Robert Laidlaw found little success as a breeder of silver foxes, while his wife tried to anchor the family by selling furs at a Muskoka resort. Munro has talked about this situation in her memoir *Work for a Living*,[3] where she tells us about her father's stoicism, her mother's determination and grit to pull through heavy odds.

From her early life, Alice Laidlaw had visions about her future. She "knew what she wanted to be very very famous" (Ross: 15). As a child, she dreamed of becoming an actress and at one time planned of a Gothic novel to be called *Charlotte Muir*. When her mother developed Parkinson's disease, she was forced to undertake a large share of domestic work. Nevertheless, she still found time to write. As she told CBC, Shelagh Rogers in 2004, "...although I didn't realize it, I was planning an historical novel in grade seven. It gave way to

Wuthering Heights novel, I was writing all the way through high school" (Tausky, Website citation: par. 3). So at the age of twelve she began writing stories, starting with imitative adventure stories. She also imagined herself in heroic roles as her protagonist does in "Boys and Girls". She also realized that there were: "the twin choices of my life, which were marriage and motherhood or the black life of the artist" (Tausky, Website citation: par. 3). However, writing became for her a source of great confidence. She recalls:

> I felt so buoyed up, so excited, by this writing thing that I had latched on to. It gave me in those years the most enormous happiness. I was quite stunned by what I was able to do, at fifteen or sixteen. It's just that way of being able to translate a kind of rapture that I think everybody feels—the thing is to find a way of experiencing it. And I really felt able to do that then. (Tausky, Website citation: par. 7)

Her steely resolve lurks in the fact that she wanted to be a writer, and came from a little town where nobody was interested in writing or the world of literature. Her childhood was guided by limited expectations and pervasive self-reticence. She explains this: "We were encouraged to be practical about everything. In the social background I came from, people never asked, "Am I happy? Self fulfillment wasn't a concept" (Merkin: "Conversation", Website citation: par. 10).

Munro was brought up in the United Church of Canada where she was a member of the Canadian Girls in Training. She attended the Lower School, and was a top student. As she lived on the outskirts of town, she could not go home for lunch. She therefore spent her noon hours locked in the schoolroom writing stories that she never showed to anyone, as writing was condescended in Wingham, especially for girls. These stories were intensely romantic, tales of rapes and abortions, the occult, and love that is stronger than death. In 1949, she received a scholarship to attend the University of Western Ontario in nearby London, where she studied journalism before changing to English Major. While at the university, she worked part time at the London Public

Library and at the Western's Lawson Library. In the summer between Alice's first and second years at Western, she worked as a waitress in a lodge in Muskoka.

In 1950, Munro's first story *The Dimensions of a Shadow*[4] was published in *Folio,* the university's student literary magazine. *Folio* published two other stories *Story for Sunday* and *The Widower* in subsequent issues. During the 1950s and 60s, her stories were also accepted for broadcast by CBC and for publication in various journals. Since then, many more short stories have been published regularly in prestigious periodicals such as *The New Yorker, The Paris Review,* and *Atlantic Monthly.* In the late 1950s, Munro worked on a novel alternatively titled *Death of a White Fox* and *The Norwegian,* which was never finished.

In 1951, 29 December, Alice married James Armstrong Munro, a fellow student from Oakville, Ontario. They moved to Vancouver before Munro could complete her university degree, and Jim was employed by the Eaton's department store for the next twelve years. During this period, Munro worked at the Vancouver Public Library as a part-time assistant. In September, she began to work full time. In 1953, her first daughter was born and Munro had her first magazine sale, publishing the story "A Basket of Strawberries" in *Mayfair.* Meanwhile, her mother's death from Parkinson's disease in 1959 gave her the impetus for a story, "The Peace of Utrecht". The story was well received, after being published in Robert Weaver's *Tamarack Review* in 1960. Munro's writings now showed a shift towards the use of personal materials in fiction. "In August 1955, a second daughter Catherine was born. Without functioning kidneys, she lived less than two days" (Ross: 52-53). Munro's output slowed during this period followed by a third daughter Jenny in 1957. On 8 September Andrea Sarah was born. By this time many of her stories appeared in journals as *The Canadian Forum, Tamarack Review, Queen's Quarterly,* and *The Montrealer.* Munro has attributed the reason for her low creativity to her balancing duties as a mother of three children and creative artist. In 1963, she helped her husband establish 'Munro Books', now considered as one of the finest independent bookstore in Canada. Five years later in 1968 Munro's first collection, *Dance of The Happy Shades* was published. It won her the country's highest literary prize for fiction; the Governor-General's Literary Award.[5] Munro's next book *Lives of Girls and Women* was published in 1971 and drew wide acclamation from the reading public. Marketed as a novel it may also be read as a set of inter-related stories.

Munro resided in Vancouver for twenty-two years before her marriage with Jim Munro broke up in 1973 and she moved to Norte Dame University in Nelson, BC to teach creative writing for the summer. She then taught at York University in Ontario becoming writer-in-residence at the University of Western Ontario. Here she met Gerald Fremlin, a geographer, and a co-student at the University of Western Ontario, whose fiction was also published in the *Folio*. The two moved to Clinton, Ontario and were married. Munro received her honorary doctorate in 1976.[6] During the period of 1979-82; Munro traveled extensively which included a visit to Australia, as a winner of Canada-Australia Literary Prize,[7] and a trip to China with a group of seven Canadian writers. She also visited Scandinavia during this period. In 1980, she held the position of Writer-in Residence at the University of British Columbia and University of Queensland. Through the 1980s and 1990s, Munro published short story collections about once every four years[8] to increasing acclaim, winning both national and international recognition. She now lives in Comox, British Columbia and Clinton, Ontario.

Alice Munro has also written television scripts. It includes "1847: The Irish", broadcast on CBC in 1977, and the television play "How I Met My Husband". In 1983, film version of one of her most anthologized stories, "Boys and Girls" won an Oscar for short Film in 1986. A television movie of *Lives of Girls and Women* was produced; starring her daughter in the lead role of Del Jordan. Her books have been translated into twenty languages and at 76, she shows no ebbing of her talent (Merkin: Website citation: par. 4).

Writing came naturally to Munro, and art was a reflection of her inner self. From early childhood Munro felt that she would lead two lives—one for the outer world, a life of appearances and the other, which was her true inner self. In a later interview to John Metcalf, Munro remarked: “There is probably a contradiction in many women writers in the woman *herself*...between the woman who is ambitious and the woman who...is passive, who wants to be dominated, who wants to have some one between her and the world. And I know I'm like this. I have the two woman” (Metcalf: 59). In her fiction, Munro explores through her protagonists, her own dichotomy between a writer and a woman of sensibilities and emotions. As she tells Hancock “I feel that I am two rather different people, two very different women” (Hancock: 88). Later on, she again referred this to Graeme Gibson, a decade later:

> There's the desire to give, even to be dominated, to be at least I, in many ways, want a quite traditional role, and then of course the writers stands right outside this, and so there's the conflict right there. (Gibson: 8)

Munro's choice of the short story for creativity has been more out of necessity than desire, as she had to balance her life as a mother and a creative artist. In her craft, she does not conform to the rules of short story writing. Her stories do not concentrate upon a single moment or single incident. They are more expansive in nature, expanding sometimes to even eighty-nine pages. The works also span long decades, with the narrators looking backward or leaping forward in time and space, sometimes even twenty years or more. She confides: “In my own work, I tend to cover a lot of time to jump back and forward in time, and sometimes the way I do this is not very straight forward...(She continues)...I want the reader to feel something is astonishing. Not the ‘what happens’ but the way everything happens. These long short-story fictions do that best for me” (Wikiquote: Website citation: par. 4). Munro herself was uncomfortable about calling her fiction ‘short stories’ and preferred to define them only as ‘stories’. Moreover, the stories are characterized by digressions with stories interwoven within stories. Munro has always wanted to "...find out more, remember more...to flesh out where others in this form leave tantalizing gaps" (Wikiquote: Website citation: par. 4). She was interested in the happenings in the lives of people and the stories that made their lives. However, she points out, "Anecdotes don't make good stories. Generally, I dig down underneath them so far that the story that finally comes out is not what people thought their anecdotes were about" (Wikiquote: Website citation: par. 4).

For the purpose of her art, she has relied on memory and imagination as ingredients for story telling. She reminds us: "Memory is the way we keep telling ourselves our stories and telling other people a some what different version of our stories" (Wikiquote: Website citation: par. 1). Again, she says: "Sometimes I get the start of a story from a memory, an anecdote, but that gets lost and is unrecognizable in final story" (Wikiquote: Website citation: par. 8).

However, she has been unsuccessful in writing of novel but she has tried her hand at it. She tells us: "I've tried to write novels. They turn into strange, hybrid stories. I haven't read a novel that I didn't think couldn't have been a better story" (Merkin: Website citation: par. 4).

Her choice of her vocation, the subversion of it forms and her allegiance to the genre as a vehicle for dealing with women's subjectivity has made her a groundbreaker in Canadian fiction.

Munro has often been considered a regional writer because in her work she has concentrated upon her native land, Huron County where she had spent the early years of her life. Talking about the Lake Huron, which is also known as Alice Munro country, she says: "It means something to me that no other country can—no matter how importantly historically that other country may be, how 'beautiful' how lively and interesting. I am intoxicated by this particular landscape. I speak the language" (Merkin: Website citation: par. 1). Munro's art is a picturesque presentation of the Huron landscape, where "she sees a whole geology and archaeology of meaning" (Ross: 26). Her art was aimed to present the realities of life through fiction, to expose the hidden truths of the lives of women, which she has described as "dull, simple, amazing and unfathomable—deep caves paved with kitchen linoleum" (Lives: 277). Rasporich highlights Muno's love for the locale and creation of a fictional space, when she says that "...Munro is able to authenticate a fictional female world by expanding her characters' inner lives into place, and by manipulating place as feminist inquiry" (Rasporich 122). Thus, the regional becomes a means for focusing on the universal problems of women in general.

Mother-daughter relationships figure prominently in Munro's fictional creations. In most of her stories, her mother has a haunting presence. While her mother was a source of pride in her childhood, in her adolescence Munro experienced emotional crisis as her mother suffered from Parkinson's disease and she had to take up the responsibilities of running the house at the early age of 13-14. This damaged their relationship, bringing in its wake a sense of regret which appears again and again in her stories. "My mother's illness frightened me so much", she admits, "...that I couldn't identify with her. I learned to be capable simply because I had to be" (Merkin: Website citation: par. 20). She admits of abandoning her emotionally during the period of her decline, and not going home to see her mother for the last two years of her life. As she says, "I was a person who didn't fit anywhere. I always felt I'd kind of get out" (Merkin: Website citation: par. 20). This emotional attachment reappears in Munro's stories making the ordinary experiences of life extraordinary.

Although, Munro has consistently talked about the living conditions of women, she does not identify herself as a feminist writer and has not taken any polemical stand with regard to the feminist movement. In her fiction, Munro has problematized the prominent binaries that mark patriarchal discourses. Women's voices have always been repressed in social constructs, and patriarchal hegemony has relegated them to the margin. Oppressed and victimized by society, women have long felt the need for a space to reflect their innerselves. Munro, through her fiction has dismantled the operations of patriarchal structures, gender constraints and male domination in society. Her short stories have stressed the need for social reform and reprisal of injustices towards women. The stories are silent protests, drawing attention to the untold tales of women's sufferings and may be considered as a progression of the chronicle of social history down the ages. These short stories explore the moments of crisis that arise in the lives of women in their domestic front as well as in their relationship with the opposite sex. Munro has the inordinate ability to evoke these singular moments with perfect artistry.

Munro's writing career has been a long and glorious one. A review of her fiction reveals that each of her collection has been well acclaimed, and widely appreciated.

II

Munro's first collection, *Dance of the Happy Shades* was published in 1968. It contained stories from two decades of writings. While the assortment ranged from childhood experiences to maturity, it has explored human psyche under diverse circumstances. Over and above, the stories reflect Munro's evolution towards maturity as an artist in her later stories. Thus, while her early stories such as "A Trip to the Coast" had a Gothic element, the later stories such as "Walker Brothers Cowboy", which opened the collection bear a matured tone. Set in the fictional Huron County, this story showed the influence of the writers of the American South, such as Eudora Welty and Flannery O'Connor. In interviews with Metcalf and J.R. (Tim) Struthers, Munro has given a chronology of the stories included in *Dance of The Happy Shades*, and has provided a commentary on their place in the evolution of her work. She regards the stories written from 1955 to 1959—"The Time of Death", "Day of Butterfly" as the earliest two followed by "An Ounce of Cure", "Thanks for the Ride", "Sunday Afternoon", "The Shining House" and "A Trip to the Coast" as essentially "exercise stories...the work of a beginning writer" (Interview: Metcalf 1972: 62). In summer 1959, Munro wrote "The Peace of Utrecht" that was a turning point in her career: "It was probably, to me, the most important story in the book" (Struthers: 23). In this story

Munro deals with a personal subject, her mother's illness. The choice of this material was as involuntary one. As she recalls, "That [the writing of 'The Peace of Utrecht'] came out of my mother's death. Until my mother died, though the relationship with her was a very painful, deep one, I wasn't able to look it or think about I.... It's as if up to a certain point I was much more an artist than a person I was essentially fairly tight emotionally" (Tausky: Website citation).

Munro's second collection *Lives of Girls and Women* was published in 1978. It was completed within a year. For Munro, writing of the initial and concluding chapters were difficult and took a heavy toll. Munro had begun the book with the thought of producing a conventional novel, but soon came to realize that the writing of separate but inter-linked stories suited her most. The abandoned novel, in re-written form became the middle section of the book, from "Princess Ida" through to the story "Lives of Girls and Women". "Baptizing" was written next followed by two opening stories. In an interview, she tells Struthers that the epilogue "...gave...all kinds of trouble" (Struthers: 25). Another notable fact is that most of the stories are similar to those of *The Dance of the Happy Shades*. While the content of this work is largely autobiographical, the fiction is in the form of a 'Bildungsroman' narrating the life of an adolescent, Del Jordan as she steps into world of adulthood. The fiction also provides a glimpse into the lives of women of the early forties, and is a feminist quest for women's inner selves. Munro had earlier named it *Real Lives,* as she had intended to it to be a quest into what constitutes real life. The final chapters of the novel are meta-fictional as it shows Del Jordan's intention to become a writer and the difficulties she encounters in the process. The work won her the Canadian Booksellers Award.[9]

Something I've Been Meaning to Tell You (1974), Munro's third collection presents her development as a writer. Many of these stories are fragmentary narratives, focusing on the disordered lives of women. Set in the Huron County, the stories present a diverse range of human experiences. While "Executioners" bear a Gothic element, stories such as "Walking on Water" and "Forgiveness in Families" are studies in hippie cult movements of the time. "Marrakaesh", "The Spanish Lady" however anticipates stories in *Moons of Jupiter* with its fragile human relationships. In "Memorial" and "Material", Munro explores man-women relationship and familial bonds. In the stories, "The Peace of Utrecht" and "The Ottawa Valley, the theme of mother-daughter relationship is fully examined.

Who Do You Think You Are? (1978) was titled *Beggar Maid* in the editions of America and Great Britain. Written soon after the dissolution of her first marriage and her re-marriage to Gerald Fremlin, it won her the Governor General's award for the second time. In an interview to Hancock, Munro has said that when she returned to Huron County one of the things she noticed immediately was the "class system" (Hancock: 12). This observation found its artistic expression in *Who Do You Think You Are?*, where Hanratty is far more class-ridden than Jubilee. Rose, a victim of the social order and patriarchal domination struggles to survive in such situations. Her sexual encounters makes her reflect: "...how many overblown excuses she has found, having to leave a place, or being afraid to leave a place, on account of some man" ("Simon's Luck" *Who*: 209). When her father beats her she feels that she must play her part in this, with "the same grossness, the same exaggeration, that her father displays, playing his" (*Who*: 21). The fiction ends with Rose seeking her inner voice.

The Moons of Jupiter (1982) includes stories originally meant for *Who Do You Think You Are?* A collection of unrelated stories, it highlights Munro's attempt to recover the past, as well her exploration of the frailties of old age. The collection feature more complex narratives, and wider time frames than her earlier works. Unlike her other collections, it is not dominated by Huron County but are set in Australia and New Brunswick. Its protagonists are middle-aged women, facing various troubles of life. Diverse in nature, the collection concentrates upon meditation, and a variety of settings. The title story is concerned fictionally with the death of her father in 1976, after a heart operation. At this point of time, Munro was experiencing varied emotional turbulence. This she has portrayed in her fiction.

The Progress of Love (1986) continued to feature stories set in rural southwestern Ontario or Vancouver, and is a reading into the untold tales of women's sufferings and miseries. In the same year, it was awarded the Marian Engel Award, given in recognition of an outstanding contribution to Canadian literature.[10]

Munro's 1990 collection *Friend of My Youth* is marked by her interest in re-writing history, and of reinstating the female literary tradition. It won the Ontario Trillium Book Award and the Commonwealth Writers Prize.[11]

In 1991, Munro was honoured with the Molson Prize for her contribution to Canadian letters. Three years later, her new collection Open Secrets won the W.H. Smith Literary Award in 1995. The stories are again set in the fictional town of Carstairs, Ontario and are concerned with the human relationships. The stories now take the form of longer narratives, and are novelistic in nature.

The trend continues in her next collection *The Love of a Good Women* (1998) where Munro has compressed the lives of communities of women within few pages of the story. Digressive and without any linear progression, Munro seems to build up the story, keeping in view the fact that the genre should be a house where one entered and stayed for a while. *The Love of a Good Woman* won her the Giller Prize. Summarizing the stories in this collection Coral Ann Howells comments: "Ranging over decades of time where memory, fantasy and obsession fuse with realism, this complex narratives continue to gesture towards secrets glimpsed but never uncovered" (Howells: 772).

III

Nearing six decades of writing career (1950-2006), Munro remains one of the most compelling and challenging writer of short stories. Her art has arrested worldwide attention, and since its first publication, her fiction has been analysed and critically evaluated by a host of critics and writers. Her worldwide readers and admirers have also contributed to the foundation of Munro's literary criticism.

Amongst numerous critics, who have examined the life and works of Munro, is Thomas E. Tausky. In *Alice Munro: Biocritical Essays,* Tausky has examined the life and works of Alice Munro with penetrating insight. The work has formed the groundwork for further critical studies. According to the critic, Munro's feeling of ambivalence about being a women as well as a writer is one of the several personal concerns that contribute to the vitality and emotional depth of her fiction. Through her art, Munro seeks to explore as well as discover her own emotions and feelings, as a detached observer of life. In the words of the critic, "Munro is also a gifted objective chronicler of such as the traditional values of her childhood environment, the pathos of old age, and the frantic search in our time for a vanished sense of wholeness" (Tausky: Website citation: par. 3). The critic has also observed that in spite of her seriousness towards her art, Munro has not forgotten that the aim of an artist is to give pleasure, and this she achieves through her "...remarkable powers of observation, her unfailing ear for speech of all kinds, and her capacity for the kind of wit which is unsentimental without deserting compassion" (Tausky: Website citation: par. 53).

Biographer and critic, Catherine Sheldrick Ross says that Munro has the ability to present "ordinary life so that it appears luminous, invested with a kind of magic" (Ross: 15). Ross also illustrates the artist's 'Lower Town' girlhood, formative experiences as a student in the University of Western Ontario, and also her long struggle to balance the demands of being a wife, mother and also a writer. The development of her writing, away from personal experience and towards stories based on observation and presented on a wide canvas, have also been examined.

Novelist and critic, Margaret Atwood while commenting on the fiction of Alice Munro opines that having grown up in a small town herself, Munro knew why there were so many demented people in a small town. And that, "people are conscious of gossip, rumor, the keeping up of pretension and the varying gradations of social level.... Alice's stories are so place— and time specific. What people eat, what they wear, what appliances they are using, all are important to her characters' fronts and pretensions, at what effect they are trying to achieve, and then she examines what lies underneath.... Every expectation is met; and then, there is an event, a surprise—and that's the story" (Awano: Website citation: par. 4).

Michael Cunningham, novelist, is of the view that, Alice Munro tells:

> ...large stories of people whose lives are outwardly small.... She, like Virginia Woolf, have always insisted on the particular importance of women's lives.... In so doing, Munro may be more than any other writer today, reminds us of the scope and scale possible in a short story. She intricately dissects and charts whole lives, replete with enormous changes with thoroughness we might thought only attainable in a novel. (Awano: Website citation: par. 1)

Another renowned novelist Russell banks, while assessing the narrative technique of Alice Munro says, "She is able to break off narrative then start it up later, and it's still connected". In her fiction, one "...can travel through time and space and point of view, shifting our relation to time and space, so we're closer in, or further away. Most contemporary short fiction writers capture moments in time, but Munro telescopes backward and forward.... Munro's fiction expands outward, and it shows us that while the short story form can be as compressed and hard as a diamond, it can also be as expansive as a novel" (Awano: Website citation: par. 2).

Lisa Dickler Awano, Compiler and Editor, comments: "Munro has a firm grasp on the complicated interplay between our will, our desires, and the outside forces over which we have almost no control.... There's happiness, tragedy, and everything in between, and any worldview that insists on one thing over the others is deficient or fragmentary. Mystery and surprise are crucial ingredients of every single story, and Munro is a master of the mystery that resides in the human heart.... In Munro's short stories you don't know what's going to happen to people—just as in life" (Awano: Website citation: par. 2).

Pamela Wallin, Canadian consul general to New York, points out that: "Alice Munro grew up in an era in which women were expected to be mothers, teachers, or nurses.... During the past fifteen to twenty years, the number of spectacular Canadian writers to come up has been amazing.... Munro's stories convey aspects of Canadian geography and culture as well" (Awano: Website citation: par. 1).

Charles Mc Garth, Munro's editor at *The New Yorker* from 1976 to the mid 1980's says that Munro has always been a "writer's writer...her work most closely resembles Chekhov's but she is not writing sketches. She has a novel's worth of incident and character change compressed into a fairly short story. But her stories have gotten longer, which runs a little against the current, Early on, Munro began to play with time, the stories got deeper, subtler, and richer" (Awano: Website citation: par. 1).

Walter James Miller, poet and critic regards Munro as a writer of psychological fiction. Her work delves into the working of the mind "...how we come to truths through strange pathways: how all of our mental experience—lying, concealing, denying, free-associating and rationalizing-leads to discovery, to revelation..." (Awano: Website citation: par. 5).

Assessing Munro's works on the basis on its representing of the social reality critics such as B. Pfaus suggest that Munro's fiction visualizes two worlds, as well as two sets of values: "...the chaotic, natural world or 'other country' and 'the world' or social garrison of conventionality, terms of the Munro canon supplied by the title story in her first collection 'Dance of Happy Shades'" (Pfaus: 10). Northrop Frye in his *Anatomy of Criticism* has raised this dichotomy between the outer and inner reality. Other critics like Struthers have tried to situate Munro's work within a realistic tradition. Because Munro's work explores a world of social relationship and inner experiences, her critics such as Woodcock have explained that her work has an element of 'magic realism' (Woodcock: 133). John Moss again terms it as "heightened realism" (Moss:

1981: 9), and even calls it "hyper-realism or super realism" (Moss, 1981: 215). In his monograph on Munro Hallvard Dahlie observes, Munro's fiction is intangibly rooted in the social realism of the rural small town world of her experience but...insistently explores what lies beyond the bounds of empirical reality" (Dahlie: 5).

In an article in 1976, Rae McCarthy Macdonald insisted that "the essential tension between two sets of values, two ways of seen, two worlds, is always apparent, as central in [Munro's] last book as her first" (Macdonald: 365). Macdonald, enlarging on Frye's conception of the 'garrison' culture in Canada and D.G. Jone's notion of 'alienation from a vital community', sees the tension between 'the world' and 'the other country' as an opposition which informs all of Munro's fiction (Hebel: 10).

Comprehensive discussion has been made on the narrative art of the fiction of Munro. Ajay Heble in his work titled *Alice Munro's Discourse of Absence The Tumble of Reason* draws attention to the fact that our understanding of Munro's work depends not only on what happens on the surface reality but rather on that deep within. Drawing on the structuralist and post-structuralist theories of language as well as on post-modern approaches, he studies the meanings that underlie Munro's fiction.

Feminist criticism in Munro's text, are formed on gender issues, femininity, and sex. Lorna Irvine, in "Women's Desire/ Women's Power The Moons of Jupiter" in *Sub/Version*, shows how women writers combine desire with power in their narratives: "...positing a desiring female subject, conscious of her gender, who acts in response to her own needs" (Irvine: 93). Susan Brownmiller summarizes that by championing the power of primitive and pagan women, Munro shows women's struggle against patriarchal dominance sanctioned by Christianity (Brownmiller: 24). Munro's work has also been acclaimed by Elaine Showalter. In a letter written to Joyce Johnson she writes:

> ...reading such a strong novel (Lives of Girls and Women) of female consciousness makes me feel rather like an astronomer who had predicted the existence of a

comet, and then watching it appear—it's very exciting to read beyond androgyny. (qtd. Rasporich: 12)

Beverly J. Rasporich in *Dance of the Sexes* investigates into the feminist quest by Munro's protagonists. The critic observes that Femininity is of major interest to Munro who revolts against its imprisoning effects but also understands its possibilities as a subtle brilliant aesthetic. The author's femaleness expresses itself in what feminist theorists have identified as 'writing the body' in texts that are literary extensions of female physical life.

Magdalene Redekop's *Mothers and Other Clowns: The Stories of Alice Munro* is the first study of the work of Alice Munro to focus on her obsession of mothering, and relates it to the hallucinatory quality of her magic realism. The critic outlines the aesthetics of her comic vision and thereby involves a new way of looking at autobiography and narrative sequence.

Probable Fictions: Alice Munro's Narrative Acts, edited by Louis K. Mackendrick examines the narrative art of Alice Munro. Robert Thacker in "Clear Jelly": *Alice Munro's Narrative Dialectics*, probes into the style of her writings, which "is best seen through an examination of narrative technique" (Mackendrick: 37). John Orange in "Alice Munro and A Maze of Time" looks into the evolution of Munro narrative technique over the years and finds her "use of narrative time as a structural device in the telling of her stories" (Orange: 83). Gerald Noonan's "The Structure of Style in Alice Munro's Fiction" examines her writings and arrives at the conclusion that: "In Munro's ultimate art of "disarrangement", then, the solid, detailed texture of style is muted lest the surface of the objects, the immediacy of them, be misinterpreted as a whole of reality" (Noonan: 163).

W.R. Martin, in his work *Alice Munro Paradox and Parallel* concludes that working with the familiar Canadian material and with the classical form of the short story, Munro constantly surprises and delights her readers with new truths and thereby makes immense contribution to Canadian literature.

Photography is an integrate part of Munro's narrative art. Evaluating Munro's photographical vision Lorraine M. York said "Alice Munro's magical realism, her interest in documentary expression, are parts of a larger whole: her photographic sensibility" (York: 27). Munro's vision is directly linked with photography. When asked how she manages to remember the minute details and textures of the past, Munro replied, "They just come to me when I am writing. It's a kind of seeing. Last year I saw a black-and-white photo of my high-school class that was taken in Grade Ten, and I did remember the color of everyone's clothes" (York: 27).

IV

A thorough understanding of Munro's art requires an overall view of the social conditions, especially of women in Canada of the late 1930s and early 1940s. This was a period of social transition. A major development in 1940 was that all Canadian women were granted the right to vote in provincial elections. The last province to grant this right was Quebec. However, Federal franchise had been accorded much earlier—in 1918. Thus, changes in the living conditions of women were foreseen. Munro, being a conscientious writer drew upon this fact in her work *The Lives of Girls and Women*. The voice of anticipation is echoed in the words of Del's mother: "There is a change coming in the lives of girls and women. Yes. But it is up to us to make it come..." (*Lives*: 192).

Another social crisis that often appears in Munro's fiction is 'The Great Depression of 1930s.' This period is considered as a 'black chapter' in Canadian history. Both in 1920s and 1923 there were cyclical depression of relatively short duration, but the Great Depression of the 30s shook the very citadels of society. The Depression lasted almost a decade. A serious consequence was that 23 per cent of the Canadian workforce became unemployed. Munro's parents were greatly affected by it. In her earlier works, Munro refers to this situation.

An intensive study of the critical works on Munro reveals that although research has been made on Munro from various angles, the unfathomable quality of the artist, calls for exploration of newer grounds. Much therefore, remains to be unearthed and examined. In this project, investigation has been made with the purpose of looking at the fiction of Alice Munro with fresh insight and introspection. The aim of this work is to search out the 'Inner Voice' inherent in Munro's writings. It will also seek to unravel the underlying layers of meanings and significance of Munro's fictional creations. The voices of women in Canada have remained unheard in literary history, and the prime motive of this project is to unravel the social conditions, as voiced by Munro's protagonists, in various situations of life. Munro has consistently tried to unveil the hidden mysteries of women's lives, and has shown that women are unable to articulate their inner voice under the givens of conventional society. A striking feature of Munro's art is that, it is mainly concerned with women, yet Munro does not consider herself a feminist writer. The message that she seeks to put across to her readers is that—art is not a medium for propagating ideas but is rather a subtle means to convey the mystery that underlies all human lives. To quote Munro in this context, "The complexity of things—the things within things-just seems endless. I mean nothing is easy, nothing is simple" (Wikiquote: Website citation: par. 10).

For the purpose of critical assessment and investigation, theories of narratology, photography, autobiography as well the feminist theories of criticism have been taken into study. Working on a writer, who is still publishing with worldwide acclamation, has been a challenging one. Munro continues to be one of the most recognized writers even to this day. When compared with the all time master of the genre, Anton Chekhov, she humbly refuses to acknowledge her talents "...I don't even claim Chekhov as an influence because he influenced all of us. Like Shakespeare his writing shed the perfect light—there's no striving in it, no personality. Well, of course, wouldn't I love to do that!" (Wikiquote: Website citation: par. 3).

A master of short fiction, she remains till today, an enigma to her readers and critics. Her creations will continue to appeal to all, for all times to come.

Notes

1. Nationally she has received the Governor General's Award for Fiction three times, (the most for any author); two Giller Prizes, the Trillium Book award and the Canadian book Sellers Award. In 1990, the country awarded her the Canada Council Molson Prize for lifetime contributions to the cultural ethos of Canada. Internationally, she has won the W.H. Smith Literary Prize in the U.K., the National Books Critics Circle award and the O'Henry award for continuing achievement in Short Fiction in the U.S., the Pen/Malamud Award for Excellence in Short Fiction, the Rea Award for Short Story, and the Libris Award. She has also won the Canada—Australia Literary Prize and the Commonwealth Prize Regional Award for Canada and the Caribbean. In 1986, Alice Munro was awarded the Royal Society of Canada's Lorne Pierce Medal. In 1992, she was made a Foreign Honorary Member of the American Academy of Arts and Letters. [The Rogers' Writers Trust Fiction Prize, Sponsored by Rogers Communications Inc. Awarded to a writer of a novel or short story collection. Winner. Alice Munro (Clinton, Ontario) for Runaway, <dt.05-01-2007 http://www.newswire.ca/en/releases/archive/March2005/09/c3029.html>.] Munro also honoured with MacDowell Medal. The medal is awarded annually to a person who has made an outstanding contribution to the arts. The MacDowell Colony is the oldest artists' colony in the United States. < 31-12- Archive for the 'Lit Awards' 2006. http://www.vqronline.org/blog/category/lit-awards/>.
2. Booker Prize is an International award. Annually recognizes an outstanding work of English fiction (novel) published in the Commonwealth, South Africa and Ireland; the Booker Prize (£15,000) is administered by the Book Trust. < Canadian Awards and Literary Prizes, http://www.mala.bc.ca/~soules/english/awards.htmDt.22-12-2006.
3. Alice Munro's childhood experiences are recounted in "Working for a Living", Grand Street 1, No. 1, Autumn 1981, pp. 9-37.
4. Alice Munro, "The Dimension of a Shadow", *Folio 4*, Ed. by the Authorization of the Students' Council of the University of Western Ontario, April 1950, pp. 2-8.
5. Governor-General's Literary Awards: Evolving and growing since their inception in 1936, fourteen annual awards ($10,000

each, with a specially-bound copy of the award-winning work) are now given to Canadian authors, illustrators and translators of the best English-language and French-language works in each of the following categories: Children's Literature—Text, Children's Literature-Illustration, Drama, Fiction, Poetry, Non-Fiction and Translation (of a Canadian-authored title). Launched by the Canadian Authors Association and administered by the CAA until 1971, the awards were at first non-monetary prizes; the prestige of the prizes was complemented by a small cash award of $250 in 1951, to be increased in 1966 to $2,500, in 1975 to $5,000, and in 1989 to $10,000. The Canada Council assumed sponsorship of the awards in 1959, and at the same time added prizes for works written in French. Canadian Awards and Literary Prizes, <http://www.mala.bc.ca/~soules/english/awards.htm Dt.22-12-2006>.

6. In 1976, Robert Laidlaw dies in a Toronto Hospital after a heart operation. Alice receives the honorary degree of Doctor of Letters at spring convocation at the University of Western Ontario, (qtd. Ross 12).
7. It is awarded annually, in alternate years, to an English-language Canadian or Australian writer for his or her complete works; it is supported and administered by the Australia Council and the Canada Council. Canadian winners include: 1994: Rohinton Mistry; 1992 David Adams Richards; 1989 Audrey thomas; 1987 Sharon Pollock; 1985 Jack hodgins; 1983 Mavis gallant; 1981 Leon rookie; 1979 Michael ondaatje; 1977 Alice Munro.< Canadian Awards and Literary Prizes,<http://www.mala.bc.ca/~soules/english/awards.htmDt.22-12-2006>.
8. Alice Munro's Publication: In chronological order. Dance of the Happy Shades – 1968.

   Lives of Girls and Women – 1971.
   Something I've Been Meaning to Tell You – 1974.
   Who Do You Think You Are? – 1978.
   The Moons of Jupiter – 1982.
   The Progress of Love – 1986.
   Friend of My Youth – 1990.
   Open Secrets – 1994.
   The Love of a Good Woman – 1998.
   Hateship, Friendship, Courtship, Loveship, Marriage – 2001.
   No Love Lost – 2003

Vintage Munro – 2004.
Runaway – 2004.
The View From Castle Rock – 2006.

9. Canadian Booksellers Association Libris Awards: Formerly the Canadian Booksellers' Association Book Award, these annual awards recognize excellence from the writer to the reader in Canada; current categories include—author of the Year: Awarded to the Canadian author of an outstanding literary work that is a contribution to Canadian culture, and whose work is both readable and popular and had an outstanding impact on the Canadian bookselling industry. Alice Munro won the award in 1994 & 1999 [://www.mala.bc.ca /~soules/english/awards.htm Dt.22-12-2006>.]

10. Marian Engel Award: Presented annually ($10,000) to a female Canadian author in mid-career for outstanding prose writing. Administered by the Writers' Development Trust. Winners: 1998 Sharon Butala; 1997 Katherine Govier; 1996 Barbara Gowdy; 1995 Bonnie burnard; 1994 Jane urquhart; 1993 Sandra birdsell; 1992 Joan barfoot; 1991 Joan Clark; 1990 Carol shields; 1989 Merna summers; 1988 Edna alford; 1987 Audrey thomas; 1986 Alice Munro.

11. [Commonwealth Prize: Provided by the Commonwealth Foundation and administered by the Book Trust, the Commonwealth Writers Prize is intended to reward and encourage the upsurge of new fiction by writers of Commonwealth countries and to ensure that works of merit reach a wider audience outside their own country. Two prizes (£1,000) are awarded regionally—Africa, Eurasia, the Caribbean and Canada, and South East Asia and the South Pacific—for each of the best entry for that region and the best first published book from the region; regional winners are then judged for the chief award, £10,000 (and a private audience with the Queen) for the best entry submitted and £3,000 for the best first book published. Canadian winners have included Margaret Atwood (1994 Best Book, Regional for *The Robber Bride*; 1987 Regional Winner for *The Handmaid's Tale*), Alice Munro (1991 Best Book, Regional for *Friend of my Youth*).] http://www.contemporarvwriters.com/authors/profile/?p"=auth03 D29 L0441126356917-11-2006>

Works Cited

Awano, Lisa Dickler. ed. and complier. "Appreciation of Alice Munro", *The Virginia Quartely Review* (Online only) dt. 16/12/2000 http://www.vqronline.org/articles/2006/summer/awano-munro/

Brownmiller, Susan. *Feminity,* New York: Fawcett Columbine, 1984.

Cunningham, Michael. *Appreciation of Alice Munro,* Ed. Lisa Dickler Awano, *The Virginia Quarterly Review,* Summer 2006.

Dahlie, Hallvard. *The Fiction of Alice Munro,* Ploughshares 4, No. 3, Summer 1978.

———. *Alice Munro and Her Works.* Toronto: ECW Press, 1984.

Gibson, Graeme. *Eleven Canadian Novelist,* Toronto: Anansi, 1973. qtd. Thomas E. Tausky, Canadian Literary Archives-Alice Munro Biocritical, University of Calgary Kibrary (Special Collection) 1986. <http://www.ucalgary.cal/libold/specoll/monrobiochtm (1-12) 10/25/2006.

Hancock, Geoff. "The Colonel's Hash Resettled" in *The Narrative Voice: Stories and Reflections by Canadian Authors.* Ed. John Metcalf, Toronto, Mcgraw Hill: Ryerson, 1972.

———. "An Interview with Alice Munro" with Geoff Hancock. *Canadian Fiction Magazine* 43, 1982.

Hebel, Ajoy. *The Trumble of Reason: Alice Munro's Discourse of Absence,* Toronto, Buffalo, London: University of Toronto Press, 1994.

Howells, Coral Ann. *Alice Ann Munro,* Ed. W.H. New, *Encyclopedia of Literature: Canada,* University or Toronto Press, Toronto, Buffalo: London, 2002.

Irvine, Lorna. "Women's Desire/Women's Power The Moons of Jupiter" in *Sub/Version,* Downs View, Ontario: ECW Press, 1986.

Macdonald, RaeMcCarthy. "A Madman Loose in the World: The Vision of Alice Munro", *Modern Fiction Studies* 22 (1976): 365-74.

Mackendrick, Louis K. *Probable Fictions: Alice Munro's Narrative Acts,* ECW Press, Downs View, Ontario 1983.

Martin, W.R. *Alice Munro: Paradox and Parallel,* Edmonton, Alberta, Canada: The University of Alberta Press, 1987.

Merkin, Daphne. "The Making of Alice Munro" Nov. 27, 2004. <http//www.Theage.com.an/news/Books/Munro/2004/11/25/ 1101219.12/4/2006>

Metcalf, John. "A Conversation with Alice Munro", *Journal of Canadian Fiction* 1.4, 1972.

Moss, John. 'Introduction'. *The Canadian Novel Here and Now: A Critical Anthology*. Ed. John Moss, Toronto, NC Press, 1978.

———. *A Reader's Guide to the Canadian Novel.* Toronto: McClelland and Stewart, 1981.

Munro, Alice. "Working for a Living", *Grand Street* 1, No. 1, Autumn 1981.

———. "Conversation" Htm dt. 12/4/2006http://www1. Broward. edu/--bnightin/ Sample% 20Term%PaperMunro>

New, W.H. Ed. *Encyclopedia of Literature: Canada*, University or Toronto Press, Toronto, Buffalo: London 2002.

Noonan, Gerald. "The Structure of Style in Alice Munro's Fiction", Ed. Louis K. Mackendrick, *Probable Fictions* (Downsview, Ontario: ECW Press, 1983.

Ozick, Cynthia. *A Conversation with Alice Munro*, Reading Group Center, Vintage Books, 05.01.2007 <http://www. randomhouse.coin/vintage/read/goodwoman/munro.html>.

Orange, John. "Alice Munro and A Maze of Time", Ed. Louis K. Mackendrick, *Probable Fictions,* Downsview, Ontario: ECW Press, 1983.

Pfaus, B. *Alice Munro*, Ottawa: Golden Dog. P, 1984, qtd. Ajay Hebel, *Alice Munro's Discourse of Absence*, University of Toronto Press, Toronto, Buffalo, London, 1994.

Rasporich, Beverly J. *Dance of the Sexes: Art and Gender in the Fiction of Alice Munro*, University of Alberta Press, Edmonton, Alberta: Canada 1990.

Redekop, Magdalene. *Mother's and Other Clowns: The Stories of Alice Munro*, London and New York, Routledge 1992.

Ross, Catherine Sheldrick. *Alice Munro: A Double Life*. Toronto: ECW Press, 1992.

Struthers, J.R. (Tim), "The Real Material: An Interview with Alice Munro", Ed. Louis K. Mackendrick, *Probable Fictions* Downsview, Ontario: ECW Press, 1983.

Thacker, Robert. "Clear Jelly": *Alice Munro's Narrative Dialectics,* Ed. Louis K. Mackendrick, Probable Fictions Downsview, Ontario: ECW Press, 1983.

Tausky, Thomas E. *Alice Munro Biocritical Essay*, Canadian Literary Archives, University of Calgray Library (Special Collection) 198610/25/2006. <http://www.ucalgary.ca/libold/specoll/ monrobiochtm (1-12).

Twigg, Alan. "What Is: Alice Munro" Interview with Alice Munro, *For Openers: Conversation with 24 Canadian Writers.* Madeira Park, BC: Harbour Publishing, 1981.

Wikiquote: "Alice Munro" dt. 3.12.2006 http://en. *Wikiquote. org/wiki/Alice Munro The Literary Encyclopaedia,* Documents/ Literary Encyclopaedia AliceMunro.16/1/2006 <http://www. theage.com.au/news/Books/The-making-of AliceMunro/2004/ 11/25/11/25/1101210...12/4/2006>.

Woodcock, George. "The Plots of Life: The Realism of Alice Munro", *Northern Spring: The Flowering of Canadian Literature.* Toronto: Douglas and McIntyre, 1987. pp. 132-46.

York, Lorraine M. *"The Other Side of Dailiness": Photography in the Works of Alice Munro, Timothy Findley, Michael Ondaatje, and Margaret Laurence,* ECW Press, 1988.

2

The Short Story: Patterns and Paradigms

(I)

Story telling has always been a part of human nature. Since time immemorial, people have loved to tell stories about themselves or of others. The earliest existence of this art can be traced to the anecdotes and the tales that were orally transmitted by the ancient people, before the advent of the written form.

> ...storytelling in one form is hardwired into our human discourse as if—as soon as our sense of time past and time future evolved in our awakening consciousness—we became aware we could shape the telling of our personal histories and imagine possibilities that would enchant, terrify, enthrall, admonish, titillate—and the rest of the gamut of emotions that attend a compelling story. (Boyd: website citation: par. 1)

Looked at, from its historical perspectives, it is seen that short stories and tales have existed for centuries[1] in one form or another. Boccaccio's *Decameron,* Chaucer's *Canterbury Tales,* and the *Bible,* the subplots of plays, novels, etc. are instances of this literary genre. However, the form took longer to evolve as a literary art. William Boyd has attributed the reason for this delay when he says that, "...the answer is to be found in the industrial and demographic process" (Boyd: website citation: par. 3). With the 19th century industrial development, and mass literacy of middle-class people, the interest of the reading public accrued. Many publishing houses came into being, leading to the publication of a number of magazines and journals. Writers now, keeping pace with the reader's choice started publishing numerous short fictions.

Edgar Allan Poe was the first theorist of the short story, and the first to recognize it as an independent literary genre. In his definition, Poe, formulated and outlined the patterns of this art, practiced in the course of his writings. His definition is considered as most comprehensive and acceptable to all. In his words:

> A skilful literary artist has constructed a tale. If wise, he has not fashioned his thoughts to accommodate his incident but having conceived with deliberate care, a certain unique or single effect to be wrought out, he then invents such incidents—he then combines such events as may best aid him in establishing this preconceived effect.... In the whole composition there should be no word written, of which the tendency, direct or indirect, is not one to the one pre-established design. And by such means, with such care and skill, a picture is at last painted which leaves in the mind of him who contemplates it with a kindred art, sense of the fullest satisfaction. (Poe: "Introduction", xiii)

Many of its practitioners have adhered to, Poe's principles on the art of the short story from the nineteenth century to the present day. His dictum set the norms and codes of this literary creation. It pointed towards brevity, compactness, structural unity, effectiveness of expression and the attainment of unified effect through art. In his review of Nathaniel Hawthorne's *Twice Told Tales* (1850), Poe defined this literary art as "the short prose narrative" which "can be read at one sitting" requiring "a half to one or two hours in its perusal" and where "the soul of the reader is at the writer's control. There are no external or extrinsic influences-resulting from weariness or interruption" (Poe: "Review", par. 2). The prime concern of the artist is to keep the reader's attention and interest intact, therefore, the aim of the artist should be to produce one unified effect, and complete satisfaction.

Commenting on Poe's definition Somerset Maugham states:

> To write a story on the principles he laid down is not as easy as some think, it requires intelligence not perhaps of a very high order, but of a special kind, it requires a sense of form and no small powers of invention. (Maugham: 155)

Thus, the technique of story telling is a complex one as the art demands precision, attention towards the craft, mode of narration, so that the overall effect is one of unity. Critics have forwarded various theories of the genre. According to Frank O'Connor what makes a short story is its attitude to time and that it is "a lonely personal art." (O'Connor: 15), the attitude of the artist is constrained by the exigencies of time. He further opines that: "The crisis of a short story *is* the short story, and not, as in the novel, the logical inescapable result of everything preceding it, the mere flowering of events" (O'Connor: 14). The singular aim of art is to give aesthetic pleasure and this genre, aims to fulfill this requirement to its fullest extent. In this context, Henry James opines that, in this art of fiction the craft require seriousness and care. "The private history of a sincere work looms with its own completeness" (James: ix). He also maintained that in a short story, the artist should write from his experience, "the characters must be such as might be met in actual life" (James: 8), "should have a conscious moral purpose" and that the craft of the story telling should be the artist's prime concern. Thus, exactness, precision, attention to every detail becomes important factors for the short story. According to M.H. Abrams:

> A short story is a brief work of prose fiction...differs from an anecdote...like the novel it organizes the action, thought and interactions of its character into the patterns of a plot. (Abrams: 193)

With the publication of Poe's works, short story writing became a recognized form of literary art. His precursors were

Melville, Turgenev, Chekhov, and Maupassant amongst others.

Herman Melville, whose stories also achieved totality of effect, followed Poe. His short stories are the first real exemplars of the strange power of the genre. Published in *The Piazza Tales* (1856), stories, such as "Benito Cereno" and "Barteby the Scrivener" heralded the modern concept of short story: "It is Melville who establishes the benchmark for what the short story can attain and allows us to set the standards by which all the other great writers of the form can be measured" (Boyd: website citation).

In the 1850s, Turgenev had also started publishing short stories. By 1890s, Anton Chekhov, considered the greatest writer of modern short story revolutionized the genre by his narrative art. Chekhov showed that the story should be a representation of life, without having the traditional beginning, middle and end. He further pointed out that a story should have a framework: with one or two central characters. Writers who followed his principles were Joyce, Katherine Mansfield, Raymond and others.

From 1850 onwards, the short story was mainly concerned with the realistic presentation of life, and this trend was in vogue in all countries like Russia, France, USA and UK. In Russia, Gogol's "Overcoat" was the first attempt to represent the common man in fiction. Tolstoy, Chekhov and Maupassant took up Gogol's art, and presented a truthful and honest picture of life of the common man. Tolstoy's stories[2] presented the entire range of social life. "The Death of Ivan Ilythch", "The Cossacks" and "Family Happiness" are among his masterpieces. Chekhov however took a liberal attitude towards humanity and his stories "Misery" and "The Dependents" are examples of human loneliness as well as moral probing into the nature of guilt itself. His art "probes and studies his characters, and discovers along with them the shore they struggle to reach" is of the opinion that Chekhov's art is intense with a "sense of human loneliness" (O'Connor: 83).

Like Chekhov, Maupassant's short stories too covered the wide range of human life, which accounted for the universal appeal of his writings. Maupassant too, studied life from a very close angle of vision. He "...presented characters with candour of mind, neither exaggerating nor extenuating human frailty" (Chatterjee: 32). "Boule de Suif" and "Madame Tellier's Excursion" are his master pieces. Maugham and Katherine Mansfield later on practiced this form respectively.

Edgar Allan Poe however traversed a different terrain. In his art, he explored the world of phantasm and the supernatural. His story "Ligeia" is an interpretation of the human soul. Poe's stories were welcomed by all and found a large reading public the world over. Thus, by 1890, the short story as a literary genre had set strong footholds across the globe, drawing enthusiastic readers and opening up new vistas of thought and expression.

Henry James further transformed the form of the short story. His tales were different in style from Nathaniel Hawthorne and Edgar Allan Poe. It showed his concern for the art in its relation to society. His "The Figure in the Carpet" (1896) has been taken as the quintessential self-reflexive modernist story, with its metaphor of hidden patterns in the weave of a carpet to stand for intricate design and for in-depth reading (Childs: 84). In the twentieth century, short story writing became an immensely popular form of art particularly in America. Moreover, it became a highly paid art.[3] Writers now explored a wide variety of techniques. The short story entered a new phase with its next great master, Ernest Hemmingway. Through his narrative, he established that art is the expression of the writer's inner self. Counter to the traditional form Hemmingway's stories were "...well made... usually elliptical in form, rarely tying up details in a neat bundle in order to bring the stories to a conclusion" (Mangum: 1621). Hemmingway was indebted to Mark Twain, Sherwood Anderson and Gertrude Stein and by his use of zero ending;[4] he influenced the modern short story writers.

Others who followed the modern techniques were Rudyard Kipling, R.L. Stevenson, H.G. Wells, and D.H. Lawrence.

Another writer of great prominence who wrote only short stories was Katherine Mansfield. In her art, she employed a considerable amount of free indirect discourse as her characterization operated through a blend of third and first person narrative. A singular feature of her art was the use of ellipses, and tendency to open her sentences with conjunctions, suggesting that something had gone before. "Bliss" opens with 'although', while "The Garden Party" begins with 'and'. Thus, the reader is not given any descriptive introductions or any preamble, but is directly led onto the story. Modernist art is also found in Samuel Beckett as in "Ping" (1967), where "language has broken down and the signifier without a signified...stands as a speech act freed from a language system, as a parole without a langue, in which it can operate meaningfully" (Childs: 93).

One noticeable fact regarding the popularization of the short story is the publication of magazines and periodicals. Short story writing received further impetus with the publication of magazines in Philadelphia, Boston and New York, e.g. *Saturday Evening Post 1820, Harper's 1850, Atlantic 1857, Century Magazine 1870, Scribner's 1887* (New 1987: 4). Amongst its other American practitioners, were Washington Irving, Hawthorne,William Faulkner, Katherine Anne Porter, Eudora Welty, Flanner O'Connor, John O'Hara, J.F. Powers, James Wharton, Garland, Freeman, O Henry, Jewett, Aiken, Anderson, Hemingway, Fitzgerald and others. In England, the genre took its shape and form in the art of the Victorian writers such as Sir Walter Scott, Dickens, Thackeray, Meredith, Mrs. Gaskell, Kipling, Conrad, and Wells. Others were Hoffman in Germany, Balzac in France; Gogol, Turgenev, Maupassant and Chekhov in Russia; Joyce, O'Flaherty and O'Connor in Ireland; Lawson in Australia; Machado de Assis in Brazil; Mansfield and Sargeson in New Zealand; Scott, Roberts and Callaghan in Canada and more besides.

A vital question that often surfaces in this form is how long should it be, and yet it be called a short story? It has been observed, that the short story by nature is short in length. Here the practitioners of the form are constrained by a limited space, in contrast to the novel, which provides a greater scope for expression. However, the determinant length remains a subject of varying opinions. While it can either be in the form of a slightly elaborated anecdote of perhaps five hundred words, it may be long and in complex form.[5] At times, this form has neither the brevity of the short story, nor the length of the novel and is termed as *novelette* or *novella*.[6]

For twentieth-century writers, the length of the short story is not at all a vital factor in narratives. Writers have at times either limited their art to a page or expanded it to many pages e.g., "Sargeson's work ranges from 500 to 32,000 words" (New 1987: 27). The opinion of Frank O'Connor here is significant, as it attempts to answer all queries in this regard:

> ...the length of the short story is given by its form. There is simply no criterion of the length of a short story other than that provided by the material itself...great short story is not necessarily short at all, and the conception of the short story as a miniature art is inherently false. (O'Connor: 27)

In a short story, the art of narration is very important, as the singular appeal of the story is influenced by it. The central concern of the artist is to communicate the theme in a manner that heightens the reader's interest and sustains it in the memory for a long time. The length becomes insignificant, while the mode or technique of story telling gains prominence. Thus, the artist's forte lies in the technique of presentation, which is to provide aesthetic pleasure.

A major point of difference between the short story and the novel is the basic nature of both the forms of art. While the scope of the novelist is wide and varied, the short story writer unfolds the incidents, happenings and moments of crisis in the life of the protagonist within a limited space. This in turn throws adequate light on the individual, and the social milieu. Constrained by space, the artist uses economy of words and expression, and allows no scope for superfluity. The text therefore becomes embedded with hidden layers of meaning, and conveys more than is apparent. Concentrating on the basic differences between the short story and the novel Frank

O'Connor is of the view that the novel shows the logical, inescapable flowering of events while the short story springs from the heart of a situation where "the crisis becomes a consequence of the crisis" (Connor: 14). He further says that the genre is "the lyric cry in the face of human destiny" and deals with "the profound and common interests of life" (Connor: 15).

A short story provides a limited scope for character development and for transformational change. Elizabeth Bowen is of the opinion:

> ...by reason of its aesthetics, is not, and is not intended to be the medium either for exploration or long-term development of character. Character cannot be more than shown—it is there for use, the use is dramatic. Foreshortening is not only unavoidable, it is right. (Bowen: 53)

Sean O'Faolain's observations echo this view. According to him:

> In short story writing there can be no development of character. The most that can be done is to peel off an outer skin or mask, by means of an incident or two, in order to reveal that which is...as each writer sees this 'is', the character will not change his spots; there is no time; if he seems to do so in the future the story can but glance at the future. (O'Faolain: 170)

However, within the limited scope of the genre, reflections on human predicaments and diverse circumstances of life are presented. In most stories, the progress brings about transformation in the mindset of the characters, and self-realization takes place in the end. These vital moments of revelations or epiphanies abound in the stories of James Joyce, Chekhov, Alice Munro and a host of short story writers.

The plot of the short story is an area of major concern. In this regard, Aristotle is of the viewpoint that a narrative work of art should have a beginning, middle and end. Writers such as Thomas Hardy, Somerset Maugham and others, followed this criterion. Modern short stories however, do not conform to such rules of creations. There is a continual interweaving of the main plot and the sub-plot, which at times run parallel to each other. Moreover, there is an overlapping of time sequence in most modern and postmodern writers. Here the past, present and future are juxtaposed one against the other. Intertextuality and open-endedness are other paradigmatic realms explored by writers of modern short fiction. At times, the local dialect is used to make the composition more realistic and true to life.

Creation of a narrator is another singular feature of short fiction. According to Wayne C. Booth: "Point of view should always be used 'consistently', because otherwise the realistic illusion will be destroyed" (Booth: 89). The narrative voice can either be in the first person where the reader experiences the story through the perceptions of the narrator. The narrator may again be third person omniscient narrator, and may have access to the thoughts of one or all the characters. In certain cases, the narrator maintains a distance and the stories are narrated from a detached third person point of view. Here the writer is allowed more freedom in the use of language.

In a short story, the sequence of time is most significant. Fictional time is illusory and may be either in flashback or in flash-forward method.

Short stories may be written by adopting different techniques. One prominent technique followed by writers of this art is the presenting of the story in the form of a fable. This form enables the authors to adopt the tradition of *Aesop,* in order to mask human idiosyncrasies and eccentricities. Writers such as J.E. Powys and James Thurber speak about their own times and create a new awareness by representing the comic incongruities of the contemporary life with expert artistry. James Thurber "The Little Girl and The Wolf" is an example of a fable. Parabolic pattern in short stories is another form. Here stories have a biblical reference and a simple narrative presents the truth. E.M. Froster's *The Other Side of the Hedge,* Shirley Jackson's *The Lottery* and R.L. Stevenson's *Dr. Jekyll and Mr. Hyde* are some examples. Allegory is yet another form of the short story. *In the Penal Colony,* Kafka allegorizes the concept of religion in the twentieth century.

Many writers of short fiction popularized diary form. Here the story is unfolded by means of a series of events, narrated in the form of diary entries with different dates. Ring Larder's short story "I Can't Breathe", and Joyce Coral Oates's story "The Turn of the Screw", possess the technique of this form. Angus Wilson in his "Ten Minutes of Twelve" used the form of a memorandum as the base of the story. Exchange of letters forms yet another art of story telling. Ring Lardner's story "Some like Them Cold" is one such example. This epistolary form helps the writer to develop and further the plot through a series of letters.

Human outlook underwent radical change, following the aftermath of the Great Wars. Writers now found traditional literary modes inadequate and heralded new concepts. Great thinkers and philosophers such as Frederic Nietzsche, Karl Marx, Sigmund Freud, and James G. Fraser also influenced the period. Subversion and experimentation of the traditional mode of narrative art in prose fiction led to:

> ...breaking up the narrative continuity, departing from the standard ways of representing characters and violating the traditional syntax and coherence of narrative language by the use of stream of consciousness and other innovative modes of narration. (Abrams: 199)

James Joyce, Virginia Woolf, Gertrude Stein, Ernest Hemingway, Samuel Beckett and others gave new shape to the short story, and attempted to represent real life in fiction. Virginia Woolf in her short stories *A Haunted House and Other Short Stories,* experimented with the stream of consciousness technique in art. Her stories, tended to present the discontinuous moments of human life. In *Robert Kennedy Saved from Drowning,* Donald Bartheleme presented a series of haphazard snapshots as a realistic picture of life and times of Kennedy.

This period also saw a very popular form of writing that of inter-related stories, held together by a chaining system, with a common setting or character. These cycles of stories presented the disconnected experiences of life leading to epiphanies at times. Examples of such works are James Joyce's *Dubliners,* Sherwood Anderson's *Wines burg Ohio,* Hemingway's *Our Time,* Eudora Welty's *The Golden Apples* and Alice Munro's *Lives of Girls and Women* and *Who Do You Think You Are?*

The form of the short story underwent further change with writers adopting postmodernist techniques in creative art. Here the writers presented a blend in literary genres, the serious and the playful. The use of pastiche, parody, self-reflection, magic realism, also became a favorite medium of expression of these writers.

To sum up, we may say that from the nineteenth century onwards, the short story became a distinct form of art. Poe's stress on the story being short enough to be read at one sitting, to enhance unity of effect, was taken up as a singular feature of this art. In this respect, the short story became closer to poetry. Here Elizabeth Bowen's viewpoint is significant:

> It is at an advantage over the novel, and can claim its nearer kinship to poetry, because it must be more concentrated, can be more visionary and is not weighed down (as the novel is bound to be) by facts, explanation or analysis. (Bowen: 77)

The impact of the Wars was felt in art, and it became a reflection of the critical times. Existentialism had a profound influence upon writers as they probed their inner selves to find an answer to the riddles of life. New horizons were explored, which in its turn opened up avenues for the questing mind, searching for realities of life.

II

The growth and development of the short story as an art form in English Canada, has been a gradual one, evolving down the ages to its present complex structure and form. This progression has not been linear, but the result of various forces acting upon one another synchronizing them into a unified whole. Reingard M. Nischik observes: "Beginning in the 1890s, reaching its full realization by modernist writers in the 1920s, brought to its heyday during the Canadian Renaissance starting in the 1960s, the short story has become Canada's flagship genre."[7]

The preference for this genre for literary creativity seems to be rooted in the fact that Canada had long been under colonial rule. W.H. New argues that the short story being a marginal literary genre, finds prominence in countries such as New Zealand and Canada:

> Canadian and New Zealand writers use the short story, even if unconsciously, as a kind of cultural-ideological protest, subversively, and often with a sheathing irony that remains mostly lost upon the central, dominant, and self-regarding cultures in which, financially they need to succeed. (Lynch: 1041)

Thus, the nature of the land and its postcolonial status, accounts for the choice of this genre by Canadian writers, both male and female, for literary creativity from the nineteenth century to present times. Northrop Frye views that: "Canada is the only country left in the world which is a pure colony, colonial in psychology as well as mercantile economics" (Frye, 1971: iii). Margaret Atwood too echoes similar thoughts when she says: "Canada as a whole is a victim or an 'oppressed minority' or 'exploited' colony for someone else's profit" (Atwood, *Survival*: 35). These feelings of victimization have propelled writers to create an inner space for themselves, in a genre, which is open to multiple interpretations, and implies more than that is revealed.

The short story in Canada is predominantly a post-Poe literary form. It evolved in English Canada in the middle of the 19th century and was subsequently taken up in Quebec during the early 20th century. With European settlement, the short story took its first step towards its establishment as an independent genre.

In providing an overview of the evolution of the short story in English Canada, it has been observed, that the earliest records of the short story in existed in the oral narratives of the "The First Peoples" (Lynch, Encyclo 1046). These were in the form of myths and tales: "involving the creator Raven and the trickster COYOTE, or...the INUIT legend of the sea-goddess

SEDNA" (Lynch, Encyclo: 1046). The stories differed from tribe to tribe and were either narrated or performed to the accompaniment of song and dance. Generally, the stories narrated were:

> ...other world journeys, heroic encounters with supernatural powers, animal wives and husbands, animal divinities, powerful magicians, guardian spirit guests; the ritual observance of animal corpses; belief in the significance of dreams, in the indwelling spirit of every created thing.... (Toye, 1)

The rituals however, were an association of ceremonies such as "purification and expiation...initiation, puberty and mortuary rites" (Toye: 1). The myths had "the culture hero or trickster-transformer" (Toye: 1), who was either a credulous fool, or shrewd and crafty trickster, able to change himself into animal or human shapes. Gathered piecemeal by the European settlers, fur traders, explorers and travelers, these narratives were translated into French and recorded in *Jesuit Relations*:[8]

> The texts of Aboriginal tales appear in about four separate forms: as anecdotes retold within the context of the *Jesuit Relations* and in missionary journals, often as cautionary stories; as documentary records, in the pages of scholarly bulletins, complete with annotations and footnoted variants; as child narratives, anthologized first for nineteenth century readers, and retold for modern readers often by contemporary native writers. (New, 2003: 8)

However, much of the beauty, cadence and rhythm of the language were lost in the process of translation and transcription. In the words of Maria Campbell: "It was hard, we had to change from telling a story to a group of people to being alone and telling the story to the paper" (Toye: 3).

When the Europeans arrived in Canada, and "subsequently set eye and foot on the land" (New, 1990, 34) they were overwhelmed. A sense of awe and beauty overtook them, and they described the land as 'vast' 'strange' 'untamed' and 'barren' (New, 1990: 34). They recorded this majesty and the harsh beauty of the wilderness in their narratives, which were:

> Loosely reportorial in mode...journals, letters, chronicles, documentary records...all of them designed to send impressions from the edge of civilization to an authority who stayed back home. (New, 2003: 25)

These accounts were often of a figment of their imagination, as the wilderness created a sense of awe and fear "and they read the land 'not as here, where they were, but as there, a place apart—apart' most especially, from themselves" (New, 1990: 35). Thus, their stories were a record of their encounter with the challenges of an alien land, and also served as a historical record of their settlement. The environment became the subject, as the settlers viewed the new surroundings with great interest. Clearly, the writings reflected the European mindset and desire to master the unconquered land. An interesting feature of the settler's attitude towards the existing oral art, was that these explorers seem to have regarded the native folktales "as either primitive or quaint, the forms of a peripheral culture rather than the signs of cultural sophistication and literary maturity" (New, 1986: 3).

In mapping the new land, the settlers recorded the topography, as well as the ethnicity of the country in their report writings, and this was the first serious step towards the creation of the literature of the nation.

Amongst the "finders, claimers, and multiple mapmakers, who left their names on Canadian geography" (New, 2003: 26), the French were the first to reach Canada. In 1534, French explorer Jacques Cartier reached the Gulf of Saint Lawrence. The British arrived in 1570. John Daves, William Baffin, Martin Frobisher, Henry Hudson and Luke Foxe, settled in the Hudson Bay. The next arrival was the Greek sailor Juan de Fuca, who reached the West Coast in 1592. Samuel de Champlain mapped Acadia, the Saguenay and the Richelieu in the first thirty years of the seventeenth century. Then the Jesuits traveled south into the Mississippi Basin in 1640. The Russians followed in 1741 with Vitas Bering who reached Alaska.[9]

In 1771, the land explorers—Samuel Hearne, reached the mouth of the Copper mine, while Mackenzie followed the Mackenzie River to the Arctic in 1789 and reached the West

Coast in 1793, Fraser followed the Fraser River in 1808, Thompson, the Columbia in 1811. Their writings were in the nature of journals, recording land exploration and experiences. These records and accounts of expedition "...removed from their context, could stand alone as instances of the earliest "Canadian short stories" and "are powerfully entertaining instances of the story teller's art" (Lynch: 1040). Moreover, these interpolated tales, anticipated much of the 19th century writing both in French and English Canada.

The 19th century saw the short story gaining worldwide popularity. In America, the genre had already established itself as an independent literary art in the hands of its masters, Poe, Nathaniel Hawthorne, Herman Melville and others. In Canada too, it acquired a distinct shape and character. From being a sketch, it also took the epistolary form, and was introduced by two writers—Thomas Mc Cullock and Thomas Chandler Halliburton. Important is the fact that these writers for the first time in literary history, introduced humour and satire in the art of story telling.

Thomas Mc Cullock, a Scottish emigrant and Presbyterian minister, began his writing career in the Maritime Colony of Nova Scotia in 1820, "by publishing a series of fictional letters in the *Acadian Recorder* (1821), in which the thriftlessness and unstable character of a rural Maritime community are held up for laughter and scorn" (Stouck: 1). In his creation of the character of Mephibosheth Stepsure, Cullock highlighted the economic depression of the times, and called upon the Maritimers to overcome the situation by means of their hard work and thrift. This book had an enormous effect on Halliburton's writings who also wrote at the same period.

In his series of sketches[10] for the Novascotian Halifax newspaper, Thomas Halliburton, created his masterly character 'Sam Slick' "...a shrewd outspoken Yankee who travels about the province selling clocks and openly criticizes the people of Nova Scotia, the 'Bluenoes' for their dullness and lack of industry" (Stouck: 4). A jurist and political historian, Halliburton used fiction for documentary purposes, and in his "saying and doings of Sam Slick he relied more on anecdote than on descriptive sketch" (New, 1987: 35). The stories went through several prints and were Widely circulated all over Germany, France, England and the United States.

Halliburton's art of characterization, narrative technique, humour and satire, had tremendous impact on Stephen Leacock and on "American writers from Saba Smith in 1830 through Artemus Ward to Mark Twain" (New, 1987: 36). In the following decades, this unparalleled creation was to go a long way, and have a wide impact on fiction writing. Moreover, Sam Slick's use of vernacular Yankee speech, humorous and witty dialogue, and metaphoric self-reflections captivated his readers. The cadence of Sam's garrulous speech and the realistic portrayal of social life made Halliburton's writings an influential force in the development of English Canadian fiction. Many of his phrases have become cliche, examples of which are: "...to lurk at the edges of upper crust, stick-in-the-mud, as quick as a wink, conniption fit, six of one and half a dozen of the other, as large as life and twice as natural, the early bird gets the worm, a nod is as good as a wink to a blind horse' and many more" (New, 1987: 37).

A humorist, who comically highlighted the socio-economic and political evils of his day, Halliburton's sketches have a universal appeal. David Stouck is of the opinion that Halliburton perhaps wanted his Canadian readers to take stock of their sense of humor: "British humor is class-structured, American humor involves deflating society's most cherished assumptions, Canadian humor stems from an ironic perspective on both society and self" (Stouck: 13).

With Halliburton's literary creation, the Canadian short story acquired international recognition and the series of *Clockmaker* sketches introduced a new form that of the inter-related cycle of short stories in Anglophone Canada.

The 19th century is remarkable for the emergence of another distinctive form of the genre—"the realistic animal story" (Toye: 440). The propagators of this form of fiction were Sir Charles G.D. Roberts (1860-1943), Ernest Thompson Seton (1860-1946) and William Alexander Fraser (1859-1933).

An inventor of the animal tale, Roberts's[11] first story "Do Seek their Meat from God", was published in Harper's (Dec 1892). This and other stories appeared in *Earth's Enigmas*: a book of animal and nature life. Roberts's stories were unlike the traditional stories and were concerned with the patterns of animal behaviour. In the 'Introductory' to *The Kindred of the Wild* he stated that his animal stories were: "a psychological romance constructed on a framework of natural science", one that "helps us to return to nature, without requiring that we...return to barbarism" (Toye: 406). Roberts's animal stories were of three kinds: the biographical, which examined animal conduct or personality; the action story, which emphasized plot and usually contained humans; and the sketch, "which illustrated an elemental force governing the natural world" (Toye: 406). Accused by President Theodore Roosevelt in *Everybody's* Magazine (June 1907) of being a "nature fakir"[12] Roberts argued that animals are not governed by instinct alone but by psychology. Although his animal characters were often victims of conflicting forces for survival, they remained heroic till the end. Again, in the full-length animal biography *Red Fox* (1905), an adolescent boy much like the youthful Roberts, observed these creatures. Here the fox, finds freedom by intelligently fooling his animal and human enemies. Other highly popular animal tales written during this period included *The Watchers of the Trails* (1904) and *The Haunters of the Silences* (1907). *The Heart of the Ancient Wood* (1900). In this story, a young girl's develops kinship with the forest creatures, especially with the she bear 'Kroof' who like 'Ben', the old bear in William Faulkner's novella, *The Bear* symbolized the wilderness endangered by human habitation.

Ernest Thomson Seton also made his contribution to the realistic animal story. His first collections contained the story of 'Lobo'. A number of animal stories and collections such as *The Biography of a Grisly* (1900), *Lives of the Hunted* (1901), *Monarch, the Big Bear of Tallac* (1904) and Animal Heroes (1905), followed *Wild Animals I have Known* (1898). Like Roberts, Seton too studied the behavioural patterns of animals in varied situations. He also dwelt on the human encounter with the wilderness. Margaret Atwood in *Survival* too, makes special reference to Seton's animal stories as a "central example of a tendency to identify with the hunted victim as peculiarly Canadian" (Toye: 440).

William Alexander Fraser also wrote in the same vein and his writings in a way echoed Rudyard Kipling's *Jungle Book*. Like his contemporaries, Fraser was interested in animal psychology and in "Moosa", he endowed animals with human qualities, so that they talked intelligently, had their own laws and disciplined each other.

Thus, an important aspect of the late 19th century fiction was the focus by writers on the naturalistic animal story. While the animal story reached a dead end with the dawning of the twentieth century, the realistic story continued to flourish.

Stephen Leacock (1869-1944), renowned for his humour in short fiction, occupies a distinct place in Canadian literary history. Like Halliburton, he too wrote exclusively in the form of the sketches. His writing *Sunshine Sketches of a Little Town* (1912) brought him worldwide recognition, and was "approached to write a screenplay for Charlie Chaplin".[13] Like his masters, Dickens and Mark Twain, Leacock's humor was at times genial and like Lewis Carroll, renowned for its exuberant nonsense. It also reflected Dickens and Mark Twain's growing concern for human progression and material advancement of society.

Duncan Campbell Scott's writings too depicted the changing times and the social reality. His *The Village of Viger, The Witching of Elspie* (1923), *The Circle of Affection* (1947) marked the first real break in the frontier tale and the local colour story.

The year 1928 heralded a new phase in Canadian literary history as it saw the publication of Raymond Kinster's anthology *Canadian Short Stories*. It received considerable acclamation from B.K. Sandwell, editor of *Saturday Nights*, for highlighting the stories of the great Canadian prose stylists, Roberts Thomas, and Gilbert Parker. Now for the "first time in Canadian literary history the new urbane writers of the 1920,

Morley Callaghan in particular, Thomas Murtha, and Knister were introduced to the reading public" (New, 1986: 9).

Like Knister, the stories of Callaghan[14] revealed his deep interest in human psychology. Moreover, influenced by the American writer Sherwood Anderson (1876-1941), his writings were marked by simplicity of style, syntax, as well as diction. As Gadpaille remarks: "He frequently uses short declarative sentences, anchored whenever possible by copulative verbs, or by the plainest, punchiest action verbs—go, come, do, put, ask, look—and incorporates the idioms and rhythms of everyday speech into the narrative voice" (Gadpaille: 22).

With these writers, the art of delineation in short fiction underwent great change, as the emphasis was laid more on society and character, rather than on plot. Instead of using omniscient narrators, these writers used the 'free indirect discourse'[15] in their stories. Stress was now laid on the depiction of the life of the ordinary people, and their local speech rhythm in art.

This was the beginning of a revolutionary change in the writing of fiction. For the first time socialistic views made its entry into literature. Moreover, language, structure and style, heralded the way towards modernist and postmodernist techniques in art, which would be explored in the next four decades.

This period also saw the rise of another form of short fiction, that of writing in a "mixed genre, combination of 'the memoir, the spiritual autobiography, the nature sketch and short story'" (Lynch: 1043). The writer who brought distinction to this genre, was, Fredrick Philip Grove (1879-1948). In his cycle of short stories, *Tales from the Margin* edited by Desmond Pacey, as well in other stories, Grove used this style of expression. Many of his writings were really character sketches or anecdotes—attempt to document the rural human life. In his naturalistic fiction, he also featured the prairie landscape and the realistic prairie life, an area that would later on be explored by Sinclair Ross in his fictional works.

The 1930s were the years of the Great Depression in Canada. Writers of short stories were critically aware of social conditions arising out of the fall in economy. Albert Laberge, Harry Bernard, Louis Dantin, Ted Allen, and A.M. Klien, reflected this terrible social situation in their writings. As the 1930s and 1940s progressed, the bitter realities of life, such as drought, depression, war, class division, poverty, and machines, surfaced. Writings now mirrored these stark realities.

The 1930s also witnessed many social, political and economic transformations. These changes had its impact on literature and the result was that, by the 1950s the writers were accommodating the language to suit the changing times. The writings of Dyson Carter recorded the economic history of the day. Sinclair Ross too, in his earliest 1930s stories pictured the prairie deprivation. A.M. Klein, "...in his 1936 stories published in *The Canadian Forum* and the socialist journal *New Frontier,* addressed the facts of joblessness and beggary in fierce ironic parable" (New, 1987: 78).

Literature thus, focused on the social realities, and along with it, the language of the texts changed. In 1944, John Sutherland, whose editorial column dominated the next decade, pointed out in *First Statement,* that literature, language as well as vocabulary should reflect social and political crisis. He wrote "Against a background of social chaos of which the war is only the violent and morbid symptom...social pressure is reflected in the cry for social function in art..." (New, 1987: 78). The form of the short story was thus experimented and innovated by writers. The age was also marked by the publication of journals and magazines which gave a new fillip to the wide spread popularity of the genre.[16]

With the twentieth century, literary productivity became diverse. It saw innovations in narrative techniques. The use of internal monologues, third person narratives, autobiographical modes, diary forms, multiple narrators, and sequential discontinuity, etc. were repeatedly used in short fiction. Realism became the watchword and the representation of the social, political and economic situation was the theme of the writers. In addition, the Depression, and the World Wars, revolutionized the very mindset of all. Literature now became closely associated with power politics, and the chaotic social condition was reflected in art.

Eminent writer, Sinclair Ross, who wrote and published short stories during the Depression and War, used the diary form in his works, *The Lamp at Noon* (1938), *The Painted Door* (1939) and One's *a Heifer* (1944). "His stories usually deal with two ruling conflicts: one between man and his own failure in human relationships.... The strength of...stories lies in their powerful evocation of solitary men and women lost in a vast inner and outer wilderness, a dilemma that is seemingly fated to crush life and sprit" (Gadpaille: 32).

During this period that Hugh Garner (1913-79) also began publishing. He belonged to the tradition of Callaghan and wrote in the style of Hemingway and other American writers. Garner became the most widely read writer in Canada. Awarded *Governor General Award* in 1963, more "than fifty of his stories appeared in almost every popular Canadian magazine, including *The Canadian Forum, Chatelaine, Saturday Night* and *The Canadian Home Journal*—and were also broadcast on in CBC's Anthology Series" (Gadpaille: 28).

Another noted writer, James Reaney (b. 1926), in his short stories in the 1940s and 1950s, established the style of writing that has since been known as *Southern Ontario Gothic* (Toye: 393). In addition, he was the first Canadian writer to use "...first person narrator and 'magic realism' in his works, which would later on influence Alice Munro, in her works" (Gadpaille: 35). Joyce Marshall (b. 1913) published a single collection, *A Private Place* 1975, which showed precise control over the language as well as presenting conflicting emotions. Malcolm Lowry (1909-57), explored the lyrical parabolic narrative in his stories. *The Bravest Boat,* which appeared in the *Weaver* anthology, is a "...somewhat pallid evocation of the triumph of human spirit over great physical and spiritual torment, a struggle imaged here by the survival of a frail-balsa-word boat in the storms and currents of the Pacific" (Gadpaille: 36). W.O. Mitchell (b. 1914), worked in the tradition of presenting the realistic prairie story. Mordecai Richer (b. 1931) worked in the urban tradition of Callaghan and Garner. In his work *The Street* (1969), he depicted the wartime Montreal Jewish neighbourhood surrounding St. Urbain.

The works of Hugh Hood (b. 1928), a new form of the short story was discernable. Here realism and allegory were united in art. In *Flying a Red Kite* (1962), the kite becomes the symbol not only of the kite of a child, but also the emblem of human soul soaring to spiritual heights. Hood was one of the founding members of a group called *Montreal Story Tellers,* which sought to promote the reading of short fiction. Ray Smith (b. 1941), in his collection *Cape Bretonis Thought Control Center of Canada* (1969) used the iconoclastic form and content.

The short story acquired new paradigm with John Metcalf (b. 1938), editor and anthologist of *New Canadian Stories & Best Canadian Stories.* Metcalf came to Canada from England in 1962. He produced three collections, viz., *The Lady Who Sold Furniture* (1970), *The Teeth of my Father* (1975) and *Adult Entertainment* (1986). Episodic structures, juxtaposition of images and scenes, rather than narration, and a dialogue that concealed more than it revealed characterize his work. Thus, Metcalf aimed for metafictive effects through his art.

A renowned writer of short fiction in Canada is Clark Blaise (b. 1940). His collection of short stories include, *A North American Education* (1973), *Tribal Justice* (1974), *Resident Alien* (1986), *Man & his World* (1992) and *The Selected Stories of Clark Blaise vol I: Southern Stories* (2000). His work, *I had a father: A post-modern autobiography,* is a singular blend of memoir and fictional sketch. "At times appearing as connected stories, at times novels, his fiction generally deals with lengthy, episodic narrative replete with social and cultural detail" (Toye, 41). Blaise's writings also reflected a sense of displacement and alienation which was subsequently taken up by Alice Munro in her fiction.

To sum up, the contribution of male writers to the evolution of the short story in English Canada, it has been observed that from the nineteenth century onwards writers have explored the various dimensions of this art. Different paradigms were set to suit the tastes of the reading public, and to make story telling more effective. From documentary sketch, writers turned to the writing of humorous stories. It gained widespread popularity not only in Canada but also had its impact on American writers such as Mark Twain. The next innovative step in Canadian literary history was the debut of the animal stories. However, the form was discontinued in the subsequent years.

The 20th century saw the dawn of the realistic fiction, when the sordid and hard truths of life were presented in fiction. Language, structure, and style of presentation, were innovated by writers. The art of narration became a complex one. With the two great wars, radical changes were evident and narrative art was revolutionized.

III

Women writers of short fiction in English Canada, have a long lineage[17] in the literary history of the country. From the early days of settlement, they have recorded their observations on the pioneer stories of adventure, myths and the wilderness. Canadian short story has been written predominantly by women writers, who have "thrived on the fringes of patriarchal society, and who were pioneering something of a twice—marginalized Canadian literary culture" (Lynch: 1042). These short stories by women, written from the historical-cultural contexts exemplify the dominant patriarchal setup as also the problems faced by the woman artist. The voice of women therefore, becomes doubly marginalized, and their stories become a reflection of their subjective selves. In addition, the very nature of the form, allowed these writers greater scope to question the impositions and restrictions of society. In this context, Jameela Begum opines:

> Both in content and form, of all genres, the short story becomes a privileged vehicle for the self-expression of a woman because its protean and undefinable nature lends itself readily to paradoxes, probings, self-reflexivity, and questionings. Since there are few firmly established conventions, the woman writer gets a limited freedom to

> play with the language, form and content, and revive the age old forms of storytelling—myths, fairytales, legends and folktales. The short story therefore imbibes an orality within it and the written form becomes the perception of the woman writer. (Begum: 148)

Thus, it has been observed that writers such as Gertrude Steih, Jane Bowles and Collette have written stories in a "language that was female" (Begum: 147). Stouck observe: "Canada's best writers have from the outset been women" (Stouck: 257). Coral Ann Howells explores a strong sense of affinity between the Canadian situation and women in Canada. Women's experience of the politics of gender and the constraints of patriarchal mindset, finds its parallel in Canada's position vis-a-vis the great powers, United States and the United Kingdom. According to her:

> ...This feminine awareness finds interesting parallels in the problematic concept of Canadian national identity, which has notoriously escaped definition, being variously described as 'negative', 'plural', or 'decentralized'. All of these adjectives relate to historical problems of Canada's double inheritance and its relationship to the United States, as well as reflecting the internal tensions of a linguistically divided culture of great ethnic diversity and conflicting regional interests. (Howells: 25)

For Lorna Irvine too, the female voice "politically and culturally personifies Canada" (Irvine: 11). Thus, the feminine quest for self as well as distinctive national identity becomes a common feature in Canadian women short fiction. A singular aspect of Canadian literary writings is that, wilderness is often used as a metaphor in women's writings for mapping the female consciousness. Howells points out, "Canadian writing has always been pervaded by an awareness of the wilderness.... Throughout the Canadian literary tradition wilderness has been and continues to be the dominant cultural myth, encoding Canadians' imaginative responses to their landscape and history as an image of national distinctiveness" (Howells: 11).

Canadian women's writings from early settlement up to present times feature this wilderness myth as an image that reflects the Canadian landscape as well as the female psyche. Wilderness figures in the writings of Margaret Atwood. *Surfacing, The Edible Woman, Lady Oracle,* and the short story *Bluebird's Egg,* all reflect the landscape. Again *Marian* Engel's *Bear,* Joan Barfoot's *Gaining Ground,* Margaret Lawrence's *The Diviners* and Alice Munro's *Lives of Girls and Women* are other such examples. Thus, Canadian short fiction is characterized by "interplay of multiple codes of cultural and literary references" (Howells: 13). This is in contrast to the American or Australian fiction, where the masculine voice[18] predominates.

The Canadian female literary tradition is marked by women's attempt to create a private space and subvert the traditional socio-cultural forces that have tried to repress women's sensibilities. Thus, an attempt to search and explore the inner selves is reflected in their narratives. Women have redefined their subjective selves, and here the short story, because of its very nature and scope, has opened up possibilities for self-discovery. As Alice Munro remarked, Canadian women's writing is characterized by "...those emphasis that throw the story line open to question, the disarrangements which demand new judgments and solution" ("Simon's Luck": *Who,* 177).

Women writers, to present the female world of marginalization, and their alienation from the mainstream have also coded Canadian wildernesses with its vast geographical stretches. Jancy James has summarized this situation as:

> The pervasive influence of the wilderness, the dominant cultural myth of Canada, proves to be the most fertile element for the female imagination to revise, restructure and demythify in order to chart out a private fictional world for the female identity to occupy as its own exclusive realm. (James: 100)

For the Canadian woman writer, the geographical and topographical boundary becomes a symbolic space for exploring the female psyche. In Atwood's *Surfacing* the

"...transitions between Toronto and Quebec exploits both the environmental and mythic aspects of wilderness in its story of a female physic quest" (Howells: 16). In other writers too, the ravines, and pockets of wilderness became the state of mind for the protagonists which they cannot shut out from themselves. This theme resonates in their stories. In Margaret Atwood's *The Edible Woman*, the pockets of wilderness were alternated with the urban milieu. The fictional creation of Laurence's prairie town of 'Manawaka' or Alice Munro's south-west Ontario towns of 'Jubilee' and 'Hanratty' are the enclosed dark spaces, created by the writers to counter the wilderness myth. For Munro and Laurence, the locale and the particular, projects the universal, and becomes a miniature of the universe. In their fiction, all these writers explore the regional, thereby opening up of the garrisoned space of the lives of women. Linda highlights the regionalist focus, with it's "...concern for the different, the local, the particular...in opposition to the uniform, the universal, and the centralized" (Hutcheon: 19).

Thus regionalism becomes an essential feature in women's writings. In this context W.J. Keith remarks "...in Munro the universal is always incarnate in the local and particular" (Keith: 161).

Writing in the feminine, and using the self-referential mode makes most of the female writers explore the postmodern techniques of expression. The works of Jane Rule, Audrey Thomas, Margaret Atwood, Alice Munro and others delineate the play with language, shifting of generic boundaries as well as shifts in perspectives, the lack of unified self, multiplicity of identities, the use of magic realism, and other postmodern episteme. Jameela Begum opines that:

> ...the postcolonial Canadian women writer creates a female space with the full realization that there are no absolutes and that no text is an independent entity but a step in the continual process of re-writing texts. She uses the short text, the truncated form of the novel to challenge the authority of the modern ideology...it offers her an elastic space to analyze the process of narration in relation to female experiences that are constantly being

> reshaped within the postmodern epistemology. (Begum: 158)

In the works of most of these writers, the form used is generally the 'Bildungsroman' patterns of narrative. Here the unfolding of the various stages of the protagonist's life, and the quest for inner self is revealed. Moreover, an overlapping of genres mark the fiction of Munro, Atwood and Laurence. The sequence stories or linked stories in the works of Alice Munro of have "the effect of a novel" (Keith: 160).

Thus, it is seen that the voice of women in Canada is a multiple one. The feminine text is interwoven with multiple narratives, and an open-endedness of form. Moreover the choice of this genre opens up possibilities of the exploration of the inner voice of women. Margaret Atwood says in this regard: "The true story is vicious and multiple and untrue after all. Why do you need it? Don't ever ask for the true story" (Atwood, *True Stories*: 11).

To concentrate this study now on the woman writers from the 19th century onwards, we observe that, the documentary sketches of pioneer settlement were the first exercises of the genre. The favored forms of these writers were diaries and journals, in which they recorded their experiences of settlement. Many of these writers were women, who had left their motherland with their husbands, taking up the challenges of settling in an alien land. Narrative in form, their writings were jottings of day-to-day experiences of domestic life, as also the difficulties of settlement. In this context, David Stouck observes:

> Books about emigration describe for the prospective settlers the trip to the New World and the difficulties encountered during the first years and much practical information on such topics as food, clothing, weather, and recreation. (Stouck: 15)

One of these women writers was Elizabeth Postural Simcoe (c. 1762-1850), the wife of John Graves Simcoe (1752-1806), the first Lieutenant-Governor of Upper Canada, who arrived in 1791. In her diary she complained of her life in the wilderness and recorded every detail of her day-to-day life.[19] Like

Mrs. Simcoe, Mrs. Jarvis too in her diary recorded her discontent with her setting as well as her inability to cope with her surroundings. She complained:

> This is one of the worst place for servants that can be—they are not to be on any terms We cannot get a Woman who can cook a Joint of Meat unless I am at her Heels...I have a Scotch girl from the Highlands Nasty, Sulky, Ill Tempered Creature (New 2003: 52).

Such diaries were also maintained by Susan Allison (1845-1937),—*A Pioneer Gentlewoman in British Columbia* (1976), Elizabeth Goodie's (b. 1902) *Woman of Labrador* (1973); and narratives of Georgina Binnie Clark (1871-1955) and Monica Storrs (1888-1955). Amongst others were, Anna Jameson's *Winter Sketches and Summer Rambles* (1838) and Emily Carr's autobiographical accounts of her journeys as a painter, through the forests of British Columbia between 1898 and 1930s.

With the economic depression in Britain, between 1825 and 1840, the number of immigrants to Canada increased. Most of them were writers in their motherland, and therefore the natural surrounding stimulated their creative instincts. Amongst them were two sisters—Catherine Parr Trail and Susanna Moodie. Their writings were of great significance as they ushered in a new form of narrative in Canadian literary history. Written mainly in the form of sketches, their works were the memoirs of their impression and reaction towards an alien land. Both the sisters, had immigrated to Canada with their husbands, and had settled near Peterborough, Ontario. A remarkable feature of these writings was that, both the sisters differed widely in their narratives. Epistolary in nature, Mrs. Trail's works were thirty in number, which included *The Backwoods of Canada* (1836), *The Canadian Settler's Guide* (1854) and *Canadian Wild Flowers* (1868). *The Female Emigrant's Guide, and Hints on Canadian House Keeping* (New 2003: 54). In her letters home to her mother, Mrs. Trail made settlement in Canada an attractive proposition and encouraged settlers to venture into the New Land. It also provided an insight into the domestic life, and explained how to make soap, how to make tea from local plants, and other domestic advice.

In sharp contrast to this spirit, Susanna Moodie's version was a warning to prospective emigrants coming to Canada. She drew their attention to the fact that unless they were ready to face hardship of all kinds, they should not undertake such dangerous propositions. *Roughing It in the Bush* (1852)[20] is a grim, dismal account of discomfort and hardships of settlement. In addition, her writings voiced a yearning for her motherland:

> Dear, dear England! Why was I forced by stern necessity to leave you? What heinous crime had I committed that I, who adored you, should be torn from your bosom, to pine out my joyless existence in a foreign clime? Oh that I might be permitted to return and die upon your wave-encircled shores, and rest my weary head and heart, beneath your daisy-covered sod at last. (Stouck: 21)

As a short fiction, the work was documentary, romantic in nature, and heralded the beginning of women's self-reflection in literary art. In this context David Stouck observes:

> Susanna Moodie's cautionary tale *Roughing It in the Bush,* is not a polished work of art, but the narrator's personal drama of rejection and exile, and her search for a refuge from an uncaring world is very central to what is imaginative in the Canadian experience. (Stouck: 28)

Mrs. Moodie episodic narratives were published in the *Literary-Garland Montreal* from 1839, until it folded in 1851, mainly for economic reasons. However, *Roughing It in the Bush* has "dramatic force as narrative and a perspicacity of observation rare in the literature of emigration and settlement" (Toye: 337).

The short story was given new directions by two women writers, viz., Isabella Valancy Crawford (1850-87) and Susie Frances Harrison (1859-1935). Their stories presented local-color story, and was a projection of real life in fiction.

Reputed for her narrative poems, Isabella Valancy Crawford wrote a number of short stories and novelettes, mainly for American magazines. Her *Selected Stories of Isabella Valancy Crawford* (1975), *Fairy Tales of Isabella Valancy Crawford* (1977) and *The Haton Boy* (1979) were melodramatic in nature with colourful diction, resembling Dickens with "...twins and doubles, mysterious childhood disappearances, stony-hearted fathers, sacrificial daughters, wills and lost inheritances and recognition scenes" (Toye: 94). Susie Frances Harrison, wrote under the pseudonym 'Seramus', and contributed literary and musical reviews, articles, essays, poetry and short stories to Canadian, British and American newspapers and literary magazines. Her first book *Crowded Out and Other Sketches* (1886) attempted to capture the characteristic psyche of the immigrants to Canada. In her stories, she presented the romantic local colour, and at the same time echoed Edgar Allan Poe with "haunted disturbed characters, first person narrative and weird events" (Toye: 204).

Sara Jeannette Duncan (1861-1922) took up the issues of women's problems in her works. A novelist and a writer of short fiction, an editorial writer and book reviewer for Washington Post, her works were regularly published in the *Week*. Though she was not directly involved with the Suffrage Movement, her writings were concerned with women's rights and liberties:

> Sara Jeannette Duncan was motivated by the desire to create a new literature in Canada, and took encouragement from the fact that the new cultural experiment welcomed all practitioners. (Sullivan, 1984: x)

Duncan's masterful creation *The Pool in the Desert* (1903) brought her fame and equated her with Henry James in her exploration of psychological realm of human life. The voice of her stories was that of an "...intelligent, independent, penetrating female: critical, appreciative an above all alive" (Gadpaille: 16). This voice would again be heard in Ethel Wilson writings in the late 1930s, to be followed in the 1970s by Margaret Atwood. The age witnessed the burgeoning of popular magazines[21] which opened up new avenues for the female creative writer, and enhanced their creativity. By this time, magazines and journals were finding an open market, and the names of Canadian writers were familiar in American households, and the world over.

The 20th century saw socio political changes in Canada with the suffrage movement[22] gaining ground. Women's writings reflected these changing times as well as introspected on women's conditions in social life.

Ethel Wilson (1888-1930) was writer of great prominence. An author of six novels and several short stories, she occupies an important position in Canadian literary history. Her first story appeared in 1937, "I Just Love Dogs", while her other collected stories *Mrs. Golightly and Other Stories*, in 1961. "Wilson's stories are clearly modernist in their ironic tone, and their sophisticated control of narrative voice. Their innovative approach to first-person narration differentiates them in technique from anything before in the Canadian short story" (Gadpaille: 26). Dealing with the middle class gentility, she was interested in the multiple levels of psychological setups of human beings. "The recurrent story in her work is that of a woman who withdraws from familiar surroundings and sets out on a lonely quest of self-discovery" (Stouck: 82). In some of her stories, like D.H. Laurence and David Garnet, she used animal motifs to construct psychological fables that explored deep-seated emotional emotions. In her well-known article "A Cat Among the Falcon" she pointed out that the most important thing about writing was the reflection of the author's voice.

In 1919, the short fiction entered the feminist phase, with the writings of Sime Jessie Georgina (1868-1958). In her collection of stories *Sister Woman* (1919) she recorded the social set-up, and the plight of immigrant working women of Montreal.

> Sime was an early modernist and realist, in her fiction and non-fiction directing attention to the social, economic, and emotional difficulties of working-class women and the urban poor. (Toye: 444)

Another writer, Gabrielle Roy (born in Manitoba 1909), wrote both in French and English. In her fiction, she explored the women's situation, presenting strong individual women characters. Her writings which were episodic in nature, revealed her artisanship as well as her style, which was at once simple, direct and poetic. Her three Manitoba books were written in French and were, "translated by Binsse" (Toye: 416). These stories were in the form of linked short stories. *Where Nests the Water Hen* (1950) gives a poetic account of settlement in northern Manitoba; *Street of Riches,* again translated by Binsse is the account of a young girl growing up from childhood to adolescence. In *The Road past Altamont* (1966) Roy explored the geology of the three generations of women where the "journeys always lead back to their beginnings" (Tbye: 416).

The English-Canadian short story tended to focus on individual psychology in the art of Sheila Watson (b. 1909). Turning to myth and symbol, Watson probed into other structures of reality. In *Antigone,* she explored psychological realms and interwove myth with reality to give the genre a new outlook. *And the Four Animals* presents a combination of the realism of the land and fantasy of the mind. "Deeply rooted in the image of the Coyote, the trickster god, the story is a gruesome subversion of the story of Genesis, and is encapsulated within a 'realistic-fantasy'" (Begum: 148).

Similar attitudes were reflected in the stories of Audrey Thomas (b. 1935). In her twin stories *Green Stakes for the Garden,* and *Initram,* she played with the notions that are no absolutes, which may be represented in art. For Audrey Thomas reality is at best a mirror image, which one is incapable of presenting in fiction. In her collection *Ten Green Bottles* (1967) Audrey, experimented with a completely new form and explored a new area of female sensibility. She used the stream of consciousness narrative to map the relationship between art and fiction. Audrey also made use of the postmodern technique of disrupted sequences, elements of fantasy, magic realism, etc. that were new to Canadian Fiction.

Marian Engel (1933-85), in her stories *Inside the Easter Egg* (1975) and *The Tattooed Woman* (1985) opened up female experiences for analyses and study. Gadpaille described them: "...short, playful stories that sometimes descend from playfulness to the depths of bitterness and the grotesque" (Gadpaille: 107).

Elizabeth Spencer and Mavis Gallant also made psychological probes in their art, which focused on the territory of relationships, and woman's attitude to love and marriage. Gallant's "'The Moslem Wife' explored, with wise irony, the facts of a relationship over decades: physical need and revulsion, affection and fear, pride and guilt, admiration and resentment" (Sullivan: xv). Gallant's stories was also set against the background experiences of the Second World War, where the events of life led the narrator in quest for existence.

Sandra Birdsell in her short stories took up the problems of women in small rural towns and the intricate workings of human heart. Like Alice Munro, Birdsell's stories too are a series of "linked by setting (the fictional Manitoban town of Agassiz) and by characters (the numerous Lafreniere family)" (Gadpaille: 109). While sexual oppression was one of the prime concerns of the author, erotic love also finds its place in her fiction. Her first collection of stories, *Night Travellers* (1982, rpt. 1987) was based on the fictional town of Agassiz, followed by *Ladies of the House* (1984) which contained a more varied set. Like the narrator of a Munro story, she discovered the world's hostility towards expressions of love and beauty that were not been sanctioned by society.

Edna Alford's collection of stories *The Garden of Eloise Loon* (1986) is made up of well crafted fourteen stories which are at times fragmented and hallucinatory in nature. Moreover they deal at times with the mental setups of human beings. *A Sleep Full of Dreams* presents ten linked stories, where a single protagonist, working as a nurse in a nursing home for old and terminally women, struggles to survive, Jane Rule (b. 1931) has explored lesbian themes. A writer of both novels and short stories, her work deals with the joy and pleasure of intimacy with women. A prolific writer of short stories, she has published three collections: *Themes for Diverse Instruments* (1975), *Outlander* (1981), and *Island Passage and Other Stories* (1985). In her works, she has explored women's relationships as a natural and acceptable form of expression. The mid-20th century saw the flourishing of popular magazines and weekly supplements to newspapers such as "*MacLean's Magazine, Liberty, Mayfair, Canadian Magazine, Star Weekly, Saturday Night* and *Canadian Home Journal* and many French periodicals" (Lynch, Encylo: 1043).

The age saw another milestone, with the setting up of *The Canadian Broadcasting Corporation* and *Radio Canada.* With the broadcasting of programmes, the radio became a medium of art and information. The short story too, now saw many changes in its form, as it was read on air, reaching the household of millions. The person responsible for initiating such major changes in society was Robert Weaver (b. 1921). He founded *Tamarack Review* and edited several *Oxford Short Story Anthologies.* Roberts joined the *CBC* in 1948. In 1954, he developed a number of programmes, viz. *Anthology, CBC Wednesday Night, Canadian Short Stories, Critically Speaking, Stories with John Drainie.* Through this programme he encouraged short story writers to read their literary works on air. These positive steps, lead to the immense popularity of the genre. It validated Canadian speech sounds and accents, and projected different cultural perspectives. The short story writers who read their works on air were, Mordecai Richer, Alice Munro, Joyce Marshall and Mavis Gallant. This reading of texts was a new experience for writers, as a listening audience was needed to be kept in mind. Mavis Gallant observes:

> There is something relentless about a story being read aloud. Lack of rhythm vagueness and faulty characterization are glaringly obvious because you can skip and you can't reread.[23]

Thus, nineteen sixties are regarded as period of great literary productivity. Donald Stephens while summarizing the achievements of a decade of short-story writing in Canada, stated that it was the age when "the dam burst" (qtd.

Gadpaille: 99). To analyze the various literary developments that took place from 1960 to 1985, it is observed that many steps and measures were introduced by the Canadian Government to encourage creative writings. In 1957, the Canada Council came into existence, which empowered publication and research in art. The National Library was also set up during this period. The first edition of *The Literary History of Canada* and *The Dictionary of Canadian Biography* (New, 2003: 188) was also published. For research and publication, agencies of support such as The Ontario Arts Council were established. In the 1970s, the report on *The Status of Women in Canada* chaired by Florence Bird (New, 2003: 204), began slowly to influence legislation, publication, education and social policy. In the field of science and technological advancement the age saw rapid expansion. The age also felt the need for a literary canon, which would seek order and coherence in all literary works.

Northrop Frye (1912-91), took up the arduous task of defining a canon, and from 1950 to 1960, contributed "more than any other critic in establishing the criterion by which Canadian writing might be judged" (Toye: 151). In *Anatomy of Criticism* (1957) and *The Bush Garden: Essays on the Canadian Imagination* (1971 rpt. 1995), Frye collected the works of writers over the past quarter of a century. Frye was to a considerable extent influenced by Carl Jung, James Fraser and he strove to find the impact of the Bible on literature. With the thematic and myth poetic criticism of Northrop Frye, the study of Canadian literature took a new direction and tradition.

The seventies are regarded the "The Golden Age of Canadian Literature" (Stouck: 302). It was an age when literary activity flourished in every respect and reached the highest level of the country's cultural history. Many publishing concerns such as *House of Anansi* (1967), *Oberon* (1966) came into being. This encouraged young, promising writers to publish their writings. While the *House of Anansi* published the works of Margaret Atwood, viz. *Survival: A Thematic Guide to Canadian Literature* (1972); *Power Politics* (1971) and Frye's *Garden Bush* (1971); the *Coach House Press* published the early books of poetry by Michael Ondaatje. Moreover, the "Canada Council sponsored the growth of Canadian Literature through individual writer's grants and a writer-in-residence program" (Stouck: 302). In addition, the interviews with renowned writers, appearing in popular magazines created widespread interest in literary art. The programme also stimulated interest in writing, publications and academic support. In literature and culture, probably the greatest amount of attention in this decade was focused on Canada's women writers, and a large number of works by women were published.

This era also saw the short story reach its zenith, in the hands of three eminent women writers—Margaret Laurence, Margaret Atwood and Alice Munro. It may be recorded here that the former two were both novelists as well as short story writers, while Alice Munro's distinction lies in the fact that she is a writer of short stories Margaret Laurence (1926-87) was born in the prairie town of Neepawa, Manitoba, which inspired her fictional 'Manawaka'. More of a novelist than a short story writer, Laurence spent a major part of her life in Africa, where she started her writing career. Her first short story collection *The Tomorrow Tames* (1963) is set in Ghana, while *A Bird in the House* (1970) is a collection of linked stories with 'Manawaka' as its background. The stories enabled Laurence to see for herself, the true values of the inherited past, and thereby acquire a true perspective within which to locate the present. Speaking of her Manawaka setting, Laurence is more concerned with the fictional creation of her setting. The writings of Laurence were however considered to be outside the mainstream of Canadian literature, because of their African setting. But *The Voice of Adamo* and *A Gourdful of Glory* were included in "Robert Weaver's *Canadian Stories*, Second Series 1968" (Gadpaille: 105). Laurence's fiction was generally inter-linked stories. *In A Bird in the House*, Laurence reveals the world of the child Vanessa Mac heeds, struggling to free her from the domination of her rigid Scott grandfather. It is the story of a woman's journey towards self discovery and inner freedom through reconciliation with the past. Laurence believed that one needs to come to terms with the past in order to acquire an adequate and true perception of the self, as well as of the nation.

In marked opposition to Laurence's stance, gender politics constitutes a major thrust and preoccupation in Margaret Atwood's novels and short stories. Unlike Laurence, Atwood problematizes the feminine search for self-identity within a feminist framework and postulates a feminine discourse, against patriarchal hegemonic power structures. Moreover, she perceives a resemblance between women's powerlessness and passivity vis-a-vis male subjugation.

Atwood, in her art has experimented with various techniques of expression, and her short fiction is an in-depth study of the human psyche. In *Dancing Girls* (1977 rpt. 1988), the protagonists are psychologically complex individuals, suffering from an utter sense of alienation and mental disorder. In *Polarities,* Atwood again examines the abnormal states of mind, and madness becomes a subject matter, both inside and outside mental institution. Atwood shows that the insane proves to have deeper understanding of the general psychosis of modern society. *The Grave of the Famous Poet* is Atwood's compassionate study of the failure of relationships. *Bluebeard's Egg* (1983, rpt. 1984), contains several autobiographical stories, including *Significant Moments in the Life of My Mother* and *Unearthing Suite,* which accounted Atwood's own childhood experiences and her family life. *Wilderness Tips* (1991, rpt. 1998) included the story *Isis in Darkness* (1992), a distinguished tribute to Gwendolyn Macewen, her friend and contemporary poet.

IV

A distinguished short story writer of Canada is Alice Munro, popularly known as the 'Canadian Chekhov'. With her narrative technique, the short story took a new direction. Remarkable for its style, paradoxical expressions, and the artist's painstaking effort to delineate life in its minute detail, distinguishes her from other Canadian short story writers.

From her first collection to her recent writings, Munro has presented a complex narrative structure, spatial, rather than linear. Her art accommodates the entire gamut of human emotions and presents a realistic picture of life. In her works, Munro exploits various forms of the short story to suit the changing demands of her themes, and therefore the reader is accosted with a wide variety of expressions, viz., the epistolary form, dream-sequences, the stream of consciousness and inter-related cycle of stories.

As materials for her stories, she relies largely on family lineage, photography, story telling within the story, and at times to gossip even. Interwoven with multiple layers of narrative art, her texts are implicit with hidden meanings, which the readers have to search through to get at the heart of the matter. As the narrative structure unfolds itself in a digressive pattern, the boundaries of fact and fiction seem to merge into one another. However, at times, the narratives become discontinuous and the reader is lead through maze of happenings where the past and the present co-exist. After traversing in Munro territory for some time, the reader is jolted by the sudden twist at the end of the narration. Often the stories lead to Joycean epiphanies or sudden revelations by the narrators. "Her art is often seen as metafiction, keeping pace with the development of the short story in Europe, Latin America and North America" (Gadpaille 1988: 58).

Munro is very much interested in the manner in which people live their lives, and this features as the subject matter in all her works. The focus of her art is always on her own region, Ontario. In her interviews, she has admitted, that it was the place she really knew. Her forte lies in her depiction of real life, unveiling the truth that lies hidden behind the mask and this seems to be the prime motive of her creativity. Munro's first collection *Dance of the Happy Shades* (1968) was followed by *Lives of Girls and Women* (1971). It is considered an episodic novel, as the inter-linked stories of Del Jordan traces the stages of her growth from adolescence to maturity. Her next collection, *Something I've Been Meaning to Tell You* (1974) was followed by *Who Do You Think You Are?* (1978).

Like *Lives,* this work also traces the life of her protagonist Rose, whose experiences in life are juxtaposed in a haphazard manner to present a holistic picture of life. Next in order come *The Moons of Jupiter* (1982), *Progress of Love* (1986), *Friend of my Youth* (1990), *Open Secrets* (1994) and *Selected Stories* (1996), where Munro takes twenty-eight stories from the earlier books and arranges them in chronological order. *Love of a Good Woman* (1998) reveals the complexity of Munro's art, with story embedded within the story. "In *Love of a Good Woman* the women on whom the stories focus behave in ways that others judge moralistically, but Munro's characters do not regret. Having come to terms with their actions, at the time or in later life, they placidly move on. "The stories' careful style, invites the reader not into understanding, particularly, but into awareness, a state that permits, finally, recognition" (New, 2003: 299).

Writing and publishing until date, she has won worldwide recognition for her short stories.

In her art, Munro is concerned with the lives of women in their different stages of life. She examines human relationships, with its associate emotional bindings—the joys, fear, hopes, desires, and the pangs of sufferings brought by loss and death. Autobiographical in content, Munro's texts are a realistic presentation of life, drawn from the author's personal experiences, and embody her vision of life. Munro's choice of this genre seems to be a deliberate one, as it helped enormously in her paradoxical and ambivalent expressions. Moreover, the protean character and open-endedness of the short story seemed for Munro an apt means for voicing female sensibilities against patriarchal discourses.

From the above discussion, we may say that the short story continued to be a favored literary form in Canada, having a large number of practitioners, and readers. It has gained an international forum, and is being read, appreciated and evaluated.

To conclude we may say that from being mythical in nature in the oral narratives, the written form of short story in English Canada begins with the European settlement. It took the form of journals and memoirs, recording the first experiences of the settlers in a new land. Personal in nature, these writings were accounts of the wilderness, the inclement weather conditions, and the tough endurance that the settlers had to undergo. As a matter of fact, these writers were mainly women, who had come to Canada with their husbands and had taken up the arduous task of raising families in an alien land. The Canadian short story in English became a recognized form of art in the 19th century, when it was an established genre in England and America. Forms, introduced during this period were humorous sketches, the animal stories as well as the realistic stories. With the dawning of the twentieth century, the structural patterns and technique of presentation underwent changes. The two great wars of the century had left its imprint in the attitudes and mindset of the people, with the result that writers now adhered to more and more complex forms of narrative. The genre thus became more and more divergent. Prominent were the diary, the epistolary forms, and the inter-related cycle of stories. The modes of expression were generally humorous, witty, and at times satirical in nature. Modernist and post modernist strategies of narrative were also favored as the short stories become more and more realistic.

Women's writings continued to dominate the literary scenario down the ages. This female voice represented Canada more than the male voice. The women's quest for the inner self in their writings may be related to the Canadian quest for self-identity. The writings of Isabella Valancy Crawford, Susie Frances Harrison and Sara Jeannette Duncan highlighted women's voice in literature. This was later on echoed in the works of Ethel Wilson, Margaret Atwood, Alice Munro, and a host of other women writers. The age also saw the consolidation of the position of the Canadian short story, with the publication of its first anthology and programming on air the short stories by renowned writers. This brought the genre to the homes of the millions. Regionalism became a feature of Canadian short fiction. Thus, we may agree that the short story as a literary genre acted as a "force for exploration, understanding, and healing, and to create a literature out of everyday life that compels immediate recognition and identification" (Gadpaille, 1988: iii).

In providing a broad historical outline of the Canadian short story in English Canada covering the 19th and 20th century, certain observations with regard to some of its major male and female writers have been made. As has been seen, a majority of writers in Canada have chosen this marginal form for literary creativity. This may be explained by the fact that Canadian writers have always felt themselves to be marginalized by the European and US cultures. Questions as to whether there is a Canadian literature or not, and who is a Canadian have always perplexed the nation. Moreover, the country's having two national languages, English and French, as well as the constitutional status, have all accentuated the country's quest for self identity. This finds its expression through the medium of an art form that is itself open to multiple meanings and offers a heteroglossia of voices. The writers of short fiction, while telling their stories have tried to reconstruct the national cultural history from their angle of vision. Also to be noted is the fact that, Canada has always had numerous women writers, writing in this genre. Their writings show an inclination towards postmodern techniques, with its defiance of closure, free play of language and a crossing of generic boundaries. Thus, the voice of the women writers manifests a quest for the inner voice, and therefore is a personification of Canada itself. This quest is more evident in the works of Alice Munro, where she questions the traditional rules of compositions and sets new trends in art. In the subsequent chapters, Munro's innovations in the art of story telling, which sets her as a groundbreaker in Canadian literary history, will be observed.

Thus, we may conclude by saying that Canadian short story has rich diversity and a long literary tradition which expresses the multiple voice and mosaic character of Canada.

NOTES

1. The short story in both verse and prose is the oldest and most wide spread of literary forms e.g. Egyptian Tales, Jatakas, Panchantantra Arabian Nights The Hebrew Bible Old

Testament, New Testament, Greek Homer Aesop's Fables. Episodes in Ramayana and Mahabharata have the character of short stories. The most important contribution in Sanskrit is, however, in the form of large collection of fables and tales Sanskrit, etc. Folktales are also found abundantly in India. (Krishna 3).

2. Tolstoy's vision of life was keen and he portrayed life at all levels. Soldiers, Serfs, aristocrats all enter his pictures without loosing any essential elements of their character. His vision of life and nature has an elevating appeal, extending as it does to a metaphysical view and the consciousness of the strife between good and evil. (Modern English Short Story 31).
3. In the 1920s, the *Saturday Evening Post* for a single short story paid Scott Fitzgerald$4000. [WilliamBoyd.*ProspetMagazine*, 15/6/2006, 15/6/2006,<http.//www.prospectmagazine.co.uk/article_details.php?id=7447>
4. Hemingway's "zero ending", goes counter to the traditional "well made ending". His fictional work, *Three Stories and Ten Poems* (1923), *In Our Time* (1924) [Enlarged Edition 1925]; *Men Without Women* (1927); *Winner Take Nothing* (1933); *The Fifth Column and the First forty-nine Stories* (1938); *The Snows of Kilimanjaro and Other Stories* (1961); *The Nick Adams Stories* (1972) amongst others. [Mangum 1621].
5. A novel form of the modern short story is the "suppressed narrative" Twentieth century writers such as Nabokov, Calvino Borges and Rudyard Kipling wrote in this form. Dickens in *Christmas Specials* used the mini-novel form while Dylan Thomas, D.H. Lawrence and J.G. Ballard explored the poetic mythic story. The present age has also seen a transmutation of the short story, which originated in America in the 1990s. The biographical story however its exponents in Dave Eggers, David Foster Wallace, and William T Vollman. However, the Chekhovian form is more dominant than the events plot even to this day. (Prospect Magazine/Internetdxs8).
6. The form *novelette* or *novella* was used by Heinrich von Kleist and many other German theorists, where it was introduced by Goethe in 1795, and indicated by the name *Novelle* (Abrams, pp. 194-95).
7. Reingard M. Nischik is professor and chair of American Literature at the University of Constance, Germany. *The Canadian Short Story. Interpretations* Ed. Reingard

M. Nischik. <http://www.boydell.co.uk/ 71131272. HTM google.>

8. Jesuit Relations: "Jesuit missionaries in New France were required to present an annual account of their activities to the superior at Québec, who then put these reports together with a suitable preface and sent them on to the provincial in Paris. The provincial edited them for the Jesuit order's general in Rome and after 1632 for regular publication in Paris. The published *Jesuit Relations* appeared under the name of the superior but occasionally reproduced an entire report under the name of its original author.... The Relations began with Pierre Biard's letters from ACADIA in 1611, became firmly established with the some forty volumes that the Sebastien Cramoisy press in Paris issued between 1632 and 1673 (these volumes properly constitute the Relations des Jesuites de la Nouvelle-France), and thereafter appeared in occasional separate volumes published in Paris, Lyons, and Rome, and sometimes in journals such as the *Mercure francais*. (*Jesuit Relations*, Cornelius J. Jaenen, W.H. New, Ed. *Encyclopedia of Literature in Canada,* Toronto Buffalo London: University of Toronto Press, 2002 (pp. 548-49).
9. Almost all these explorers left observations and record. (Cartier's are not extant, although a work attributed to him does exist: Giovanni Ranusio's, 1485-1557, narrative Italian translation of Cartier's account of his navigations to New France appeared in 1556, and John Florio's, c. 1553-1625, English translation from Ramusio's Italian came out in 1580.) Such records vary markedly in literary quality. The exploration narratives collectively indicate not just that the explorers thrived on their enjoyment of adventure, but also that the explorations were less a demonstration of Renaissance curiosity than offshoots of a desire for political control, whether economic, religious or simply territorial. Exploration, therefore, linked with combat, settlement and trade. (W.H. New, *A History of Canadian Literature,* 2nd ed. Montreal & Kingston. London. Ithaca: Mc Grill-Queen's University Press, 2003. pp. 26-27.)
10. The sketches of 'Sam Slick' stories ran for several years serially in Joseph Howe's paper, 'The Novascotian', starting in 1835, and were later collected in eleven volumes (the three series of *The Clockmaker,* 1836, 1838, 1840, the two series of *The Attache,* 1943, 1944; *Sam Slick's wise Saws and Modern*

Instances, 1853, and *Nature and Human Nature*, 1855 became widely popular.

11. Roberts stories reflected Canadian nature in literature, but in doing so they perpetuated a rural illusion of Canada that subsequently reinforced by the wilderness landscape mythologies of Emily Carr and other writers. (*Dreams of Speech and Violence,* p. 61.)
12. Qtd by, Toye, William, ed. *The Concise Oxford Companion to Canadian Literature,* Oxford New York: Oxford University Press, 2001, p. 406.
13. *Ibid.*, p. 272.
14. Callaghan's publication in American magazines (numbering more than eighty), marked his transatlantic debut, the beginning of an era in the history of Canadian literature, when the short story "became simultaneously serious and profitable, a twin recognition substantiated by European reception and American book publication" (Ref.: Michalle Gadpaille, *The Canadian Short Story,* Toronto: Oxford University Press, 1988, p. 25).
15. Hans Bertens has defined free indirect discourse. According to him: "In free indirect course the narrator's descriptive reportage can so gradually give way to the reflections of one of the characters that at a certain point we honestly can no longer say to whom we are supposed to attribute what is being thought or through whose eyes we see what is being described (with whose 'point of view' we are dealing, in traditional; terms). (Hans Bertens, Literary Theory: The Basics. London and New York: Routledge, 2001, pp. 74-75).
16. The magazines published in the 19th century included: *Montreal's Literary Garlan* (1838-51), Susanna and Dunbar Moodie's *Victoria Magazine* (1847-48), *Canadian Monthly and National R.* (1872-82), *The New dominion Monthly* (1867-79), *The Canadian Illustrated News* (1869-83). Also widely popular and highly influential magazine of this period was *Week* (1883-96). The later 19th century, saw the rise and demise of the relatively long running magazine *Grip* (1873-94), published a great number of parodies, sketches, satires, bringing international fame to Stephen Leacock and others. The 'Confederation Group' began to publish in the 1880s, and with the growth of American magazine market, Canadian writers appeared in the *Atlantic Century Magazine, The North*

American Review, Scribner's Monthly—as well as in Toronto periodicals, e.g. *The Week,* (1883-1939), editorially fostering patriotism and mutual understanding. (Ref: Gerald Lynch, pp. 1043-44).

17. At least 470 early women writers have contributed to the development of short stories of Canada. *List of authors indexed in Canada's Early Women Writers* <http://www.lib.sfu.ca/womw/authors.html>
18. United States and Australia has a masculine tradition. "Australia had its beginnings as a penal colony where the lives of men and women were officially separated, while the great American movement west with its convoys of covered wagons and Indian Wars represented massive exercise in aggressive male confrontation with wilderness. Neither of these phenomena has a parallel in Canadian history". (*Private and Fictional Words,* p. 22)
19. Her diary (1911, re-edited in 1965, as *Mrs. Simcoe's Diary,* by Mary Quayle Innis (1899-1972), records many details of household duties and scenic, but judges them sharply against an English norm. (Ref New, 2003: 52).
20. Moodie, Susanna. *Roughing It in the Bush; or, Life in Canada.* London: Bentley, 1852. Several later editions including an abridged version (London: Nelson, 1932). Reprint, abridged, in McClelland and Stewart's New Canadian Library, No. 31 (Toronto, 1962).
21. The names of the magazines are *Edward Thompson's Toronto Globe, Boston Youth's Companion,* Norman Duncan with the *'New York', 'Evening Post', Marjory MacMurchy* with the *Canada Educational Monthly, CA. Fraser* with the *Montreal Star, Robert Barr,* with *The Globe, The Detroit Free Press*, and *Jerome K. Jerome 'The Idler'.* (*Dreams of Speech and Violence,* p. 43).
22. The Suffrage Movement in Canada had its origin in Quebec. Between 1809 and 1849, propertied women held the right to vote, but lost it when the legislature inserted the word 'male' into the "Quebec Voting Act" Women were granted municipal voting rights but were far off from universal suffrage. In 1916, Manitoba women were the first to win the right to vote and hold office in provincial elections; Saskatchewan and Alberta, later in the same year, followed by British Columbia, Ontario next year Nova Scotia in 1918, New Brunswick (with

restrictions in 1919, Prince Edward Island in 1922, and Newfoundland in 1925). (New 2003: 103). Moreover the Wartime Elections Act 1917, gave the vote to Caucasian women in the armed forces and to women with male relatives in the army, but it removed the vote from all naturalized citizens. In 1918 all adult women acquired federal voting rights, and in 1919 the right to run for federal office. The right to run for provincial office was however kept withheld until 1934, in New Brunswick, while in Quebec provincial voting rights were denied until the campaign of Therese Casgrain leading to an act of enfranchisement in 1940. [New (New, 2003: 103].

23. Quoted by W.H. New in his essay. "Tense/Present/Narrative: Reflections on English-Language Short Fiction in Canada". Ed. E. Arnold Davidson. Ed. *Introductory & Critical Essays: Studies on Canadian Literature,* The Modern Language Association of America, New York: 1990, p. 47.

Works Cited

Abrams, M.H. *A. Glossary of Literary Terms,* Sixth Edition Bangalore: Prism Books Pvt. Ltd., 1993.

Atwood, Margaret. *True Stories,* London: Cape, 1982.

———. *Survival: A Thematic Guide to Canadian Literature*. Toronto: Anansi, 1972.

Baily, Tom. Ed. *On Writing Short Stories*, Oxford University Press, Oxford, New York: 2000.

Begum, A. Jameela. "Postmodern as Feminist Text: A Reading of the Short Text of Canadian Women Writers", *Postmodernism and Feminism Canadian Context*. Ed. Shirin Kudchedkar, Delhi: Pencraft International, 1995.

Booth, C. Wayne. "Distance and Point of View an Essay in Classification", *Theory of the Novel.* Philip Stevick, New York London: The Free Press Collier-Macmillan Limited. 1967.

Bowen, Elizabeth. *Afterthoughts,* London: Longmans Green and Co, 1962.

Bryant, Mangum. "Earnest-Memingway", *Critical Survey of Short Fiction,* Ed. Frank Magill, Salem Press, 1982.

Chatterjee, Krishna. *Modern English Short Story: A Critical Introduction*, Mnerva, India, 1991.

Childs, Peter. *Modernism: The New Critical Idiom,* London and New York: Routledge, 2002.

Connor, O' Frank. *The Lonely Voice: A Study of the Short Story.* London: Macmillan, 1965.

Davidson, E. Arnold. Ed. *Introductory & Critical Essays: Studies on Canadian Literature,* The Modern Language Association of America, New York, 1990.

Faolain, Sean O'. *The Short Story,* London: Collins, St. James' Place, 1948.

Frye, Northrop. *The Bush Garden: Essays on the Canadian Imagination,* Canada: Anansi Press, 1971.

Gadpaille, Michalle. *The Canadian Short Story,* Toronto: Oxford University Press, 1988.

Hutcheon, Linda. *The Canadian Postmodern: A Study of Contemporary English Canadian Fiction,* Toronto: OUP, 1988.

Howells, Coral Ann. *Private and Fictional Words: Canadian Women Novelists of the 1970s and 1980s,* London and New York: Methuen, 1987.

Irvine, Lorna. *Subversion: Canadian Fiction by Women,* Toronto: ECW Press, 1986.

James, Jancy. "Canadian Paradigms of Postmodern Feminism", *Postmodernism and Feminism Canadian Context,* ed. Shirin Kudchedkar, Delhi: Pencraft International, 1995.

Keith, W.J. *Canadian Literature in English,* London and New York: Longman Group Ltd., 1985.

Lubbock, Percy. *The Craft of Fiction,* Great Britain: John Dickens & Co Ltd, 1963.

Lynch, Gerald. "Short Story and Sketch", W.H. New, Ed. *Encyclopedia of Literature in Canada,* Toronto Buffalo London: University of Toronto Press, 2002.

Mabbot, J.O. Ed. "The Selected Poetry and Prose of *Edgar Allan Poe*". New York: The Modern Library, 1951.

Mabbott, Thomas Ollive Ed. *Collected Works of Edgar Allan Poe: Tales and Sketches* (vol-111831-1842), The Belknap Press of Harvard University Cambridge, Massachusett, London, England, 1978. p. xviii.

Magmun, Bryant, *Ernest Hemmingway: Critical Survey of Short Fiction,* Salem Press, 1982.

Maugham, Somerset. *Points of View.* London: Heinemann, 1960.

Munro, Alice. *Dance of the Happy Shades,* Toronto: McGraw, 1968.

——. *Lives of Girls and Women,* Toronto: McGraw-Hill Ryerson, 1971.

——. *Something I've Been Meaning to Tell You: Thirteen Stories,* Toronto: McGraw-Hill Ryerson, 1974.

——. *Who Do You Think You Are?* Toronto: Macmillan of Canada, 1978.

——. *The Moons of Jupiter.* Toronto Macmillan of Canada, 1982.

——. *Progress of Love.* McClelland and Stewart, A Douglas Gibson Book, 1986.

——. *Friend of My Youth.* Toronto: McClelland & Stewart, 1990.

——. *"What is Real?" Making It New: Contemporary Canadian Stories.* Ed. John Metcalf and (Tim) Struthers. Erin ON: Porcupine's Quill, 1993.

——. *Selected Stories.* Toronto: McClelland & Stewart, 1996.

——. *Love of a Good Woman.* Toronto: McClelland & Stewart, 1998.

——. *The Love of a Good Woman.* Toronto: McClelland & Stewart, 1998. Reprinted Harvest/HBL edition. San Diego: Harcourt Brace Jovanorich Publishers, 1999.

——. *Women and Writing,* ed. Michele Barrett. New York: Harcourt Brace Jovanovich, 1980.

——. "What is Real?, *Making It New: Contemporary Canadian Stories,* Ed. John Metcalf. Toronto: Macmillan, 1978.

——. "Simon's Luck", *The Beggar Maid: Stories of Flo and Rose,* London: Penguin, 1980.

New, W.H. *Canadian Short Fiction: From Myth to Modern,* ed. Vancouver: University of British Columbia Press, 1986.

——. *Dreams of Speech and Violence: The Art of the Short Story in Canada and New Zealand,* Toronto: University of Toronto Press, 1987.

——. "Tense/Present/Narrative: Reflections on English-Language Short Fiction in Canada. Ed. E. Arnold Davidson. Ed. *Introductory & Critical Essays: Studies on Canadian Literature,* The Modern Language Association of America, New York, 1990.

——. Ed. *Encyclopedia of Literature in Canada,* Toronto Buffalo London: University of Toronto Press, 2002.

——. *A History of Canadian Literature,* 2nd ed. Montreal & Kingston. London. Ithaca: McGrill-Queen's University Press, 2003.

Poe, Edgar Allan, review of Nathaniel Hawthorne's Twice-Told Tales, http: //ban2.uibk.ac.at/sg/poe/works/critics/twice—to html, dt 02/08/2006

Stouck, David. *Major Canadian Authors,* 2nd ed. Lincoln & London: University of Nebraska Press, 1988.

Sullivan, Rosemary, Ed. *Stories by Canadian Women,* Toronto: Oxford University Press, 1984.

Toye, William, Ed. *The Concise Oxford Companion to Canadian Literature,* Oxford, New York: Oxford University Press, 2001.

Woodcock, George. *A Place to Stand On: Essays by and about Margaret Laurence* Edmonton: NeWest Press, 1983.

3

The Maze of Munro's Narrative Discourse

Wherever there are humans, there appear to be stories.

(Cobley: 2)

(I)

Narrative discourse represents human experiences and events of life in literary art, like "the motion pictures...moving in space and time" (Krishnaswami: 172). Gerald Prince is of the opinion that: narratology studies the nature, form and functioning of a narrative. More particularly, it examines what all and other narratives have in common, as well as what enables them to be different from one another. Narratology further attempts to account for the ability to produce and understand its working.

A narrative differs from story and plot. A story consists of all the events that have taken place, the plot chains or links up these events in relation to each other. The narrative, on the other hand shows these events, as also the mode of its representation. A narrative moves from a starting point to its end. It is bound up by the sequence of space and time. These play vital roles in fictional works. The French theorist, Paul Ricoeur, in his three volume work *Time and Narrative*, offers his views on 'time'. Commenting on Ricoeur's concept of time in narratives, Paul Cobley observes that "...time is not just a part on the narrative apparatus; in fact, he understands time and narrative as being on intimate terms precisely because narrative is the human relation to time" (Cobley: 17). The sequence of time may be 'objective' or 'subjective', and are intricately linked up in a narrative. It is not bound by linear concept but is related to "expectation and memory" (Cobley: 19). Another important aspect of narratives studied by narratologists is 'dechronologizing'[1] where sequence and time are not regularized. This is evident in most of the modern and postmodern narratives.

In a narrative, the plot governs the succession of the events in a story.[2] To quote Wake in this context: "the most obvious way in which story and plot relate is in terms of time" (Wake: 17). The importance of the study of plot dates back to ancient Greece.

In the fifth and sixth century B.C. Greeks studied the development of prose literature. Questions about fictional representation, its difference from the world of reality, as also the nature of fictional truth were looked into. Plato in his *Republic* distinguished between 'logos' (what is said) and 'lexis' (the way of saying it). He divided lexis into three types: 'diegesis', or simple narrating; 'mimesis or imitation', and the combination of both, as in epic and in other styles of poetry. The distinction between mimesis (showing) and 'diegesis' (telling) in Plato's *Republic* was taken up Aristotle in his *Poetics* and has remained a base for the study of narratology. According to Aristotle, mimesis is a fictional representation that, when composed correctly, improves its readers both intellectually and emotionally. He contended that distinction exists between the dramatic and narrative mode, and that the plot or 'mythos' is a significant element in narrative as it provides the groundwork of a story. He further maintained that good stories must have a beginning, middle and end. The aim of stories is to give pleasure and that the overall effect of the story depends upon its plot construction. For Aristotle all narratives develop longitudinally, from beginning to middle and end.

With the advent of the written form, narrative art became a network of relationships. The form became complex, as it involved the workings of various concepts into a homogeneous entity. Stories revealed interwoven connections and unfathomable depths. Thus, it became "...form of representation implementing signs...bound up with sequence, space and time" (Cobley: 3). Narratives are endowed with a text, a narrator, a listener or a reader. The discourse may be either a descriptive, expository or an argumentative.

The study of narrative art is rooted in structuralism, and Todorov (1969) the French structuralist, was the first to propose the name *narratology* to the study of narrative. Narratological studies proliferated after the 1960s and since then various French, German, Russian and American theorists and researchers have forwarded their concepts, for the study of narrative structures in all literary genres. Vladimir Propp, A.J. Greimas, Claude Levi Strauss and Northrop Frye are amongst many others.[3]

Thus, we may agree, that narratology is the set of general statement on narrative genres, the systematic narrating of a story, and on the structure of plot.

In the first half of the twentieth century, the Russian formalists made a profound impact on the study of narratology. According to them, there were two aspects of narrative: 'fabula' [story] and 'siuzhet' [plot]. Story was a series of events linked together by temporal succession, whereas plot was the artistic arrangement of the events in text. It had a different chronological order and was without casual dependency. Plot also included other artistic elements of structure such as digressions and comments.[4] The formalists based the study of narrative on Russian poetry and folklore.

The Russian formalist, Shklovsky, who concentrated on the internal terms of plot construction, observed that in narrative different categories of plot construction existed such as "staircase", "hook like" and "double plotting." In contrast to Shklovsky, Boris Eikhenbaum laid emphasis on the narrative voice in a tale, which he referred to as the 'skaz'.[5] This he described as a "special type of discourse oriented in its lexicon, syntax and intonation towards the oral speech of the narrator" (Makaryk: 55).

Vladimir Propp gave a comprehensive outline on the working of narratology. In *Morphology of the Folktale* (1928), Propp studied the morphology of 100 folktales and opined that there are 31 functional units in a plot. He showed that no plot contains all the 31 functions. In this context, Wake is of the opinion that in Propp's theory "...all tales can be summarized in terms of the functions that they contain and which, he claims, always appear in the same order" (Wake: 16). Thus, it is seen that Propp was interested in identifying the underlying structures within which the story assumes meaning.

Thus, the Russian Formalists were concerned with the literary qualities of texts. In focusing on the formal aspects of literature, its forms and its use of language, they suggested that "...literature distinguishes itself from non-literary language because it employs a whole range of 'devices' that have a defamiliarizing effect" (Bertens: 49).

The later school known as the 'Prague structuralists'[6] followed the ideas of the Formalists, and pointed out that a literary text is a structure in which all components are interrelated and interdependent. They also emphasized the fact that each text has a function. A text's function is determined by its orientation. Moreover, they replaced the term 'defamiliarization' with 'foregrounding' that drew attention to it. Thus, each structure is seen as inter-related and thereby contributes to the totality of effect.

Until the late 1960s, Propp's theory was largely neglected. It was reviewed by the French structural anthropologist Claude Levi-Strauss, whose discussion of myth in *Structural Anthropology* (1963) identified 'mythemes' the smallest unit which created the myth. He opined that, it is impossible to combine or produce a narrative without reference to an implicit system of units and rules. The guidelines of Propp enabled the French structuralists to theorize on plot structures and their effective workings. Narrative art thus, became not only a representation of life but also a code of culture.

Mikhail Bakhtin, in the late 1920s, formulated his concept of the "polyphonic"[7] novel, which not only meant that a novel has multiple voices and multiple points of view within it, but also referred to the fundamental meaning conveyed through form in the novels of Dostoevsky. In his view, the fundamental unit of language is not the sentence but the concrete utterance, which is shaped by the expected listener as well as the speaker. For Bakhtin, the novel is an interesting form of narrative, as it is "heteroglossic"[8] made up of different voices or 'heteroglot' representing various social situations and characters.

While the Russian Formalists and the Prague Structuralists were preoccupied with form, the French structuralists were concerned with the structure of texts, which they considered more fundamental than form. Structuralism had its origin in the thinking of the Swiss linguist Ferdinand de Saussure (1857-1913). According to Saussure, language has a systematic or (synchronic) as well as a historical or (diachronic) form. He distinguished 'language' (langue) from 'human speech' (langage) and 'speaking' (parole).[9] He was also of the view that human utterance is an individual act, whereas language is a social product. Thus, language is a sign system adopted by a given community for the purposes of oral communication. Saussure maintains that meaning is arbitrary, relational, and is attributed to the object or idea by the human mind, constructed and expressed through language.

Saussurean concept of language and its applicability was subsequently studied and developed by various twentieth century thinkers and critics. Amongst them were the most influential literary critic and semiologist Roland Barthes.[10] His *Mythologies* (1957) is considered a milestone in narrative discourse. His statement, "...narrative is international, transhistorical, transcultural: it is simply there, like life itself (Barthes, 1977: 78) has remained invaluable. According to Barthes, a work is like an onion, with infinite layers. Culler has pointed out that in Barthes theory, a narrative is: "a construction of layers (or levels, or systems), whose body contains, finally, no heart, no kernel, no secret, no irreducible principle, nothing except the infinity of its own envelopes—which envelope nothing other than the unity of its own surfaces" (Culler: 69). Barthes opines that writing is to be disentangled and that the structure can be followed like thread of a stocking, from one point to another. In *S/Z* (1974), Barthes analyzed "Sarrasine", a short story by Balzac, where he identified a set of five codes through which the matrix of the text may be underlined. This analysis not only provided an explanation of structural analysis but also "intertextual construct, the product of various cultural discourses" (Culler: 71). According to Barthes, there is the 'proairetic', code which is the code of actions, and binds the sequence of events within the story. Next is the 'semic' code, which defines objects and places, and is useful for grouping a number of signifiers. This is followed by the 'symbolic' code, which represents a code of binary opposites. The cultural code represents "the form of good and evil, humanity and bestiality, day and night" etc. (Krishnaswamy: 176). Finally there is the hermeneutic code, which has a dual function in relation to time and space. Also understood as 'detours', which create delays, suspense, etc. in the narratives, its function is to push the narrative forward as well as sometimes impede its progress.[11]

Another French structuralist who made significant contribution to the study of narratology was Gerard Genette. "Drawing on Todorov's distinction between 'story' and 'discourse', Genette goes on to distinguish three aspects of narrative reality: 'story' (histoire) meaning the signified or narrative content; 'narrative' (récit), meaning the signifier, discourse or narrative text; and 'narrating' (narration), meaning the narrative act itself" (Waugh: 275). Genette, in his *Narrative Discourse* (1972; trans. 1980) introduced new concepts in terms of relation and presented the existing theories with fresh insights. Firstly, he pointed out the way in which the 'fabula' or chronological sequence of events and action is presented in the 'syuzhet' or story. Here the narrative may be presented in 'analepsis' (flashback) or 'prolepsis' (flash-forward) when it may run ahead of time. Secondly, Genette focused on concept of 'duration' of events. This concept is concerned with the relationship between time taken by an event in reality, and the time that it actually takes to narrate that event. "Equal duration of event and narration may occasionally create unexpected and arresting effects" (Bertens: 72). The third concept is the relationship between the 'frequency', that is the number of times the event happens in actual life and is actually narrated in fiction. For Genette, an event may occur repeatedly but is in fact narrated only once. He uses the term 'iterative' for this narrative technique.

Another area dealt by Genette was the point of view used by the author. In a work of fiction there is the first person narrator 'I' who narrates the story from inside. At other times, there are the third person narratives, in which the narrator would seem to be absent. From Genette's viewpoint, a third person narration must have a narrator and that this narrator is always present in the story. This third person, invisible, implied narrator in a narrative, is not identical with the author. Genette thus by implying an invisible narrator in a third person narrative enables one to see first and third-person narration in terms of the relation of binary of opposites between narrator and character. Genette uses the term 'homodiegetic' for a narration where the narrator speaks in the first person. When the narrator tells us about third person, Genette calls it a 'heterodiegetic' narrative, which is the self versus the other. Genette coins the term 'focalization', which deals with the complicated relationship between narrator and the world that is being narrated.

Genette's narratology enables us to study the principles that govern texts, and helps in its interpretation: "It allows us to map how exactly actual stories are embedded in other stories, how focalization shifts during the course of a story..." (Bertens: 75). Thus, structuralists have analyzed prose narratives, and have related the text to some larger structures, with a network of interconnections.

Wayne Booth in the *Rhetoric of Fiction* (1961) systematized the narrative theory in the U.S.A. Booth introduced the notion of the implied 'author' who embodied the meaning, norms and values of the text. In his theory, Booth differentiated between the real author and the implied author, and showed that the latter is a creation of the former, a persona, deliberately constructed. As regards rhetorical study, Booth defined it as:

> ...all the ways in which stories manage to get themselves told: how authors make them able to do it, and how we mange to play our role in the drama. Authors/texts/readers: we need criticism centering on each of the three, but the full subject is the transaction among them. (Booth: 442)

Other structuralists who made significant contribution to the study of narratives are Edgar Allan Poe, Henry James, Joseph Warren Beach, Percy Lubbock, Norman Friedman, E.M. Forster from England, and Jean Pouillan, Claude-Edmonde Magny in France.

Post structuralism is both a continuation and rebellion against structuralism. In 1966, the French philosopher Jacques Derrida, at a conference at John Hopkins University presented a paper "Structure: Sign and Play in the Human Sciences",[12] where he undermined the Structuralist notion of arbitrary relationship of signs and systems that organize meaning in a text. He argued that in these modern times there has been a radical breakaway from the past, and the decentering of our intellectual universe. Earlier the existence of a norm or centre was taken for granted. However, following the World War and holocaust these centres were destroyed. Sometimes this disintegration also took place because of scientific discoveries, such as the notion of relativity, and the absolutes fixed notions of time and space, or intellectual and artistic revolutions. Derrida pointed out that there are no absolutes only 'free play'.[13]

The post-structuralist critics have also shown that the notion of play is present in the structure that structures undergo change, and also there is more than one structure in a structure. Thus, narrative is pluralistic in nature, and produces pluralistic meanings. This gives rise to the concept that there is inter-textuality in a narrative. Post-structuralists search for the underlying thought or "textual subconscious" (Barry, 73), where meanings may be contrary to surface meaning. They also show that the text is characterized by shifts and disunity, repressed meanings; and produces multiplicities of meanings.

In the study of narratology, psychoanalytical criticism is of great importance. Here, the attention is centered in the telling and interpretation of stories. Freud's notion is that dreams have surface as well as underlying meaning, and this helps in furthering the plot and story. Freud's theory has become vital in the interpretation of texts.

Psychoanalytical criticism was taken up by Jacques Lacan (1908-81), who opined that the unconscious is 'structured like a language', which in turn can highlight important aspects of the life of signs in human societies. Lacan's theory related the unconscious mind to literary process, as human traits find expression through language.

Historiography or historical narratology is another major area that comes under the preview of narrative discourse. History is not an amalgam of figures, but a narrative, which is presented by the historian using his creativity. While identifying the structural components of historical accounts or events, Hayden White theorized: "different levels of conceptualization in historical works: (1) chronicle, (2) story, (3) mode of emplotment, (4) mode of argument, (5) mode of ideological implication" (White, 1973: 5). Historiography thus, becomes the study of historical narratology and its study has been associated with critics such as Erich Auerbach, Roland Barthes, Northrop Frye, and Roman Jacobson.

The early twentieth century saw a different form of narrative, where the multi-faceted human consciousness and experiences were presented through texts. James Joyce's *A Portrait of the Artist as a Young Man* (1916) and Virginia Woolf's *To the Lighthouse* (1927), exemplified the 'modernist' concept, that a number of forces working together determine human consciousness. A modernist narrative is allusive, and complex. In addition, it also features an attempt to explore human identity, and a quest for inner self. In the postmodern epistemology, "...fragmentation is an exhilarating phenomenon, symptomatic of our escape from the claustrophobic embrace of fixed systems of belief...postmodernism rejects the distinction between 'high and popular' art which was important in modernism, and believes in excess, in gaudiness, and in 'bad taste' mixture of qualities" (Barry: 84).

The study of narrative is also concerned with the various narrative levels in a story. In the first place, is the 'metanarrative', where there is more than one level in the story, and is often characterized by a story within the story. Here the character at times assumes the role of a narrator in the story. Genette defines it as: "...a narrative within the narrative" (Genette, 1980: 228). Metanarrative is not a concept of the twentieth century, but is seen in Laurence Sterne's, *The Life and Opinions of Tristram Shandy* (1769-70) and Miguel de Cervantes' *Don Quixote* (1605-15).

Another mode of narrative is 'free indirect discourse', where narrative is presented as a mixed mode of mimesis and the narrator's voice. Here the "voice of the character becomes embedded in the voice of the narrator; thus, the character's habit of speech is present, but direct imitation and quotation marks are not" (Cobley: 231).

Narratives may be 'hard-boiled narrative', prevalent in thrillers and crime fiction. Ernest Hemingway popularized it from 1920 onwards. Here the narrative is devoid of adjectives, adverbs, and has brief sentences. The language too is of the common everyday use.

Metafiction is another form of writing fiction, usually associated with postmodernism. It "...involves one narrative mode being 'ruptured', 'undetermined' or 'invalidated' by another, as when a narrative mode such as *discours* may throw into question a passage of *histoire*" (Cobley: 235).

Narratology has also been associated with feminist studies, and the role of gender in construction of narrative discourses. It has also been applied to postcolonial theory, Marxism, deconstruction, and even film theory. To quote Lyotard in this regard: "Narration is the quintessential form of customary knowledge" (Lyotard, 1984: 19). Thus, we may say that the study of narratology is an essential branch of critical theory and has been incorporated in every form of literary art.

II

To re-read Munro's short stories within the context of narratological theories, and to situate her narrative art against any particular theoretical framework, it is observed that Munro has not followed any set rules of composition. The structure of her work cannot be categorized within any particular narrative theory; rather it incorporates in itself the varied theoretical concepts of modern times. In fact, Munro has established a new narrative form in Canadian fictional literature.

In her fiction. Munro has experimented with various narrative techniques and she has not told the story in the traditional pattern with chronological sequences and conclusive ends. Like Chekhov, her stories do not follow any vertical progression with a beginning, middle and end, but develops horizontically where the events are juxtaposed one against the other. This makes the story appear fragmentary and disjointed. In each story, there are multiple narratives, with one story overlapping the other. Moreover, the progression of the story is not a linear one, but rather a juxtaposition of the time sequences, where the past and present intermingle. While evaluating the craftsmanship of Munro, John Moss has called each story a "jigsaw puzzle" and that, "The elusive genius of a Munro story lies in its refusal to be still, to convey meaning" (Moss: 181). This complex representation of events provokes the reader's mind and defies understanding. In this context, John Moss opines that:

> Each piece seems arbitrary in design, each is an episode, or a thought, a feeling an image, a discreet and separate entity from all the others. As you read, patterns take shape, perimeters fall into place; the patterns change. Munro leaves out just enough pieces that, in the end when you tilt her narrative to the light to admire your readerly craft, it collapses. (Moss: 181)

Munro has not conceptualized her work within a concrete narrative pattern framework, but has framed her narrative to present the complexities of life. She has followed the demands of situation and adjusted the form to the content. Talking about her art Munro has said:

> I seem to turn out stories that violate the discipline of the short story form and don't obey the rules of

> progression for novels. I don't think about a particular form, I think more about fiction, let's say a chunk of fiction. What do I want to do? I want to tell a story, in the old-fashioned way.... What happens to somebody... but I want that 'what happens' to be delivered with quite a bit of interruption, turnarounds, and strangeness. I want the reader to feel something is astonishing...not the 'what-happens' but the way everything happens. These long short story fictions do that best, for me. (Reading Group Centre: Website citation: par. 1)

Again speaking about her art, to Tim Struthers, she remarked:

> I don't think about writing at all. I think very little about writing. I have practically no coherent.... I have no idea or theories about it that I can ever put together.... I don't proceed from any thinking about writing, which may have something to do with the books that influenced me. (Struthers: 13)

Munro was greatly influenced by the writers of the American South; such as, Maxwell, Clark Blaise, Beth Harvor, Audrey Thomas, John Metcalf. Hugh Hood, and Shirley Faessier. However, it was Eudora Wetly who made the greatest impact on Munro. Munro in the *Lives of Girls and Women* adopted Welty's narrative technique and the structure of *The Golden Apples*. She has admitted to Metcalf:

> A very big influence, though, I wouldn't say that I was conscious of the structure being modeled on hers.... It wasn't really modeled but I have to acknowledge an enormous debt to her.... I think more in this matter of vision. (Metcalf: 57)

Her technique of story telling is complex where meanings are oblique and paradoxical. Munro has subverted narrative art, as her fiction is characterized by metanarratives where the plot is complicated by the presence of stories within the story. In her art one finds a piling of layers one on top of the other, where the narrative is revealed through the layers of a variety of retellings.

Munro has also described her narrative art in similar words:

> What I want...is a lot of overlap. I want things to come in as many layers as possible, which means the stories have to come from as many people as possible, with their different baggage of memories. And then I have to hold them still in one frame. (Macfarlane: 53)

Moreover, each sentence in a Munrovian story is embedded with layers of implicit meanings, which the reader has to scan through to arrive at the inner truth. In this context, Beverly J. Rasporich opines that her art has "onion-skinned layers of multiple meanings and levels of reality" (Rasporich: 164). A close reading of her fiction reveals that, Munro explores the secret selves inside the roles and public masks we wear only to discover even deeper and often unfathomable depths to the human personality.

What Munro seems to imply is that human experiences cannot be placed "into neat packages of meaning" (Orange: 89), neither can it be narrated within a definite framework. This results in the story being told in series of events, presented in a disjointed and discontinuous manner to represent the discontinuity of life itself. Carol L. Beran is of the opinion that: "Each reader must construct Munro's story out of fragments of the story and the fragments of the marginalia" (Beran: 266). This presentation of the momentary events of life is a composite feature of Munro's narrative art. Ross is of the opinion that Munro's greatness as an artist lies:

> For stories written with such emotional honesty, compassion, and intimacy that in them the readers recognize their deepest selves. For stories so rich they seem like compressed novels, juxtaposing past against present, and one point of view against another. For creating an indefinable "Munro Country" based on her own experience of Huron County, Ontario. For presenting ordinary life so that it appears luminous, invested with a kind of magic. (Ross: 15)

An immaculate artist, Munro has through her art sought to represent life in its true perspectives. Her narratives convey her vision of life, as also her reflections on the paradoxes of human existence. However, she voices her concern at not being able to truthfully represent life in fiction:

> And even as I most feverishly practice it, I am a little afraid that the work with words may turn out to be a questionable trick, an evasion...an unavoidable lies. (Osachoff: 62)

This attitude summarizes the artist's seriousness and need for perfection in the art and craft of story telling.

A pertinent question that frequently perturbs the readers and critics is why Munro had limited her range to a lesser genre, the short story form. The answer probably lies in the fact, that the protean nature of the genre allowed Munro ample scope to project the marginalized lives of women in its totality. Being a woman, she was sensitive to the varied problems faced by women in their familial and social lives, and this she reflected in her works. Munro's choice of the genre for creativity was therefore a deliberate one, as the enclosed space of the short story became the structure for drawing the limitation of women's space in patriarchal setups. In addition, it provided a platform for voicing her silent protest against the male structures, and the art became a macrocosm within a microcosm. In an interview with Alan Twig, she revealed her interest for this particular form:

> I've never known why I've chosen the short story form. I guess in a short story you impose discipline rather soon. Things don't get away of other forms where things just flow *out*...something about that makes me very uneasy. I could never do it.... I'm not afraid spontaneity would betray me because I've done some fairly self-exposing things. But I'm afraid it would be repetitious and boring if I wrote that way. It's as if I must take great care over everything. Instead of splashing the colors out and trusting they will all come together, I have to know the design.... I really wanted to write a novel of [the story in 'Something I've Been Meaning to Tell You']. Then it just sort of boiled down like maple syrup. (Twigg: 16)

Recently she again said that she cannot write a novel:

> I lose interest...God knows I still keep trying. But there always comes a point where everything seems to be getting really flat. You don't feel the tension. (Twigg: 15)

For Munro, the short story was not simply a straight road, but a house, where one entered and stayed on for a while:

> ...so when I write a story I want to make a certain kind of structure, and I know the feeling I want to get from being inside that structure.... There is no blueprint for the structure. It's not a question of "I'll make this kind of house because if I do it right it will have this effect." I've got to make, I've got to build up, a house, a story to fit around the indescrible "feeling" that is like the soul of the story, and which I must insist upon in a dogged, embarrassed way, as being no more definable that. (Hancock: 332)

Thus, the soul of the story is of vital importance for Munro. This attitude towards her art reflects her artistry, as well as her mission to represent life in its true perspectives.

Talking to Gibson of her particular choice, she expressed the view that she wrote: "on...a single string, a tension string...I don't write...as some people say a true novelist does, manipulating a lot of strings" (Gibson: 258).

Again, she said:

> I don't like writing novels... I get lost doing them and bored, and I don't know how to do them. That's what terrified me that people would just get bored with the detail of very small incidents. (*The Globe and Mail:* 1)

It seems that, writing of short stories allowed Munro to have a firm grip on the design, narrative structure of her work as well as enabled her to manipulate the language of the text to suit her artistic requirements. Moreover, it became a text, which provided a reading into women's lives. The aim of her writings was not only to project life in its totality, but also to, "...insistently explores what lies beyond the bounds of empirical reality" (Heble: 4). Munro's writings therefore embody a search for the existential truth of life.

Like Hemmingway's, the stories of Munro are elliptical in form, rarely tying up the loose threads of narrative into conclusive ends. Metaphorical in nature, the stories abound with paradoxes and parallels. An important mode of narrative technique employed by Munro is the use of parody in her writings. Her collection *Who Do You Think You Are?*, is in the form of picaresque novel, and is a female quest for the inner self. In addition, it presents a dichotomy between the world of fantasy and reality.

Munro's stories are historio-cultural discourses, where the artist re-writes history giving it a fictional touch. The Great Depression of the thirties figures in most of her stories where Munro questions the given facts of history, and fictionalizes the events. Moreover, her stories contextualize the socio-cultural setup, and looks at the lives of the women from a close angle. Each story, questions the conventional norms imposed on women, and presents women's growing consciousness and the reflective self. Thus, we see that her protagonists, mostly girls and women, experience multiple challenges in the course of their lives from childhood to maturity, and this in turn provides scope for the evolution of the self. The cultural norms, which govern women's lives, are previewed through her art of storytelling and narrative skills. Munro's art problematizes women's subjectivity, their inability to articulate their latent desires and emotions, in their situated lives. Moreover, she very subtly conveys the view that it is difficult to comprehend the happenings in life. The aim of art is to present reality, and for Munro, art becomes the perfect vehicle for probing lives, which are, in Munro's own words: "Solitary and meshed.... Buried and celebrated" (York: 50).

As for the focalization of her stories, it is observed that like Katherine Mansfield, Munro uses the 'free indirect discourse', that is the blend of a first person and third person narrator. *Lives of Girls and Women* has a first person narrator, while *Who Do You Think You Are?* has an omniscient narrator, narrating the events that take place in the life of the protagonist. In these two collections, Munro uses the interlinked or chaining form of narrative with chorological sequences. In other collections, there are multiple narrators narrating in both the first and third person.

Another important aspect of Munro's narrative art is that, it delves into the human psyche, and tries to unravel the hidden self in human beings. Almost all her stories can be re-read from a psychoanalytical approach. While the childhood and the adolescent mind is examined in many stories in *Dance of the Happy Shades,* Munro shifts her focus to the evolution of the mind in its stages of progression from adolescence to maturity in her interconnected collections. *Lives of Girls and Women* and *Who Do You Think You Are?* Others traverse into adulthood, maturity and even impending death. Narrated either in the first or third person viewpoint, these stories present an "emotional depth" and intense range of feelings of "ordinary people" (Toye: 344) as they overcome the challenges of life.

As a structural device, Munro uses the letter and diary form, as also dream sequences, poems and family history to draw up her stories.

In the collection of her stories, Munro has not adhered to one narrative technique. As is observed, there is a progression from simple narrative techniques in her first collection to more and more complex forms in her later art. Talking about her technique of story telling, she tells Tim Struthers that the technique requires to be changed over and again, to make the story telling more 'effective' and more 'appropriate'.

> The technique probably has to change to keep you interested in working.... I think, for change in technique, not that there's necessarily a development but that it maybe assists you to a fresh perception. What I think is important is the fresh perception, which, again you may delude yourself that you are getting, but you wouldn't keep on working unless you thought you were getting it. (Struthers: 13)

This results in the story being unfathomable and open-ended. In this context, Magdalene Redekop is of the view that:

> Munro's stories are notoriously resistant to interpretation because they are like gossip: the best

> response is an answering story.... For that feeling you have when reading a Munro story that you are reading about your own life.... Like Homer, Munro is a genius at deploying the formulas and commonplaces, that make up our lives. (Redkop: 26)

As for the subject matter, Munro has set her stories in her native hometown Ontario where her roots really were. Her art documents the small town of South Western Ontario where she had spent the major part of her life. In this context Rasporich observes "Alice Munro's Ontario, is the source of her vision and the poetics of her prose, it is also an expression of her first truth that place is the psyche's fortress'" (Rasporich, 158). The fictions "...offer social chronicles...with precise attention to domestic surfaces and social decorum, though they also retail socially unspeakable events and their scandalous stories of transgression and desire as well as provocative speculations on the mysteries and secrets hidden within ordinary lives" (Howells: *Encyclo,* 770).

For Munro, memory plays a key role in fictional narratives as it has the power to shape our lives. In her own words:

> Memory is the way we keep telling our stories—and telling other people a somewhat different version of our stories. We can hardly manage our lives without a powerful ongoing narrative. And all these edited, inspired, self-serving or entertaining stories there is, we suppose, some big bulging awful mysterious entity called THE TRUTH, which our fictional stories are supposed to be poking at and grabbing pieces of. What could be more interesting as a life occupation? One of the ways we do this, I think, is by trying to look at what memory does (different tricks at different stages of our lives.) and at the way the same (shared) experience. The more disconcerting the differences are, the more the writer in me feels an odd exhilaration. (Reading Group Center; Website citation. par. 1)

A typical Munro story is a ramble that includes sudden shifts of time, place, and subject, the reasons for which are often not immediately clear. In her art of story telling, Munro uses the conversational style, and there is a sudden shift in the sequence of the story. In *Dance of the Happy Shades,* the narrator says in the midst of her narration: "To change the subject..." or "I have forgotten to say what the foxes were fed" (Dance: 118). Munro seems to adopt this strategy to create the impression that what we read, are events taken from our own lives. It is observed that, Munro's narrators, while narrating their stories do not come to any conclusive ends, but rather leaves the stories open-ended for the readers to arrive at their meanings. Through her narrative art, which is at once paradoxical and ambivalent, Munro portrays life realistically in its minute details. In this context, Gerald Noonan says that the "Structure of stories...juxtaposes the complexities of life in life and art" (Noonan: 177).

As for the mode of narration, it is seen that, Munro uses both the first person "I" as also the third person omniscient viewpoint. The third person narration offers the reader a view of the setting of the story, and the flickering of thoughts, emotion, etc. in the mind of the narrator. In the later stories, we find that there is a shift to third person narration. In *Who Do You Think You Are?* Munro presents a third person narrator, who narrates the experiences of Rose, the protagonist, her thoughts, sensations and view of life.

Munro has artistically employed time sequencing as a narrative device for plot development. She manipulates the time sequence, and thereby synchronizes the past and the present along parallel lines. Thus, we find a departure from the traditional method, as well as a linear progression in the art of story telling.

A remarkable feature of Munro's art is that she consciously avoids a didactic and rhetorical direction. She did not believe in moralization of art but rather the perfection of the form so that it presented real life in art. In the Foreword to the *Dance of the Happy Shades* Hugh Garner says:

> Not only do real people, situations and places—yes, and our memories of those we have known—become the paint and clay of the artist in words but they come to

> life in the hearts and minds of the readers. (*Dance*, "Foreword": p. ix)

An analysis of the collections, show that Munro's narrative art underwent gradual transition from a casual depiction of incidents of life in the first collection, to a portrayal of the complexities of human nature, relationship and diverse situations of life in the subsequent works. Munro's concept of flux in life, and the significance of the past as it alter and remake the present, are evident here. Her art of making the narrators traverse back and forth in memory is a technique, which she adopts in most of her narratives.

Dance of the Happy Shades (1968),[14] Munro's first publication, which brought her the Governor General's award, was structured, as she told Struthers—to show not progression, but...

> ...for variety. I think that my editor and I arranged [them] so that you wouldn't be getting a big lump of stories with this 'I' person who obviously wasn't always the same person, so that the reader wouldn't be led to expect that this was a kind of segmented novel or something. (Struthers: 20)

Thacker is of the opinion that the fifteen stories in this collection, "brings her two separate narrative approaches together within one story" by "a commingling of...first-person commitment and third-person detachment" (Thacker: 50). Stories in *Dance of the Happy Shades* are therefore multi-voiced, incorporating diverse experiences of life. The stories in this collection provide the groundwork for Munro's later works. Ajay Heble opines:

> While the stories here are more accessible, more conventional than the stories, which appear in her recent collections, while the plot may be more easily discernible and the strategies of narration more straightforward, there are...suggestions of absent and potential relationships.... (Heble: 19)

The critic also remarks that the opening story in the collection "...operates, in many ways, as a microcosm for the whole of Munro's work. The concerns which run throughout her fiction are presented in this piece..." (Heble: 20).

In an interview, conducted several years after the publication of *Dance of the Happy Shades,* Munro said that the art of fiction was concerned with "the whole business of how life is made into a story by the people who live it" (Struthers: 33). The quest for inner self, by the protagonists, and their inner voice speaking out, or trying to speak out in various situations of life is also initiated in this collection, and which will recur in her subsequent stories.

The first two stories "Walker Brothers Cowboy" and "Images" are written on similar thematic pattern, where Munro presents a child's initiation into the adult world of experience. In the stories, the perception, critical assessment and inward thoughts of the child narrators become the prime theme. A common feature in both the stories is the retrospective technique, where the narrator now an adult recaptures the childhood days. Narrated in the first person, both the stories present the change and growth towards maturity of the young narrators.

In "Walker Brothers Cowboy". Munro presents the psychological changes that the child narrator undergoes as she observes the adult world of her father. For her, the metaphorical change and the difference between the reality and appearance, perturbs her observant mind, and she understands that the grownup world is full of lies and deception, which remain strange and mysterious. She observes:

> I feel my father's life flowing back from our car in the last of the afternoon, darkening and turning strange, like a landscape that has an enchantment on it, making it kindly, ordinary and familiar, while you are looking at it, but changing it, once your back is turned, into something you will never know, with all kinds of weathers, and distances you cannot imagine. (*Dance:* 18)

The story thus brings to the mind of the reader, the fact that events and happenings are a composite part of life and that one cannot know the entire truth of life. W.R. Martin is of the view that, "Walker Brothers Cowboy"

> ...combines the vividness of the child and the maturity of the adult perspective in the same narrative, moves the protagonist through the pattern of the spiral, from the strange to the familiar and then back again to the mysterious, and at the same time conveys intensities and profundities in the child's experience. We are moving into the world of *Lives of Girls and Women.* (Martin: 51).

The story thus sets the groundwork for Munro's later works. The quest for the truth of life and existence, which forms the fundamental of all Munro's work, finds its first expression here.

"Images", however differs in a small way, as here too the perceptive child observes the out-door world in contrast to the narrator in the first story, who senses difference inside the house. Here too, the father's name is Ben Jordan, and a similar sense of insecurity grips the mind of the child, as she tries to come to terms with life. The dramatic progression of the story can be observed, towards the end, as the narrator feels "our fears are based on nothing but truth" (*Dance:* 43).

The final paragraph of "Images" like that of "Walker Brothers Cowboy" sums up the child's attitude to the grown-up world:

> Like the children in fairy stories who have seen their parents make pact with terrifying strangers...but who come back fresh from marvelous escapes and take up their knives and forks, with humility and good manners, prepared to live happily ever after—like them dazed and powerful with secrets, I never said a word. (*Dance*: 43-44)

Taken as a whole, both these stories delve into child psychology and present the story from a child's perspectives.

"Boys and Girls" is yet another story, where Munro probes into the child's consciousness as also its reactions to the adult world. In this story, Munro through her narrative presents the minute details of a girl child's insight into life. The story also appears to be an eye-opener on the social complexities and obligations imposed upon the female from the early formative years of her life. It shows the evolution of the conscious self towards the realization of the inner self. Written in the first person narrative, the story presents flashback technique, where the now adult woman, looks back at her childhood experience. Read as a feminist text, "Boys and Girls" is one of Munro's masterpieces. Here the author presents a binary of opposites in life. The narrator's father is a fox farmer who raises silver fox in pens, pelts fox fur and trades with the "Hudson Bay Company or the Montreal Fur Traders" (*Dance:* 113). At the beginning, a contrast is presented between the life of the Mother and that of the Father. While the world of the mother was concentrated, within the house, the father's world was on the outside, in the barn. The young narrator was more akin to the world of her father and had a tremendous dislike for the life within the house. A note of revolt is thus evident in the attitude of the narrator, as she tries to defy the social codes set for girls and thereby tries to assert her independence of mind. Like the narrators of "Walker Brothers Cowboy" and "Images", the young girl here too suffers from a sense of insecurity. The story however takes a dramatic turn towards the later part. Munro suddenly maneuvers our attention towards the central action of the story. It culminates in the action of setting Flora free, by the narrator and thereby save the horse from being slaughtered by her father. "Instead of shutting the gate, I opened it as wide as I could. I did not make any decision to do this; it was just what I did" (*Dance:* 129). This story, presupposes that the narrator by acting to her own impulses reveals her subconscious desire for freedom.

> The word girl had formerly seemed to me innocent and unburdened, like the word child; now it appeared that it was no such thing. A girl was not, as I had supposed, simply what I was; it was what I had to become. (*Dance:* 121)

Here, the urge to break the patriarchal binaries and self-reflexivity of the narrator is focused by Munro in her art.

In other stories of the *Dance of the Happy Shades,* "Thanks for the Ride", "Red Dress-1946" and "Ounce of

Cure", Munro is concerned with the emotional upheavals that adolescents encounter during their teenage. The acute state of restlessness and dejection that characterizes adolescence is evident in "An Ounce of Cure". Munro's narrative art acquires new dimension here. Her protagonists have appeared here as participant and as observers in the act of narration. Through the interaction of these two modes, Munro is able to present coherently the whole significance of a story's dramatized event.

In "Thanks for the Ride", Munro initiates a newer technique, that of bringing in both the first person and the third person narrator. The protagonist Dick is the sole male narrator in this collection. The story centers on Dick, who is both an observer as well as a detached participant. It is interesting to note that throughout the story, Lois does not utter more than a dozen lines. Herein, Munro through her art shows that silence at times conveys more meaning than articulation. "Dick is, as the reader can see, observing, describing, participating, and remembering, seemingly all at once" (Thacker: 52).

Munro achieves great heights in her artistry with "Thanks for the Ride". The retrospective narrative technique conjures up a situation that is simple enough, but it conveys the intricacies of relationships and adolescent character—wayward and defiant, while the mother remains a passive observer.

In "Day of the Butterfly", Munro reverts to the terrain of child's consciousness, with its typical reminiscent art. Robert Thacker is of the opinion that this is the "first story which reveals a remembering narrator actively shaping the stuff of her memories...presenting an impression of immediacy and a detached understanding...and that in it Alice Munro is moving towards being able to fuse observer and participant within one narrative voice" (Thacker: 43). In the subsequent stories "The Shining Houses", "The Office" and "Postcard", Munro takes up the problems of adult women, who are in the prime of their lives. Here, the experiences of the narrators are complicated by social conditions, and individual requirements. "A Trip to the Coast" is one of the longest stories in this collection. Munro is quoted to have told Metcalf that it is "a throwback to the almost formula stories" (Metcalf: 58). Here, the grandmother of the independent and self-reliant May, meets her sudden end, when a young man hypnotizes her to death. Munro juxtaposes a contrast of life and situations, and two different attitudes towards life. While the grandmother is stern and rigid, the young May longs her freedom. Yet when she ultimately gets it, with her grandmother's death, she sits "with her legs folded under her looking out at the road where she might walk now in any direction she liked..." (*Dance:* 191).

"The Peace of Utrecht", is considered Munro's first autobiographical story. In an interview to Metcalf, she revealed "...first really painful autobiographical story...the first time I wrote a story that tore me up" (Metcalf: 58). Referring to this work of art Martin observes:

> At the end of "The Peace of Utrecht" the ironic snapping of the trap on Maddy is almost in the manner of Maupassant or Maugham...", "The Peace of Utrecht" is Alice Munro's *Mansfield Park*. In it, like Jane Austen in her novel, she does not achieve her highest technical brilliance, but she does probe and explore new themes and with greater profundity, and in ways that lay a basis for her mature work. (Martin: 44-45)

A reading of the story shows that there is a close resemblance between the events narrated in the text and the author's life.

Munro has herself, laid great significance to this work. She says:

> Half the stories in the first book [Dance of the Happy Shades] are sort of beginning stories and then they start getting closer and closer to autobiography]...["The Peace of Utrecht"] was very close, and from then on this was the only kind of story I wrote". (Gibson: 31)

Munro thus emerges, as a more matured writer, and the sensibilities, emotions, etc. that forms the foundation of her works, will now be examined in her subsequent writings.

Lives of Girls and Women, Munro's second fiction was intended to be a novel, but was later written in the form of inter-related stories. Narrated in the first person, the stories are told retrospectively by Del, as a matured woman, looking back at the early childhood and adolescence experiences of her life. The work traces the various events of Del's life as she steps into adolescence but leaves out the later period of her life. The setting of the stories is again the small Southwestern Ontario town of Jubilee, where Del grows up, and dreams of becoming a writer. Written in the form of a *Bildungsroman*, the work traces the different stages of her mental, emotional, educational transition and growth. The work is divided into eight sections, with separate titles, each showing the different stages of Del's life, and its associate experience.

> The title signals Del's insistently pluralized vision as she moves between real and invented worlds. 'The Flats Roads' offers a child's view of some of the eccentric characters who live on the borders of Jubilee, while 'Heirs of the Living Body' is concerned with family history and inheritance; 'Baptizing' tell of Del's first passionate love affair and her resistance to traditional female plots; 'Epilogue: The Photographer' offers a comment on the writer's problems of representing real life within fiction. (Howells: *Encyclo*, 770)

Although, the stories are arranged chronologically, each section is self-contained, and can stand on its own. Munro's narrative now undergoes a transformation from her earlier art Notable is the fact that, the point of view here is presented simultaneously, by a child and an adult. Memory and imagination play significant roles, as the narrator recapitulates the incidents of childhood, recollects them, and then narrates those experiences at a later stage in life. In this process, fact and fiction co-mingle in art. Moreover, the narrator remains all throughout a detached observer of life. When questioned about this device, Munro said:

> The adult narrator has the ability to detect and talk about the confusion [of the child]. I don't feel that the confusion is ever resolved. And there is some kind of a

> central mystery, as in "Walker Brothers Cowboy", that is there for the adult narrator as well as it was for the child. I feel that all life becomes even more mysterious and difficult. And the whole act of writing is more an attempt at recognition than of understanding because I don't understand many things. I feel a kind of satisfaction in just approaching something that is mysterious and important. Then writing is an act of approach and recognition. I believe that we don't solve these things—in fact our explanation take us further away. (Thacker: 54)

Munro's narrative art thus delves deep into the recess of human heart and seeks to reveal its strange workings.

Talking about the composition of *Lives of Girls and Women,* Munro told John Metcalf:

> I didn't begin [Lives of Girls and Women] at the beginning. I began it with the Princess Ida section and I wrote it right from there to the end of 'Baptizing' and then...I went back and wrote the first two chapters which I think have less vitality.... I think the middle and the later parts of the book...except for the epilogue...are the best parts...there is another section that I'm not happy about either, that I didn't get to work properly... the one on the girl's religious experiences when she was young. (Metcalf: 60-61)

The question of whether *Lives of Girls and Women* is a novel or linked stories. Munro asked Metcalf:

> ...would you say [Lives of Girls and Women consists of] organically linked stories? Here is the similarity to [Eudora Welty's] *The Golden Apples,* which I would think of in my mind as a novel but many people wouldn't. ("A Conversation": 60)

Some years later Munro said:

> ...I see [Who Do You Think You Are?] definitely as linked stories, and lives as an episodic novel. If [Who Do You Think You Are?] is going to be judged as a novel it doesn't work because it doesn't explain enough, whereas

'Lives' explains enough for that period of Del's life". (Carole Gerson: 4)

Again she told Metcalf that she was "...not even very clear on the distinction" ("A Conversation" 60). In the same interview, she complained that the short story "wins one so little respect" (Metcalf: 61), and that "I don't feel that a novel is any step up from a short story" (Gibson: 258).

Although , the *Lives of Girls and Women* is a more matured work, than *Dance of the Happy Shades,* and brought Munro acclamation of consummate artist, yet she was dissatisfied with the concluding chapter "Epilogue: The Photographer". This she expressed to Graeme Gibson. Again she told Metcalf that she wrote this "over an over again", but that "it doesn't satisfy me at all. It doesn't express what I wanted it to.... I was trying to deal with something fairly complex there" (Metcalf: 60).

Munro had once intended to name her next work, "Real Life", though it was later on published as *Lives of Girls and Women.* In this book, Munro has given an accurate depiction of life of Canadian women in the 1940s and their socio-economic and religious situations, within a narrative structure where fact and fiction seems to coalesce.

Something I've Been Meaning to Tell You,[15] Munro's next 'multi-voiced collection' presents the artist's mastery of the narrative technique, and her ability to present superbly, the complex situations of life in fiction. Instead of presenting the stories in conventional linear form, Munro in this volume uses time sequences more freely and flexibly, to suit the demands of story. Like her previous collection *Dance of the Happy Shades,* these stories are fragmentary narratives, based on momentary events in life of various individuals. Each narrator here is a matured individual, who look back at the past experiences, with irony and renewed interest, and narrates them from a new angle of vision. It is a re-construction of the past, in the light of the present. What Munro seems to emphasize here through these narratives is that life is a continuous process of flux and change, and that events acquire new meaning and significance with the passage of time. In addition, through the process of storytelling, the happenings of the past are made fictitious as they are coloured by the narrator's imaginative powers. Thus, a blend of realism and fantasy is evident in these narratives. Another singular feature of these unlinked stories is that, here the narrators' shuttle back and forth in time, with the consequence that there is sometimes a gap of twenty years or more between the actual happening and the narration. This retrospective technique accounts for the ambiguous nature of the stories, and the difficulties of interpretation.

A Munrovian story, when deconstructed is open to multiple meanings, as each sentence is paradoxical in nature. The use of inter-textuality by Munro also adds to the ambivalence of the narration. Moreover, there are abrupt shifts in time and settings. John Orange has categorized the entire collection under three narrative heads. In the first place, Munro employs the 'conventional narratives' containing familiar themes and settings (Orange: 88), where she follows a linear progressive art. The stories in this category are; "How I met My Husband", "The Found Boat", Executioners", "Winter Wind", "The Ottawa Valley", and "Forgiveness in Families". In the second group, Munro tells the stories in a disjointed manner and the narratives are never completed, leaving the impression that the pain and sufferings that the women undergo cannot be fully expressed. In addition, one cannot provide a full explanation of their occurrence. This group includes "Material", "Tell Me Yes or No" and "The Spanish Lady". A close reading of these stories leaves the mind disturbed, as it fails to explain the unresolved mysteries of life. In the third group, the narratives become more and more complex as the narrators are "unable to control their memories, let alone understand events in their present lives" (Orange: 89). These stories are "Something I've Been Meaning to tell You", "Walking on Water". "Marrakech", and Memorial" (*Something*: 89). Narrated in the third person, these stories reveal intricate workings of the human heart, the failure and misfortunes of life, and the existence of a secret self beneath the mask.

In *Something I've Been Meaning to Tell You,* Munro reveals the complexities of human relationships and familial bonds. In the title story, Munro presents an intricate relationship amongst two sisters Et Char and Char's husband Arthur. Into this triangular relationship, there is Blakie their friend, who was at one time attracted to Char. An ambivalent relationship pervades amongst the two sisters, as Et seems to be jealous of Char; the mysterious death of Char, and Et's failure to tell Arthur of her true inner feelings—leaves a gap in the narrative. This barrier of communication, the inability to express oneself, becomes the base of her other stories as well.

In "Material", we see that the narrator intends to write a letter to her ex-husband 'Hugo', which she can never complete. *"This is not enough, Hugo. You think it is, but it isn't. You are mistaken Hugo"* (*Something:* 44). Told in the form of a confession, it tells us of the past life of the narrator, her relationship with Hugo, her former husband. The memories of her past come to her mind as she comes across the autobiography of Hugo, who was a writer of repute. She realizes that his story reveals only the half-truth, and that he had used the story of Dotty, the daughter of their former landlady as material for his work, which he had manipulated for his own ends. For the narrator, art should always reflect the truth, which was the moral duty of the artist to represent. The narrator thus shuttles back and forth between her past and present, to narrate the story of her life. Now, as she recapitulates the past she feels strange to realize: "...that we shared, still shared, the same bank of memory, and that what was all scraps and oddments, useless baggage, for me, was ripe and usable, a paying investment, for him" (*Something*: 43).

The same thematic device of doubt and uncertainty, as well as difference between appearance and reality, dominates the other stories in this collection. In "How I Met my Husband", an airman, trifles with the narrator's feelings and flies away with the promise that he would write to her soon. "I'm going to write you a letter. I'll tell you where I am and maybe you can come and see me..." (*Something*: 60). The narrator waits for the mail, but no letter ever comes. Then it dawns upon her "No letter was ever going to come" (*Something*: 65). The story ends with the mailman telling his children of how he met their mother. The narrator puts it in this way:

> He always tells the children the story of how I went after him By sitting by the mailbox every day, and naturally I laugh and let him, because I like to think what pleases them and makes them happy. (*Something*: 66)

In "Tell Me Yes or No"; the narrator begins the story by saying 'I persistently imagine you dead' (*Something*: 106). The story narrated in the sequence of flashback, where the narrator retrospect and tells us of her life, twenty years back. Here, the whole story is addressed to the narrator's lover, whose death she comes to know from a news caption. She then visits his city, where his present wife hands her a packet of letters. She goes through them and is shocked to learn of his betrayal of her trust and love. The story ends with the narrator's statement that she had taken recourse to the strategies of fiction to tell the story of her life:

> I invented you, as far as my purposes go. I invented loving you and I invented your death. I have my tricks and my trap doors, too. I don't understand their workings at the present moment', but I have to be careful; I won't speak against them. (*Something*: 124)

In this context. Gerald Noonan comments on the mysterious working of the human heart, as the "half fraudulent artifices of literature": In the course of Munro's canon of short stories, a similar development occurs: the early importance of "detail and solidity" is overmastered by "tricks" and "trap doors" of fiction (Noonan: 176).

The mystery of human heart again forms the subject matter of "The Spanish Lady". Here we are faced with the puzzle, as to how to define reality that is illusory, and the difference between reality and fiction. The narrator tells us the story that she had once met a Rosicrucian, who could tell her of her previous births: "One hundred and forty-four years. That is the span from the start of one life to the next" (*Something*: 185). He also tells her that she was a Spanish Lady in her previous birth. The mysteries of life and death continue to puzzle the reader as the story progresses. At the end of the story, the narrator is shocked into a "message" (*Something*: 190). As she sees the sudden death of an old man on a slum bench in Hastings Street, it dawns on her that:

> What we say and feel no longer rings true, it is slightly beside the point. As if we were all wound up a long time ago and were spinning out of control, whirring, making noises, but at a touch could stop, and see each other for the first time, harmless and still. (190-91)

Suspense, mystery, doubt, recognition and acceptance of the mysteries of the universe, continues to be the theme of all the stories in this collection. "The Ottawa Valley" which closes this collection is autobiographical in tone. Here Munro reminisces of her dead mother, who appears in a dream. This appearance of her mother becomes a recurrent phenomenon in most of her later stories. As she says:

> And she is the one of course that I am trying to get; it is to reach her that this whole journey has been undertaken. With what purpose? To mark her off, to describe, to illumine, to celebrate, to *get rid,* of her; and it did not work, for she looms too close, just as she always did. She is heavy as always, she weighs everything down, and yet she is indistinct, her edges melt and flow, which means she has stuck to me as close as ever and refused to fall away, and I could go on, applying what skills I have, using what tricks I know, and it would always be the same. (*Something*: 246)

In *Who Do You Think You Are?*[16] Munro returns to the story-cycle form, which she employed in *Lives of Girls and Women*. Dedicated to her second husband, Gerald Fremlin, the book was released under the title *The Beggar Maid: Stories of Flo and Rose* in the United States and the United Kingdom. It had a reference to the legend of King Cophetua who, like Lord Henry, Brinthrop, married a beggar maid.

During the period of writing of this book. Munro had come to Huron County to live in Clinton. Talking about the source of this work of fiction, Munrd said that her husband Gerry provided the material for the opening chapter "Royal Beatings", when he was reading the local newspapers, as part of his newspaper preservation project. The incident was recorded in Clinton, around 1885, when a man suspected of incest, was dragged out of his house into the snow around midnight and horsewhipped by a vigilante group, with blackened faces. The man left the town for London, where he died of pneumonia, in the YMCA. Munro said that she wanted the incident to be there, despite the readers who say, "Why write about anything so depressing?" and towns people who feel that "use of this story is a deliberate exposure, taunt, and insult" (Metcalf & Struthers: 225-26). In another interview to Struthers, Munro said that she was interested in "...how life is made into a story by the people who live it, and then the whole town sort of makes its own story" (Struthers: 33).

Written in ten sections, the work, like *Lives of Girls and Women,* records the diverse episodes in the life of Rose, the protagonist, as she traverses through life. These linked stories, illuminate one aspect of Rose's life at a time, in chronological order. However, each section is compact in form and can be read on its own as a short story, without its loosing meaning or coherence. In this aspect, Munro's view is that the art of story writing should be such, that:

> ...I can start reading them...anywhere; from beginning to end, from end to beginning, from any point in between in either direction. So obviously, I don't take up a story and follow it as if it were a road, taking me somewhere, with views and neat diversions along the way. I go into it, and move back and forth and settle here and there, and stay in it for a while. It's more like a house. Everybody knows what a house does, how it encloses space and makes connections between one enclosed space and another and presence what is outside in a new way. This is nearest I can come to explaining what story does for me and what I want my stories to do for other people. (Metcalf & Struthers: 332)

This structural code is followed here, as the stories can be read as individual units, while at the same time it has the extended form of a novel. Narrated in the third person, it recounts Rose's experiences, as she looks at life as a detached observer in order to find an answer to the riddle of life. The structural pattern of the story here is of paramount importance, as Munro through her narrative art juxtaposes the different episodes in the life of Rose in order to present a symmetrical pattern of her life, as she moves from young age to maturity. Reading the events, one is therefore required to fit in, or rearrange the pieces as in a jigsaw puzzle in order to draw a holistic picture of Rose's life. To present these complicacies of life in an artistic manner, here too, Munro, as in her previous creations, breaks up the time sequence, and shifts abruptly, between the past and the present. "The juxtopositioning of episodes from different times also adds an ironic commentary, and character and reader alike have to shift perspectives of reality as we move through life" (Orange: 96).

A reading of the text reveals that the first chapter "Royal Beatings" deals with Roses's childhood, as she grows up in West Hanratty, Ontario. Here she lives with her father and stepmother Flo, and her "half brother" Brian. We also come to know that she is many a times flogged by her father, "cracking the belt at her when he can, then abandoning it and using his hands" (*Who*: 21). The part of the town where they lived was inhabited by "bootleggers and prostitutes and unsuccessful thieves" (*Who*: 5). During the pre-World War-II, Rose grew up on the other side of the bridge in West Han ratty which was a place of "legendary poverty" (*Who*: 6). For their neighbor they had people like Becky Tyde who was "big-headed loud-voiced dwarf.... A twisted neck that forced her to hold head on one side...had been sick with polio as a child..." (*Who*: 7). The chapter is drawn to a close with a reference to a T.V. interview with Mr. Wilfred Nettleton of Hanratty a horsewipper in the Wawanash Country Home, where Flo will be taken later on after the loss of her mental balance.

Munro in this fiction presents the darker aspects of life with characters that are either deformed or ill or maimed. Throughout the book, there are many such creations, as 'Franny McGill', senile and old in "Spelling"; Milton Homer, the town fool, Ralph Gillespie, who skillfully imitates Milton Homer. We are also lead to tragic situations as Rose's father dies of lung cancer; and her lover Simon dies of cancer of the pancreas.

In the next two chapters, "Privilege" and "Half a Grapefruit" Munro highlights Rose's early schooldays, her encounter with three big girls in the entrance class, and the fierce boys who later joined the army during the war. At the high school, Rose wants: "badly to align herself with towners as against her place of origin" (*Who*: 38), and is very sensitive about the "country phrases", "the country habit of teasing" (*Who*: 51). She is also ashamed of the coarseness of Flo and her cousin Billy Pope, who "worked in butcher shop" and who "used to actually live at the slaughterhouse" (*Who*: 46). During this period, she would bring home a pile of books to read every night (*Who*: 44). She reads *The Garden Party,* and is angry because "...she was sure Katherine Mansfield was never obliged to look at stained underwear"; the fact that she imagines herself not acting Lady Macbeth but "she imagined herself *being* her, being Lady Macbeth" (*Who*: 58-59).

In "Wild Swans", Rose leaves home alone, for the city of Toronto. Prior to her departure, Flo cautions her about "White Slaves" (*Who*: 67) and "people dressed up as ministers" (*Who*: 68), who get after her money. Rose ignores her. However, in the train, a man claiming to be from the United Church minister sits down beside her, and under the pretext of reading the newspaper, slides his hand under her skirt and starts groping and touching her body. "The minister's hand was not or not yet, at all welcome to her. It made her feel uncomfortable, resentful, slightly disgusted, trapped and wary. But she could not take charge of, to reject it. She could not insist that it was there, when he seemed to be insisting that it was not" (*Who*: 75). Munro's description of the scenery outside and the molestation inside the compartment is embedded with double meaning. "As the train crossed the Niagara Escarpment" to "exploding from it taking to the sky" (*Who*: 76-77).

The middle of the fiction is made up of "The Beggar Maid", "Mischief", "Providence" and "Simon's Luck".

In "The Beggar Maid", Rose joins the University, falls in love with Patrick Blatchford, a student of history and finally makes up her mind to marry him. Her first meeting with Patrick had been a dramatic one, as he had saved her from a leg-gragger in the library. Rose's country accent, her coarseness, makes Patrick cast her in the role of a Beggar Maid, and himself presumably as King Cophetua in Burne-Jones painting. Patrick's background, his belonging to an affluent Vancouver family seems to Rose an escape from her poor middle class connections, from Hanratty, which was a source of embarrassment for her. She therefore decides to marry him. However, she soon realizes that she had made a wrong choice. She tries to break off the engagement only to re-engage herself.

"Mischief" is the story of Rose's marriage to Patrick and her affair with Clifford. Rose had met Clifford and his wife Jocelyn in the maternity ward of the North Vancouver General Hospital. Her attraction towards both of them was prompted by Jocelyn's sophistication, and Clifford's lifestyle, his association with "musicians and journalists and lecturers at the University" (*Who*: 99). Rose who had always wanted to shun her connections, now thinks that this environment is her identity. As an actress, she feels an attraction towards a violinist, both being creative artists. Clifford on the other hand, is more matured and sensible. He takes the decision of calling off their plan of spending the night together. "It's only mischief" he says. "What we're doing. It's not some big necessary thing. It's ordinary mischief" (*Who*: 151). Later on, he says:

> It's absolutely true I've wanted out ever since I got in. And it's also true that I wanted in, and I wanted to stay in. I wanted to be married to you and I want to be married to you and I couldn't stand being married to you and I can't stand being married to you. It's static contradiction. (*Who*: 157)

Rose on the other hand had been planning to leave Patrick. At the end of the chapter she "resolved never to see them again and to write them a letter.... By the time she had the letter written...in her head, she...had calmed down" (*Who*: 164). In an interview with Hancock, Munro has said that "Mischief" was the part she liked most, though she added, "But I don't think I've got it quite right" (*Who*: 84).

In "Providence", Rose leaves Patrick and takes a job on a radio station in the Kootenay mountains rather than on Vancouver Island, in order to be closer to Calgary and Tom, a teacher at the University of Calgary, with whom she is "*a little bit in love*" (*Who*: 167).

In "Simon's Luck", Rose returns back to Ontario. She is by now a renowned actress and had matured considerably. Here she meets Simon, a teacher in the classics department. She falls in love with him, and has a passionate physical relationship with him. To her, he is very different from all the men that she had known. A strong willed person, he shared her passion for acting, as he too had played various character roles—"The Humble Workman: The Old Philosopher, and Others" (*Who*: 201). Accomplished in all respects, he could tackle every crisis in life. For the first time in her life. Rose "was in that state of happiness which seems perfectly natural and unthreatened" (*Who*: 201). In her delight, she cries out, "Oh Simon, you idiot, you're the man for my life!" (*Who*: 204). However, this relationship was suddenly brought to a close by the mysterious disappearance of Simon from her life. The entire affair had left Rose distraught, and only when, "A year or so later" (*Who*: 213), when she was working on a full time job in a television series, she got the news of Simon's death. He had died of cancer of the pancreas. He had this disease for quite some time, and had presumably left Rose, to die a lonely death. The news left Rose shocked and immobile. "Simon's dying struck Rose as that kind of disarrangement. It was preposterous, it was unfair..." (*Who*: 215).

Simon's story, thus leaves the impression that the story of human life is a path of misfortunes, where "...the story line open to question, the disarrangements, which demand new judgments and solutions, and throw the window open on unforgettable scenery" (*Who*: 215).

The last section is made up of two stories. "Spelling" and "Who Do You Think You Are?" Here Munro brings about denouement to the narrative, with the "homecoming" (Martin:

119) of Rose, after a long travel, where she had experienced life, from diverse angles, and had come to a realization of her inner true self. She feels calm within her, as the diverse experiences of life teach her acceptance and reconciliation. Rose's quest for identity had begun when she had left for Toronto and she returns to her native place, from where she had begun her life's journey. "Spelling", provides a grim picture of her home, of Flo, who was now mentally deranged, and required to be shifted to the County Home. Flo, who had been so energetic throughout her life, was now in a pathetic state. She was incapable of recognizing her surroundings and even Rose. Her own son Brian and daughter-in-law Phoebe, who lived in Toronto, had failed to take care of her. Later, when Rose had her admitted to the Home, she relapses back to her past life and questions Rose "Are you and Brian behaving yourselves? Don't fight, it gets on your father's nerves..." (*Who*: 233). The story also provides a realistic and dismal picture of the people who spend the weary remaining days of their lives, in the 'Home', people who have either lost their power of speech, who can only spell out their lives. These senile patients are only "bodies [to be] fed and wiped.... Taking in oxygen, giving out carbon dioxide" (*Who*: 226).

The final story reverts to Rose's childhood days, and we are acquainted with Milton Homer and Ralph Gillespie through Rose's memories. *Who Do You Think You Are?* "...it is a composition of remembered episodes, making up a sort of meditation, an expressive of a state of mind—the mind of Rose, who is now mature and whole" (Martin: 122). She has realized herself, that her achievement as an artist, as a television interviewer was only superficial, and that her true self was what mattered.

Rose's meeting with Ralph Gillespie, her childhood acquaintance, after a very long period, and who had worked in the Navy, posted in Halifax, awakens in her strange feelings. She realizes his "life, close, closer than the lives of men she'd loved, one slot over from her own" (*Who*: 256). The novel ends with a news item reporting the tragic death of Ralph

Gillespie. Rose does not talk about this to anyone, feeling that none would understand her true sentiments.

Who Do You Think You Are? presents Munro's vision of life, which though apparently fragmentary and unconnected, as a matter of fact, presents a holistic view of life. She tells Hancock that her collections of stories were "just like a tray with a lot of different sandwiches on it". She further adds "And what on earth is this feeling that somehow things have to connect or they have to be part of a larger whole?"

The Moons of Jupiter,[17] presents women, who are in their middle age, especially in their forties, who make uncomfortable discoveries about themselves, and like Lydia in "Dulse", are "Up and Down" (*Moons*: 59). "Many of them are caught in the voluptuous delight, hysterical eroticism, tearful recriminations, and power struggles involved in love relationships. Creating a sense of life's randomness, the stories focus on the different ways that people get through the unexpected turns of their lies, cope with defeat, survive or not, and go on" (*Ross*: 86). As in *Something I've Been Meaning to Tell You,* the stories are records of disjointed, fragmentary and diverse experiences of women's lives. "'If *Something I've Been Meaning To Tell You*' is a cluster of small constellations, *The Moon of Jupiter—as* the title suggests—has a tighter organization and is more like a single system" (Martin: 128). Of the eleven stories in this collection only the first and the last have the same narrator, while the rest "...represent a star map of many women's lives as the focus shifts continually between particularities and universal patterns of female experience" (Howells, *Encylo*: 771).

Dedicated to Bob Weaver, [Munro's friend, who had introduced her to the Canadian Broadcasting Corporation] Munro in the 'Introduction' to the book spells out her thoughts on the writing of this collection:

> The story is a kind of extension of myself, something once attached to me and growing out of me, now lopped off, exposed and abandoned...some of these stories are closer to my own life than others are, but not one of them is as close as people seem to think.... When you

> start out to write a story many things come from distant parts of your mind and attach themselves to it. Some things you thought would be part of it fall away; others expand. So with hope and trepidation and frequent surprises you put the whole thing together. (*Moons*: xiii-xiv)

An analysis of the stories reveals that Munro has here shifted the setting of her stories. The opening story "Chaddeleys and Flemings", written in two parts: 1. Connection. 2. Stone in the Field; has two settings: Dalgheish, in Ontario, and Vancouver where the second part of Connection is set. "Dulse" is set in the Maritimes, "the southern coast of New Brunswick" (*Moons*: 36); "Accident" in Hanratty; while "Bardon Bus" is shifted to as far as Australia. The rest are in Toronto.

The theme of this constellation is "change and possibility" (*Moons*: 29) in human lives. Munro was very much interested in people's ways of living. As she says:

> I like looking at people over a number of years, without continuity. Like catching them in snapshots.... I just see people living in flashes from time to time...mostly in stories I like to look at what people don't understand. (*Hancock*: 89-90)

Narrated both in the first and third person, here again human relations form the pivotal point of creation. As in *Something I've Been Meaning to Tell You,* here too Munro provides an in depth study of relationships, between daughter and father or mother, wife and husband; between friends; between lovers. "Perhaps all the stories can be said to be about—Passions hopelessly conceived, affections betrayed, marriages made and broken: the joys, fears, loves and awakenings of women echo throughout these twelve unforgottenable stories laying bare the unexceptional and yet inescapable pain of human contact" (*Newsweek*, qtd. in *Moons*, CP).

An important feature is that Munro here deals with the progression of age in ascending order. At the beginning of the collection the narrators are in the prime of their life, while towards the middle and the end, they advance towards maturity and old age. Leaving aside the first two stories, the theme is sexual passion and then it is elevated to something beyond physical obsession.

In "The Turkey Season", love is presented in gross and vulgar terms as the two sisters, Lily and Marjorie, talk about sex, while they gut turkey: "They said that ninety percent of the young girls nowadays drank, and swore, and took it lying down" (*Moons*: 67). However, in "Visitors", the couple is mellowed and has settled for a complacent life. In an interview to Carole Gerson, Munro put this question and provided an answer to her attitude towards love and life:

> Whether you settle for a kind of freedom and happiness that (doesn't necessarily contain erotic love, whether there is such a thing, or whether in choosing freedom you have to deliberately put that kind of happiness behind you, or whether everything's possible.... I think it is, sometimes. (Gerson, *Review-Interview*: 5)

In the next five stories: "Dulse", "Accident", "Bardon Bus", and "Prue", Munro examines emotional involvements, sexual relationships and friendship. Here the women picturized are in their thirties and mid forties, facing the challenges of life.

The last five stories of this volume, "Labor Day Dinner", "Mrs. Cross and Mrs. Kidd", "Hard-Luck Stories", "Visitors", and the "Moons of Jupiter" deal with the love and attachment in elderly women. Here the strong physical desires, and yearnings for love present in earlier stories are completely missing and a matured outlook is observed.

"Mrs. Cross and Mrs. Kidd", is a story, based on two octogenarians, the oldest protagonists in the volume, who meet after a long time in the 'Hilltop Home'. The two women feel strong attachment towards one another, as the differences of their early days have now been ruled out. In an interview on the CBC radio, programmed, "Morning side" (21 Oct. 1982), Alice Munro told Peter Gzouski that the story is "about love".

In the title story, which closes this volume, Munro deals with old age, to its culmination with death. The story is connected to the first two stories in this collection, with its common narrator, Janet, who has now reached her middle age, and is divorced from her husband, Richard. Her children too are now grown-ups: "Judith, the younger was living with a boy named Don" (*Moons*: 221), in Toronto, while Nichola, who is the favorite of Janet, and of whom Judith is jealous, wants to remain "incommunicado" (*Moons*: 221) in Toronto.

The story opens with Janet visiting her father in the "Toronto General Hospital" (217), where he was admitted following a severe heart attack. He lay there in bed with "wires taped to his chest" (217), and seemed calm and optimistic, in contrast to the previous night when he was brought in "pale and closemouthed" (217). Now, coming face to face with death he seemed to regain his composure, and was in his typical jovial mood; making fun of himself, calling the large machines to which he was "hooked up to" as "doohickeys" (*Moons*: 217); his tranquillizers as "the happy pills" and the doctor as "young fellow..." a bit too eager to operate, "bit knife happy" (*Moons*: 219). At first, he is reluctant to be operated upon "Think of the risk at my age, and what for? A few years at the outside. I think the best thing for me to do is to go home and take it easy.... That's all you can do, at my age. Your attitude changes, you know. You go through some mental changes. It seems more natural" (*Moons*: 220). But by the fourth day he changed his mind. "'Well, it looks like I'm going to have it'.... He had done a complete turnaround overnight" (*Moons*: 224).

The story deals with father-daughter relationship, and their bonds of love and dependency. As he says "You know those years you were growing up-well, that's all just a kind of a blur to me. I can't sort out one year from another" (*Moons*: 222). Now as a mother she too experiences similar feelings. He also counsels her "keep out of your children's business. I tried not to say anything. I never said anything when you left Richard.... It wasn't any of my business.... But that doesn't mean I was pleased" (*Moons*: 228). A man of great consideration, he does not want Janet to inform Peggy, his second daughter about his condition, as they would have to cancel the trip to Amsterdam, where her husband Sam would be attending a conference. In his calm acceptance of death he recites: "Shore less Seas", Behind him lay the gray Azores,/ Behind the Gates of Hercules;/ Before him not the glot of shore,/ Before him only shore less seas" (*Moons*: 225).

On the day before his operation, Janet visits the Planetarium, and observes the planets in the Solar System. Next day when she visits her father, she enthusiastically narrates the event. He is equally interested, and goes on to name the Moons of Jupiter, though not the "bunch of new ones" (*Moons*: 232). He narrates that "the moons of Jupiter were the first heavenly bodies discovered with the telescope" (*Moons*: 232), the girlfriends of Jupiter. Before he goes under anesthesia, he calls out to her "Ganymede wasn't any shepherd He was Jove's cupbearer" (*Moons*: 233). Those were his last recorded words. Acclaimed for its brevity, compactness of expression, it touches the reader because of its emotional intensity. It deals with grand themes, without any rhetoric or melodrama. Its construction is strong, and on a typically Munrovian pattern. The story provides a fitting end to the volume as like the "Moons of Jupiter", which holds up the entire solar system, this story too holds the others in a constellation. The collection thus ends with the ultimate reality of life, which is death.

Munro's creative talent reached the zenith in *Progress of Love*.[18] Here, Munro worked upon intricate patterns of narrative structure. Each story is made up of multiple threads, offering parallel versions of a situation observed from different angles. Moreover, there is the re-telling of stories within the story, as the narrative shifts from the voice of the narrator to that of her mother. "Although the pieces collected in this volume are not, for the most part, overtly metafictional, although they do not engage in the kind of self-consciousness,...for example, in 'The Ottawa Valley',... 'Winter Wind' and 'Home', they do nevertheless render problematic our ability to keep apart experience and narration" (Heble: 143).

In the title story, the distinctive features of Munro's art becomes remarkable as the artist works on an 'allegorical structure'. The story summarizes the social history and ethos of three generations, where the narrative constantly shifts from the present to the past and back. Phemie, the narrator is a young woman, belonging to the present generation. Marietta, the mother, tells us of her past and of her life in her father's home. The story opens with a phone call from the narrator's father, informing her, about the death of her mother. The story next reverts to the past, and we are told of Marietta's childhood, her mother's suicidal attempt, and of her hatred of her father. Years later, as a mother, she tells her daughter "Hatred is always a sin.... One drop of hatred in your soul will spread and discolor everything like a drop of black ink in white milk" (*Progress*: 6).

We also learn that Marietta had gone against the wishes of her family, taken some education and finally became a teacher. She had also paid back her father every cent that he had spent on her. Again, the story reverts to Phemie's narrative and we know of the visit of Aunt Beryl, and her 'man friend' (*Progress*: 14). Mr. Florence. As the story progresses, we are told of the startling fact that Marietta had burned the three thousand dollars, a legacy left to her by her father, while her husband watched. When Phemie's mother narrates this incident to her sister Beryl there is no mention of her husband being present. Yet in Phemie's version of the story, which she relates to her friend Bob, years later in her matured life, she re-tells a very different story, where her father had stood besides her mother, watching her drop "the bills into the fire" (*Progress*: 30). She then questions herself: "Why, then, can I see the scene so clearly, just as I described it to Bob Marks (and to others—he was not the first)?" (*Progress*: 29). Thus, the matured Phemie, in order to re-live the past fabricates the truth, to suit her own purpose.

In this story, Munro problematizes the very art of story-telling and narrative structure, which is to a large extent coloured by a figment of imagination. The process presents not the reality itself but a photographic representation of life. In addition, an allegorical form of the progress of love towards hatred is evident in the story. Martin views that, like D.H. Lawrence's "The Rainbow", though in a much smaller scale, with remarkable artistic compression, the story presents the history of society of the twentieth century. "Alice Munro depicts the social change of our time, and the dynamics that bring them about. What we admire is the cubic capacity and the architectural richness of her modest-seeming edifice" (*Progress*: 179).

Complexity of style and expression is apparent in the next few stories of the volume. In "Lichen", parallel stories of David's past, present and future life overlaps one another. David and Stella "were married for twenty-one years. They have been separated for eight" (*Progress*: 34); and like the protagonists in Munro's later collections, Stella "has transcended the vanities and vagaries of merely sexual passion". Her life centers around her 'home', her 'community', where she leads a "busy and sometimes chaotic life" (*Progress*: 35), Here she is writing her "memoir." In sharp contrast to her, is drawn the character of David, who is still untouched by age and who tilts his head so that Stella will not see that he is dying his hair (*Progress*: 44). But Stella is happily 'white-haired' (*Progress*: 32).

After years of separation, he comes to visit Stella, along with Catherine, the woman he lives with. He is seen to be still dependent on Stella and seeks her opinion, as he shows her a 'Polaroid snapshot' of his 'new girl'). To Stella, the photograph reminds her of 'lichen', 'like moss on a rock' (*Progress*: 41) as "The legs are spread wide—smooth, golden, monumental: fallen columns. Between them is the dark blot she called moss, or lichen". In the story Munro presents a contrast between David's profane attitude to love, which is in opposition to Stella who has settled to a serene life in "Nature's bounty" (*Progress*: 34).

"Miles City Montana", is yet another story written on similar structural patterns, where the period is extended to cover the narrator's childhood and her later matured years. In addition, there is theme of the interweaving of story within story.

"Fits", the next story in this collection, works on the same complex pattern of narrative art, though the theme is different from the rest. Here the story is based on an incident of a murder, which takes place on the house of the Weebles, the next-door neighbors of Peg and Roberts. Although Peg discovers the dead bodies of the wife and the husband, she was unwilling to talk about the incident. The story is narrated from Robert's point of view as he re-constructs it from the parts, he had gathered from his wife, the towns' people and from the constable's report. Peg on the other hand, tries to appear normal through out the day after her shattering discovery, and tries to keep herself busy at her works. Later on as she tells Roberts "her part of the story" (*Progress*: 124) where she does not give the exact details but only as she would like to present it. As she says, she "knew there wasn't anybody but me alive in the [Weebles'] house. Then I saw his leg, I saw his leg stretched out into the hall, and I knew then, but I had to go on in and make sure" (*Progress*: 125). However, Roberts learns the truth from the constable's report, that, the head had been severed and was lying in the hall, when Peg went in. The story thus probes into human psychology, and the nature towards insatiable curiosity, from which even Peg is not free. Instead of screaming and running away, she stepped through the remaining parts of Walter's exploded head and entered the bedroom to have a look at Nora's corpse. Although, Peg tries to suppress her natural curious instinct, in the end, it is revealed to Roberts as well as to the readers.

In "Eskimo", Munro explores letter form in her narrative. Here the protagonist imagines herself to be writing a letter to her employer Dr. Streetner, a married man, with whom she is emotionally involved.

Marry Jo, hailing from "a small town in Huron County" (*Progress*: 196), a nurse, is, at the opening of the story, boarded on a flight to Tahiti, for a holiday, which her employer had gifted her as Christmas present. On the flight, as she observes the co-passengers, she carries on an imaginary conversation with Dr. Streetner. Nevertheless, a couple whose attitudes, she finds repelling catches her attention. She then, frames in her mind, a letter to Dr. Streetner, giving him an account of the happenings on the plane. What she observes is that the man is "...probably older than Dr. Streetner, but more buoyant" (*Progress*: 196) and he reminds her of a Khan of the high valleys of Afghanistan that she has seen on TV (197-98), and she thinks that the lady must be one of his wives. Only later, she comes to know that the man and his wife are a Métis and an Eskimo, "Fellow Canadians" (*Progress*: 200). What is most disgusting about their behavior is that, as the girl leans over the man, she kisses him "She kisses his lips, his cheek, his eyelids, his forehead. He offers himself to her; he permits her. She kisses him and licks him.... Mary Jo has to keep on looking (*Progress*: 204). This draws to her mind, her relation with Dr. Streetner and she tries to draw a comparison between the two. The last sentence of the story: "This is the beginning of her holiday" (*Progress*: 207), suggests that the insight is an acquisition, which brings a renewal of her relationship with Dr. Streetner. The movement has been in the form of the spiral that characterizes most of Alice Munro's work.

In *Friend of My Youth,*[19] Munro exploits another aspect of narrative art, where she fictionalizes history, and presents a re-evaluation of the past in relation to the present. Munro, in this collection, problematizes the very art of writing fiction, where reality is at times conceptualized through dream sequence or fantasy. "The mode...is revisionist, as narrators constantly look back into family history, small-town local history and the 19th century colonial history..." (Howells: *Encyclo.* 771).

In the title story, strands of dream and reality are intermingled, to provide a complex narrative structure. The narrator begins the story by saying, "I used to dream about my mother..." (*Friend*: 1). The story thus draws largely upon autobiographical material, which Munro through her fictive imagination renders uncommon and mysterious. At the very outset, we see that the narrator's mother, who died of Parkinson disease, appears in the dream "looking quite well... not exactly youthful, not entirely untouched by the paralyzing disease that held her in its grip for decade or more before her death, but so much better than I remembered that I would be astonished" (*Friend*: 1).

In her attempt to reconstruct her mother's past, the narrator at times goes into minute details, and the reader is led through a maze of events, where the distinction between reality and dream becomes completely blurred. As the story unfolds, the narrator reminisces of her mother as a young woman, which she had seen in a photograph, on her visit to Ottawa Valley, as a child with her mother. She then tells us of her two aunts. Flora and Ellie. Ellie was married to Robert Deal, who had physical relations with Flora. Later on after Elbe's death, he married Audrey Atkinson, Ellie's nurse.

Much of these stories are narrated by her mother to the child, and which the narrator now reminiscences as an adult. It is a reconstruction of the past, through photography and story telling. Munro's art here presents a structuring of the story through interpolations, and story telling within the story. The voice of the mother at times, while at others the narrator's voice, draws comments and remarks on her mother's stories. Thus, there is a juxtaposition of the past and present, through dream sequence, letter writing and memory.

Not all the information is first hand, as much of it the mother had collected from town gossip. Later on, the connection remains through exchange of letters. However, the narrator fails to accept her mother's story as entirely true. She feels that the truth is at times fabricated: "I saw through my mother's story and put in what she left out. My Flora would be as black as hers was white" (*Friend*: 20). The mother's attempt to glorify Flora is strongly resented by the narrator. As she says, "If I could have been a writer...then I would have written the story of Flora's life. And do you know what I would have called it? 'The Maiden Lady'" (*Friend*: 19).

To the narrator, the "really mysterious person in the story...was Roberts.... But he was the one who started everything in secret. He did it to Ellie.... He must have done it to Audrey Atkinson, too, but with less disastrous results (*Friend*: 21-22). The narrator finds the notions of sex, as highlighted by the mother unacceptable, yet she justifies it by saying "What made Flora evil in my story was just what made her admirable in my mother's—her turning away from sex" (*Friend*: 22). Then again, she justifies it by saying "My mother had grown up in a time and in a place where sex was a dark undertaking for women. She knew that you could die of it" (*Friend*: 22).

At this point of time, the narrator tells us that her mother receives a letter from "the real Flora" (*Friend*: 23), where she states that she had moved to town and had taken up the job of a clerk in a store. Looking back now after many years, the narrator reminiscences on the incomplete letters that her mother had tried to write, when the terrible Parkinson disease afflicted her. A sense of guilt over takes her, at her own negligence when in one she read "Friend of My Youth". She says, "I would feel impatience with the flowery language, the direct appeal for love and pity. She would get more of that, I thought (more from myself, I meant), if she could manage to withdraw with dignity, instead of reaching out all the time to cast her stricken shadow" (*Friend*: 24). The narrator next says that she has lost interest in Flora, yet at the same time, she cannot shake off the thoughts from her mind. She now fantasizes that: "I might go into a store and find her", and then immediately recognizes the impossibility of the notion: "She would be dead a long time now" (*Friend*: 25). Again, the idea persists and she says: "But supposes I had gone into a store... perhaps a department store.... I would have wanted to tell her that I know, I know her story, though we had never met". Again, she realizes "This is a dream now; I understand it as a dream" (*Friend*: 25-26).

Fact and fancy therefore co-mingles, and the reader fails to draw a demarcation between reality and fiction. The story concludes with the mother appearing in a dream as in "the Ottawa Valley" and she says,

> Of course its my mother. I'm thinking of, my mother as she was in those dreams, saying, It's nothing just this little tremor, saying with such astonishing light hearted forgiveness. Oh, I knew you'd come someday. (*Friend*: 26)

The narrator feels "offended, tricked, cheated" (*Friend*: 26) for her dream mother seems to release herself from all bindings and control.

"Menesteung" is a superb creation by Munro, where the writer re-writes history, and revives the lost Canadian literary tradition. Delving into the life of a 19th century Canadian poetess Almeda Joynt Roth, she re-looks at the past in the mode of autobiographical fiction. An important feature of this story is that, here Munro represent the past through varied devices, such as poetry, photography, newspaper clippings, a narrator as well as the character herself.

Narrated in both the first and the third person, the story provides a constant shifting of the voice of the narration, from the poetess to that of the narrator. The story begins with the narrator coming across a book of verse "Offerings" by Almeda Joynt Roth published in 1873. The photograph on the frontispiece shows the strong feature of the poetess, and a dress, which bespeaks of the Victorian era.

The Preface to the book, quoting the voice of the poetess tells us of her father, a pioneer who settled "to the wilds of Canada West (as it then was)"; and who was a "harness-maker by trade". A 'cultivated man', he could "quote by heart from the Bible, Shakespeare, and the writings of Edmund Burke". She had lost her brother and sister in the third year of their settlement, following an attack of "prevalent fever" (*Friend*: 51), and three years later, her mother, who could not stand this tragedy. She then became the housekeeper of her father, for twelve long years, until his death. However, she had a deep love and fascination for poetry from her early years, and the household chores could not keep her engaged for long. Her subjects of interest were childhood, death and landscape, "about birds, and wildflowers and snowstorm" (*Friend*: 52). This creative space filled in the gaps and fissures of her life.

In the process of reading the past, Munro, takes into account the socio-economic scenario of the late 19th century Canada—the coming of the railways, the discovery of salt-wells and the sawmills and brickyards—all typical features of new towns built on the edge of the Canadian wilderness.

As the story progresses, we come to know about the life story of Almeda, or Meda as she was also called. She lived in a house on Dufferin Street. It was in this shelter that Almeda secluded herself, writing poems and cherishing dreams of romance and fancy. Jarvis Poulter, a widower and a loner, occupied the house next to hers. He had come to this part of the country to drill oil, and which in its turn led to the discovery of salt. Between him and Almeda developed a bond of friendship and he would escort her home from Church every Sunday. Speculations of their eventually settling down in life continued. Almeda too had fantasies about her marriage with him and dreamt of their courtship. She wanted "a man who doesn't have to be made, who is firm already and determined and mysterious to her" (*Friend*: 61).

The narrative now takes a different turn, as on a hot summer night, Almeda is roused from her sleep by shouts and yells from Pearl street:

> It's as if there was a ball of fire rolling up Pearl Street, shooting off sparks...only the fire is noise; it's yells and laughter and shrieks and curses, and the sparks are voices that shoot off alone. (*Friend*: 63)

To Almeda, these cries seem to be of pain and murder, which in reality were the sound of sex and violence. She is terrified, and early next morning she rushed out of the house, only to discover that the body lay still at the back of her house. In her horror, she ran out into the street "barefoot, in her nightgown and flimsy wrapper to the house of Jarvis Poulter. She narrated in great excitement the incidents of the previous night and sought his help. Jarvis Poulter, accustomed to the ways of the world, walked over to her house, and looking down at the body, nudged the leg with the toe of his boot, "just as you'd nudge a dog or a sow" (*Friend*: 66). As he drove the woman away, his wry comment was "there goes your dead body!" (*Friend*: 67).

The incident, situation, the behaviour of Poulter sickened Almeda, and she turned towards her house. The vulnerability and nervousness of Almeda, made Poulter conscious of her sexuality, and felt the desperate need for protecting her. He at once thought of marrying her. But he could only say "I will call on you later".... "I will walk with you to church" (*Friend*: 67), which was equivalent to proposing to her. However, Almeda turned down this proposal as inertia crept into her mind and body. She realized "an accumulation of menstrual blood that has not yet started to flow" (*Friend*: 68). So she locked the back door of her house with a note for Jarvis stuck on the outside, "I am not well, and wish to rest today" (*Friend*: 68). She then prepared a large pot of tea for herself, poured a cup, with "several dark drops of nerve medicine" (*Friend*: 68). It was in this state of complete lethargy, she spent the whole day. The only sound that pervaded the silence of the room was the "plop, plup" of the grape juice falling from its stained dark purple cloth, which she had tied for grape jelly. The closed house, the medicine, "her extraordinary languor, her perfect immobility, her unresisting surrender to her surroundings" (*Friend*: 69) worked into her and she now thought of writing a poem "The Meneseteung"; the name of the river which flows through the Maitland

> with its deep holes and rapids and blissful pools under the summer trees and its grinding blocks of ice thrown up at the end of winter and its desolating spring floods. (*Friend*: 70)

As she rose at dusk, she discovered "that she is bleeding". She walked upstairs leaving "purple footprints and smelling her escaping blood" (*Friend*: 71).

The story now takes a leap forward, as it highlights on a news caption published in the 'Vidette' which records the death of Almeda in 1903, from pneumonia, caught ironically enough, after being chased by some urchins into the Pearl Street bog. The newspaper refers to her as "a lady of talent and refinement whose pen, in days gone by, enriched our local literature with a volume of sensitive, eloquent verse", and who later on turned to be a "familiar eccentric, or even, sadly, a figure of fun" (*Friend*: 71). A year later the newspaper records the death of Jarvis Poulter in 1904. The story closes with the narrator visiting the graveyard, looking for Almeda Roth on her family plots, and finally stumbling into a small inscription "Meda". The story ends with a disclaimer, which the narrator had made up the story by inference only, thereby giving an ironic twist to the story. "And they may get it wrong, after all. I may have got it wrong. I don't know if she even took laudanum. Many ladies did. I don't know if she ever made grape jelly (*Friend*: 73).

As in a metafiction, there is a complex relationship between the narrator, character and the author and where each identity mingles into the other. "In this sense, the narrator's 'dreaming back' to the nineteenth-century woman in order to dream her forward into her own contemporary consciousness which identifies the other's eccentricity as her mystery and her saving difference" (Smythe: 8). The house of Almeda symbolizes the past in the story that the narrator is trying to recover, while the Pearl street represents the downtrodden section of the society, and the associate drunken brawls and humiliation of women in the street. Another feature here is that the father image which predominates the story. Almeda's attraction towards Jarvis is partly an attempt to re-live her father's memory. "She misses the harness of female service, misses...her father" appreciation, his dark, kind authority (*Friend*: 60). When she imagines Poulter coming to her bed "a fit of welcome and submission overtakes her, a buried gasp" (*Friend*: 60). Almeda's flow of menstrual blood which coincides with the flowing of grape juice, as well as the flow of the river "Meneseteung", all symbolizes the creativity in her, and her ability to create a new life; "a hopeful sign" (*Friend*: 70). It also symbolizes her release from the hopes of marrying Poulter, and can be taken as a sign of her continuing fertility, her potential to create future presence, rather than an indication of past failure.

Here, we may say that Almeda discovers her identity through a process of self-realization. She feels the hurt of the brutal treatment meted out to the woman on the street, and Poulter's inhuman behavior. She therefore, takes the decision to extricate herself from patriarchal subjugation. Munro has referred to her as a mad woman. However, in reality it is only a mask to hibernate herself and hide her identity. By reliving the past, Munro like Lawrence's Morag Gunn in *The Diviners*, she knows that the rejected is the mother code of women's stories.

The other stories in this collection are narrated from a third person point of view, where the past is enlivened and reconstructed through Munro's narrative art. A noticeable feature of these stories is that, majorities of these are based on various forms of lies, deceptions, and distortions and even disguises.

"Five Points", "Wig time", "Oranges and Apples", "Differently", "Goodness and Mercy" are the other stories of this collection, where Munro shows that deceptions and lies are at the core of human relationships.

"Pictures of the Ice", presents an exemplary feature of Munro's narrative art, as the underlying meaning of the story remains controversial. A great discrepancy occurs between what is narrated and what actually happens. Throughout the story, Munro narrates the events in the present tense, emphasizing on what 'could have', or 'should have' been said or done. Moreover, readers are led on to great surprises, as things do not happen as expected. The story begins with the line: "Three weeks before he died...drowned in a boating accident in a lake whose name nobody has heard him mention.... Austen Cobbett stood deep in the clasp of a three-way mirror in Crawford's Men's Wear" (*Friend*: 137).

Reading through the story one expects to know the circumstances of Austen's death, yet in the next few lines, the readers are told that Austen was going to be married in Hawaii, where his wife to be, lived. We also come to know that his former wife died a year back, and that he was retired officially, "...but was game enough to gear up for a second marriage" (*Friend*: 138). We are then told of Karin, a woman who "spends a lot of her time over at Austen's cleaning out his house, getting everything ready for his departure to Hawaii", and to whom Austen shows a photograph of "the woman he is to marry". He also shows her a postcard of the "town where he will live in Hawaii" (and) "where Austin Cobbett would walk with friendly Sheila" (*Friend*: 140),—his future wife. "By emphasizing what Austen could have, or should have said or done, Munro warns us that what actually gets said does not necessarily reflect what Austen means" (Heble: 181) for Austen "instead of saying what he is thinking, comes out with something else entirely" (*Friend*: 138). This disparity between thought and utterance, deceives the reader, and through this literary device, Munro seems to emphasize that real life can never be fully understood and that photography projects only the partial truth. Towards the end of the story, when Austen is supposed to fly to Hawaii "the first big storm of the winter began" (*Friend*: 149). Munro's use of past tense for the first time in the story "signals to us that events as they are described should not simply be taken at face value" (Heble: 181) Austen's going to Hawaii remains only a supposition. "Pictures Of the Ice", fictionalizes the turn of life's events and the 'absent meanings' (Heble: 181) of life. Looking at the photographs that "'Austen took so often' on the ice, Karin 'gets the feeling that he is in them, after all. He's a blank in them, but bright'" (*Friend*: 155). The ironic twist of the story at the end reveals that all throughout Austen had deceived everyone into believing about his forthcoming marriage, while in reality, he had only taken up this strategy to conceal and overcome his loneliness. Karin too learns about his fictitious creations, but again conceals it from Austen. She takes the photographs of Austen and mails them to his children, leaving out the sender's address, "refusing to provide Austen's family or friends with any kind of firm or determinate knowledge" (Heble: 181).

"Pictures of the Ice" ends without any conventional closure, but rather with a multiplicity of meanings. Munro's play with words, narrative techniques, renders all things mysterious, as there is a great difference between appearance and reality. Karin's closing line that she would leave one day without any address: "She just wants to make them wonder" (*Friend*: 155), problematizes the very concept of the short story as it does not provide any explanation to the mysteries of life.

Open Secrets[20] explores more complex areas of Munro's literary art, as she now rejects the conventional method of story telling, and interweaves fantasy and realism together. All the eight stories, in this collection are set in Ontario, Australia and Europe; in dangerous mountains, forbidding wilderness, familiar towns. Things that cannot be explained happen here—

and yet all seems inevitable, deeply credible and always profoundly true to the human heart.

Peter Gzowski describes these stories as "magical" in his 1994 *Morningside* interview with Munro, while Nathalie Foy, is of the opinion that in this collection "There is a shift away from her previous work...as she explores narrative in a way that seems more celebratory, less caustic, than before" (Foy: 147). In an interview for the *Paris Review,* conducted the year that *Open Secrets* was published, Munro attributed the shift to a single need for new material:

> I'm doing less personal writing now than I used to, for a very simple obvious reason. You use up your childhood.... Maybe its advisable to move on to writing those stories which are more observation. (McCulloch: 244)

She also mentioned to Gzowski that *Open Secrets* was much more "riskier" than her previous work:

> I want to move away from what happened to the possibility of this happening or that happening and a kind of idea that life is not just made up of the facts, the things that happen,...but all that happen in fantasy, that might have happened, the alternate life that can almost seem to be accompanying what we call our real lives. (Gzowski: Radio Programme)

Concerned with the depiction of life in its true perspective. *Open Secrets,* as the name suggests, unfolds the mysteries of life, from diverse angles. Each story in this collection is complex in nature, and has multiple layers of narrative threads, which overlap and intersect at various levels.

With *Open Secrets,* Munro moves further away from just presenting real life to the realization of the existence of real life. Readers are now made aware of the fact that placed in the crisis of life, an individual recognizes one's true self. Also, as Munro here is both celebrating and reverential in her stance towards fiction, 'magical' becomes an apt word to describe her fiction. It reveals as much as it conceals. Just as life itself is hazy and opaque, Munro's stories in this collection are at times obscure.

Talking to McCulloch and Simpson, Munro said: "I don't think I have this overwhelming thing that comes in and dictates to me. I only seem to get a grasp on what I want to write about with the greatest difficulty. And barely" (McCulloch: 240). For Munro life is made up of multi layered events, which exist in parallel lines. It is therefore the duty of the artist to flesh out these happenings and present them in art. Her conversation with Gzowski illuminates this aspect of her fiction.

> I do think of the story as happening, not of me making up the story. The story is happening, and I'm finding out about it.... It's as if I'm doing justice to something somewhere. (*Morningside,* CBC Radio: 1994)

An analysis of the stories of *Open Secrets,* it is observed that throughout the collection, narratives splinter, unravel, and proliferate, thereby creating parallel stories. The moments of revelation occur, when characters glimpse at their selves in parallel narratives.

In the opening story "Carried Away", Munro contemplates on unfulfilled and unconsummated relationships. Louisa, a librarian in a small town in Ontario, during the First World War, develops an emotional attachment to a person whom she actually never meets. Like the narrator in "How I Met my Husband", Louisa too waits for letters that never comes. Later on, she comes to learn about his marriage, and that he had been engaged before he went to the war. Thus, promises made, were never kept. Louisa comes to know startling facts about Jack, and gradually the mysterious happenings of life begin to unravel before her. The last section of the story serves as a turning point, as Louisa is now jolted back to reality and she muses, "Love dies all the time, or at any rate it becomes distracted, overlaid...it might as well be dead" (*Open Secrets*: 54). The last sentence finds Louisa imagining horses pulling away from the town and the factory:

> ...down the dark side roads Somewhere out in the country they would lose the sound of each other's bells. (*Open Secrets*: 51)

A dream, a nostalgia carries her away.

In "Vandals", we again have multiple narratives within the story. The movements from one plot to the other, as well as strands of threads are interwoven into the narrative. A reading of "Vandals" reveals that elements of magic, romance, memory, co-exist throughout the story. The form is epistolary, and each character has his or her own narrative, which intersects with each another. The story shows how Liza takes her revenge on Ladner by vandalizing the house of Bea and Ladner. She coldly tells Warren the reason: "I already told you what she did to me. She sent me to college!" (*Open Secrets*: 332). Thus, the "unarticulated layers, the uncut gatherings, the unspoken secrets—all remain darkened so that we may approximate Munro's sense of her work, that is mysterious and difficult" (Foy: 167).

"Wilderness Station", deals with the social history and change, recurrence in the lives of Huron County dwellers from the rough pioneer existence of the 1850s, to the developed communities of the twentieth century. "Spaceships Have Landed", shows Billy, Doud, Aurther and Lucille sell the piano factory after the death of their mother and convert the family mansion into "a home for old people and disabled" (*Open Secrets*: 304).

The Love of a Good Woman,[21] an unparalleled creation, echoes the themes of the previous collections. It works on the same narrative structure where the very art of story telling is problematized, as the narrator shifts the focus back and forth in time and space. In this collection there are five 'Sowesto' stories, while three are set in British Columbia and which "hint at murder mysteries (title story and 'Cortes Island'), sexual transgressions, blackmail, and children's games gone disastrously wrong" (Howells: Encyclo. 771).

In the title story, which opens this collection we come across a narrative in four parts, each, forming a part of the other. This puzzles the reader as it throws open the question as to whose narrative it actually is. Whether of the drowning of the small-town optometrist, or of the boys finding the body or the story of the young dying woman, who spites the energetic, practical and youthful nurse, attending her. A story of eighty-nine pages, it draws comparison with a novel. Munro here seems to exploit the possibilities of the genre as a literary art, where the length of the story is of nominal importance. Elliptical in construction, each story revolves around its main events. The result is a layered and complex pattern, which is not apparent on its first reading, in other words, something like life.

A reading of the story shows that, a young nurse takes up the task of looking after a sick dying woman, only to keep a deathbed promise to her father, and in the process sacrifices her own life. In the course of time, she is drawn towards the husband of the woman. However, the story takes a dramatic turn when the woman confesses at her dying moment that she and her husband, had committed a murder, and had deposed off the body in a river. The confession leaves the narrator shocked and astounded, as she is at a loss, whether to accept them as the truth.

Suspense, murder, confession is again the central drama in "Cortes Island", where a stroke patient discloses the deepest secrets to his part-time caretaker, of his involvement in the death of Mr. Wild of Cortes Island. The inquest report stated: "The death of Mr. Wild was ruled to be an accident due to misadventure, its cause being a fire of origins unknown" (*Love*: 157). Munro here uses newspaper clippings to bring to light the truth of the story.

Revelation of secrets of life figures in "Before the Change", where a young woman confronts her father with the open secret of his life and reveals the hidden facts of hers, but she is unprepared for the final irony of his legacy.

In "The Children Stay", Munro takes up the subject of adultery, where Pauline, a mother of two young children, develops an illicit relationship with the director of theatre group and runs away with him. The story ends with the children now grown-ups, reminding their mother of the time when she had gone away.

Munro achieves her height of excellence in the final story of this collection "My Mother's Dream". The story is based on a dream that haunted Munro recurrently after the death of her second daughter. In this story the narrator too, like her creator dreams of a child being left out in the snow all night, and of its being forgotten.

A singular feature of this narrative is that, the story is told from a baby's perspective, where the baby recounts of incidents in the life of her mother, before her birth as well as of the months that followed. From the story, we gather that, a fatal incident had taken place in the life of the baby, when the mother nearly suffocates her child to death. This is revealed to the narrator when she is nearly 50 years of age. This revelation has a great effect, as it strengthens the bond between the mother and daughter.

This compressed work spanning decades, takes the arc of a novella. It lays bare not only the strata of solitary life, but also the seamless connections and shared guilt that binds together the narrator and her mother. Further, it is observed that the story, like the fable unwinds from one sentence to another through a maze of narratives. Munro is always interested in depicting human lives in its totality, and her fiction records disruptions and disasters with exactness and precision. As Gentry puts it "in *The Love of a Good Women,* we find that human beings are bonded by love and kinship, and it also suggests people are brought together by weakness, silence and denial rather than by sweet and open communication"[22] (Gentry: Website citation, par. 1).

An overall assessment of Munro's art of story telling, and the technique that she employed, demonstrate that her works cannot be explained by any particular theoretical application. Rather it can be said to be the culmination of various narratological concepts and ideas. In fact, Munro's narrative technique is distinct in itself and she has propounded a new narrative form in this literary genre.

It has been observed that Munro had a predilection for 'change and possibility', and that her art of narration changed with every story. For her, human life is not a static one; rather it is in a state of constant flux and transformation. Her words to Wachtel "I think that [change] is the thing that doesn't change" (Wachtel: 49) is most significant. It underlies her interest in the events of human life, which not only changes with the passage of time, but also recurs in human history.

As an artist-historian of small town Ontario, Munro makes effective use of traditional values, archetypal images, figures, and myths as themes to explore the complexities of life. This ranges from human history to human psyche. The realistic world of the small town rural Ontario, is the world to which she belongs and which her life is. In an introduction to the *Vintage Edition of Selected Stories,* she says:

> I don't think I'm writing just about this life [in "the country to the east of Lake Huron"] I hope to be writing about and through it. (*Selected Stories:* xv)

However, she has not confined herself to the depiction of history alone, but has concentrated on the feelings, visions that constitute human life. She has transfigured daily life with something that gives her readers universal experiences. Her work has been a comprehensive record of the enduring condition of human lives.

Munro's revelations in this regard are worth pondering.

> I feel that all life becomes even more mysterious and difficult. And the whole act of writing is more an attempt at recognition than of understanding, because I don't understand many things. I feel a kind of satisfaction in just approaching something that is mysterious and important. Then writing is the art of approaches and recognition. I believe that we don't solve these things—in fact our explanations take us further away. (Thacker: 54)

Metaphor, symbols, paradoxes, intertextuality all abound her texts, so that it becomes difficult at times to explain the diverse nature of her fictional art.

What is noteworthy is that, a gradual transformation with regard to both theme and style is discernable as her writing career progressed. While the *Dance of the Happy Shades* set the very foundation of her fictional range—the art of depiction in this collection was rather in the form of observation and speculation. More Gotthic in nature, it meditated on the themes of strangeness and secrecy in everyday life. The second work *Lives of Girls and Women* was organized around metaphorical presentation that drew all the varied sequences to the radiant center. Here attachment and relationship acquired prime importance, but did not lead to epiphanies discoveries, as is apparent in *The Moons of Jupiter*. Moreover, the book is written in the form of a *bildungsroman* and the final chapter is strongly meta-fictional as it explores the difficulties in writing of a novel.

Something I've Been Meaning to Tell You, ventures into more complex areas of human relationships where, the narrative art becomes diversified and disjointed. Overlapping, parallel stories, shifts in time sequence, characterize this collection. With *Who Do You Think You Are?* Munro again reverts to the cycle of stories, where the arc of Rose's journey of life becomes a complete whole with her return to Hanratty.

From *The Moons of Jupiter* onwards it is seen that Munro's stories feature more complex narratives and wider time frames. The untold or untellable stories of lives of women become the theme of *Progress of Love*. Examination of the past, rewriting of history, adultery and sexual relationships are explored fully in *Friend of My Youth*. The narration too becomes longer and run over several pages. With *Love of a Good Woman*, Munro reaches the excellence of a female Canadian writer. The form becomes more complex and multi-layered. However a re-reading of the stories reveals that the strands of the earlier stories and some of the same materials are handled here with variations.

Because Munro's stories are construed in such complicated narrative techniques, and present life in all its realities, it leaves the reader as well as the critic overwhelmed. Like a projector it highlights on the dark secret mysteries that characterize human existence. Munro's narrative art focuses on the intricate working of human lives with their associate feelings of joy, pain, suffering and hopes. It also interprets the working of the levels of human consciousness, and therefore tries to establish the search for inner voice under all situations of life.

Munro's success as writer lies in her frequent use of local dialects in fiction. She had an ear for the regional idioms and phrases, and her writings resonate the words and speech of the common folks of South Western Ontario, "Particularly Canadian Irishisms" (Rasporich: 189), where her roots really were. Munro has admitted in an interview that she had picked up a strong Huron country idiom from her stepmother. This Canadian speech is recorded in "The Ottawa Valley" (*Something*). Munro's grandmother was Irish, and exerted great influence on the family. Thus, in the story we see that the fictional mother and daughter return to visit the family, whose characteristic behavior and language Munro records. Uncle James speaks with an Irish accent and is given to impulsively booming out Irish ditties: "As I was a-goen over kil-i-kenny Mountain.... But I take delight in *THE WATER OF THE BARLEY*" (*Something*: 238). Aunt Dodie uses the folk epithets "Eh?" talking of her sister she says, "Oh, busy.... She's busy scraping the chicken dirt off her boots. Eh?" Aunt Lena "Lays down the law" (*Something:* 183).

In "Walker Brothers Cowboy", we come across expressions such as "*She digs with the wrong foot*" (*Dance*: 15), folk expression used in *Dunganon* to indicate that somebody was a Catholic. In *Lives of Girls and Women,* a deranged woman is roused and attacked by a rhyme conceived and expressed through the imagery of destruction of female anatomy:

> Irene don't come after me
>
> Or I'll hang you by your tits in a crab-apple tree. (*Lives*: 8)

Again, Munro's use of language reveals the tradition and conventions of society, where the position of women had been minimized. In writing about them, Munro uses irony as "comic, liberating, and self affirming for women" (Rasporish: 114). Iris, the old maid in "Connection" (*Moons*) is dismissed by Richard, as a "pathetic old tart" (*Moons*: 17), but she happily cracks a joke about her situation and says:

> I'm with a tour, dear, did I tell you? Nine old maids and seven widows and three widowers. Not one married

couple. But I say, you never know, the trip's not over yet. (*Moons*: 15)

A vital question of feminist literary movement was the presenting of female experiences and aesthetics. In Munro's art, female sensibilities finds its expression in presentation of female psyche, use of landscape, and in a variety of ways of writing the body.

Thus, we come across, a fictional world of hearth and home, of traditional female concern and female relationships, and the domestic world. Munro's is a feminine art—that of the house, furnishing, interior decoration, food, and fashion; all of which spell out feminist comments and protests.

For Munro, words are of utmost importance. As she says, "I suppose I just experience things finally when I do get them into words" (Gibson: 244). The rhythmic flow, cadence, beauty, and enchantment of Munro's language, gives her short stories a poetic appeal. In *Who Do You Think You Are?*, one comes across many such examples: "*The cloud-capped towers, the gorgeous palaces*" (*Who*: 4) or "*Then slowly, slowly, she got up*". Again, "*Oh the buzzin' of the bees in the cigarette trees*" (*Who*: 10). All indicate the rhetorical resonance and majestic dignity of a verse, and establish Munro's genius as a writer of short fiction.

Part-II
SNAPSHOTS: THE STILL MOMENTS OF LIFE

I

Photography, as a form of visual art attempts to look at moments of life through the lenses of a camera and presents them as a series of fragmentary events that have taken place in the life of an individual. As an art form, it provides a paradoxical vision of life, as it concentrates on its subjective representation. It conceptualizes life as an amalgamation of momentary events, which are artfully captured as still-shots. In this context, Diane Arbus has observed: "[a] photograph is a secret about a secret. The more it tells you, the less you know" (Coleman: 77). Photography thus becomes the art of cryptic projection of life in all its multidimensional aspects.

The art of photography has been variously interpreted and commented upon by critics and writers. In the nineteenth century, this art was viewed as "window on the world" (York: 11). In the twentieth century, the critical focus was on its subjective nature. Ronald Barthes forwarded a comprehensive definition of this art. He was among the first to place the photograph at the center of the twentieth-century debate over perception and reality. In his *Image Music Text* (1977), he termed photography as "a message without a code". "Certainly", he wrote: "the image is not the reality but at least it is its perfect *analogon*..." (Barthes: 17). Further he pointed out that photographic message is more paradoxical and complex since "the connoted (or coded) message develops on the basis of a message without a code" (19). All these views seem to be a pointer to the fact that, as an art form, photography is open to multiple interpretations and in this respect; it is close to creative art.

The concept of photographic metaphors in narrative structures has been widely used by modernist and post modernist writers, as it tries to provide an understanding between perception, and reality. The art helps in the projection of a realistic picture of the wider variety of life. A close bonded relationship is therefore discernible between photographic imagery and the narrative art. As in narrative art, photography too assumes and draws the realistic situations of life from the artists' angle of vision. Highlighting the impact of photographical art in creative literature, Frank Webster remarks: "Because photographs are open to a variety of interpretations, they have a desperate need for words which can fix a particular interpretation" (Webster: 162). As an analog to narrative art, photography reflects life as a series of snapshots of momentary events. However, in photographical imagery only a partial view of life is recorded, as the lenses of a camera focuses only at one angle of vision at a time.

Photographic structures are paradoxical in nature, as they implicate hidden layers of meanings. This results in the process of both concealments as well as revelations. Referring to this art, Lorraine. M. York, opines that photography has a "dual relation" as it "lies" and "transforms rather than represents reality" (York: 9). A singular feature of photography is that it can be considered as an effective device for "rediscovering one's own cultural past," as it helps to "reconcile past and present" (York: 136). Thus, this art has a narrative of its own, which when decoded reveals varied interpretations. Acknowledging the importance of photographic art, Victor Burgin views: "Photographs are texts inscribed in terms of what we may call photographic discourse. But this discourse, like any other, engages discourses beyond itself...previous texts 'taken for granted' at a particular cultural and historical juncture" (144). Lorraine M. York is also of the opinion that:

> ...narrative in photographs is always implied narrative—the freezing of a moment in time because it excludes the moments before and after the exposure, irresistibly impresses upon the linearity of experienced time and our own inability to freeze time.[23] (York: 18)

As a matter of fact, photography captures the static and decisive moments of life in art. As such, modernist and postmodernist writers have seized upon it as an analogue to narrative art. Referring to this representation in literary art, T.S. Eliot terms it as: "the still point of the turning world" (Eliot: 192).

Because photographic metaphors are open-ended in nature, it helps the artists in presenting the complex situations of modern life. Further, it attempts to preserve the past, which Jean Mohr views: "A photograph arrests the flow of time in which the event photographed once existed" (Berger and Mohr: 86).

A photographic narrative when deconstructed reveals a continual deferral of meaning and significance. Thus, similarity exists between narrative and photographic art. In both situations, the artists remain a detached, passive observer of life. The lenses of the camera as well as the narrative become the medium for clipping various situational realities of life. The art therefore, becomes the most effective means for focusing on hidden mysteries of life. The use of photographic imagery in narratives has been widely advocated by writers all over the world.

II

In Canada, writers, such as Alice Munro, Timothy Findley, Michael Ondaatje, Margaret Laurence, Al Purdy, Brian Moore, Margaret Atwood, and host of others, have applied photographic technique in their fictional narratives. But it's consistent use and application is seen in the works of Alice Munro.

In her fiction, Munro continually explores the possibilities of photographic representation of the thoughts and emotions of her characters. She projects the paradoxical situation of life, the multiple adversities of fortune, predicaments, etc. that pervade human lives through photographic imagery and metaphors. In various writings and interviews, Munro has often expressed her interest in photography and photographic realism. In an "Open letter" to a small Wingham, Ontario Journal, *Jubilee,* Munro summarized her feeling about the emotional power of local detail, by referring to an Edward Hopper Painting. This canvas, entitled "The Barber Shop", is fairly static, symmetrically-composed, sunlight-flooded interior scene; yet for Munro it becomes "full of distant, murmuring, almost tender foreboding, full of mystery like the looming trees" (Munro, "An Open Letter": 7).[24]

It has been observed that in each of Munro's short story, there is an abundance of such photographic metaphors and imagery, which only reveals the artist's keen and earnest desire to provide a clear and vivid picture of life. Munro has explicitly stated that to her, photographs are very important and that she simply loved looking at them. In her words:

> "What I want to get" she claimed: "Change with different stories...some times I want to get something that is very grainy and I don't want to artifice at all" and that "the material demands a kind of luxuriance". (Hancock: 107)

Again in an illuminating conversation with Tim Struthers, Munro' claimed to be very interested in photography, but was some what hesitant about equating writing and photography; "photographs are too explicit to relate stories as far as I can see" (York: 28). However, she admitted that Diane Arbus was her "favourite" whom she admired "very, very much" (Struthers: 6).

An examination of her writings show that Munro was in fact, greatly influenced by Arbus as well as by Walker Evans, who had presented the adversaries of life in their paintings. Munro too believed that art is a perfect vehicle for presenting the realities of life which, in her own words are: "solitary and meshed...buried and celebrated" (York: 50). In all her writings one notices a picturization of the grotesque as well as the ugly, which is an integral part of human life. This presentation is done with humour and irony, which demonstrates Munro's greatness as an artist.

In fact, narrative art in Munro's fiction unfolds itself in a digressive pattern, through the medium of snapshots taken at various moments of life. Thus, photography becomes a means for presenting life in its total variety. Munro was greatly concerned with not only the depiction of life but also an understanding of it. In addition, photography provided her a means of representing not only the surface reality, but also its inner significance. For her: "surfaces were not surfaces" and that there was "a kind of magic...about everything.... A feeling about the intensity of what is there" (Metcalf: 56).

Thus, one finds in her work an underlying intensity, which penetrates deep within. This inner voice provokes the reader to search out the hidden truth beneath the translucent surface. In this context, York's observation seems to echo similar thoughts:

> Munro is always deeply concerned with describing scenes and people clearly in the mind's eye, and as in real life, so in her stories, we establish our conception of character of people first by recognizing what they look like and how they speak, and then such familiarity established, proceeding inwards to minds and feelings. The photographic element in her presentation of scenes

> and characters as visualizable images is an essential factor in her writings. (York: 135)

In fact, Munro has herself talked about the use of photography in her art. In "What is Real?", she asserts:

> Yes, I use of what is real, in the sense of being really there and really happening, in the world, as most people see it, and I transform it into something that is really happening, in my story. (Metcalf, 1982: 226)

Narrative art thus, becomes for Munro a picturesque presentation of life, where photographic imagery is of paramount importance, as it helps the story to move back and forth in time and space.

Munro was a great admirer of the North American painters, and the Canadian painters of the 1970s and 1980s such as Ken Danby, Christopher Pratt, Jack Chambers, Tom Forestall, and Alex Colville considerably influenced her writings. When asked by John Metcalf whether she was impressed by Canadian magic realists painters such as Forestall and Colville, Munro replied that she was "very responsive" to their material (Metcalf, 1972: 58). Again, in response to Graeme Gibson's question: "Do you see yourself as trying to record things, like a representational painter?" she replied: "what I admire is a kind of super-realism...." When Gibson suggested Andrew Wyeth's name, Munro responded, "that I'm trying to do this, this same thing" (Gibson: 256). In another illuminating revelation, Munro maintained that Pratt's painting formed an analogue to her own style of writing:

> That window picture is more like my stories, because you look out and you see the flat horizon and you see the shades of blue and grey, just flat bars. This one [young woman a Slip] is more claustrophobic, and may be it indicates that most of the stories are about introspective woman. (Scobie, "A Visit": 13)

Munro had the greatest appreciation for the works of Edward Hopper. "I'm crazy about Edward Hopper", she enthusiastically commented to Graeme Gibson (Gibson: 256). Her enthusiasm was more especially for the painting "The

Barber Shop". In an interview with John Metcalf she claimed that the painting such as this one, "do to me exactly the same thing that the writing I respond to does and that I would like to do" (Metcalf: 58). Munro has drawn a picture in similar manner:

> A barber shop, not yet open; the clock says seven... fresh morning light of a hot summer day. Beside the barber-shop, a summer—heavy darkness of trees. The plain white slightly shabby barber-shop, so slightly shabby barber-shop, so commonplace and familiar; yet everything about in that mild light, is full of a distant, murmuring, almost tender forebodings. Full of mystery like the looming trees. ("An Open Letter": 6)

All these emphasize, that Munro had a deep love for paintings, and for her narrative art existed as visual objects. Like Arbus's photograph, Munro's fiction involves a continual process of concealment and revelation, where the reader has to search out the inner meaning hidden within. Also like Arbus, the grotesque makes its appearance in Munro's stories in order to make us aware of what is odd and unnatural in life. In "Images" the eccentric hermit Joe Phippen, whom Ben Jordan takes his daughter to meet, is an example of the unfamiliar and uncommon.

This ability to paint skillfully the minutest detail of human life has won her wide appreciation from readers and critics alike. Alexa DeWiel, in the review of *The Moons of Jupiter,* has described Munro as a "superb chronicler of detail..." (Dewiel: 13). George Bowering has called her a "realist" (Bowering: 4), and Jean Mallinson called her a "visionary documentary writer" (Mallinson: 70). When asked how she manages to remember the minute details and textures of the past, Munro replied:

> ...they just come to me when I'm writing. It's a kind of seeing. Last year I saw a black-and-white photo of my high-school class that was taken Grade Ten, and I did remember the color of everyone's clothes. (Murch: 70)

An analysis of the short stories of Munro shows that photographic metaphors form the base of her fiction. In

Munro's style of writing, family pictures are also used continually to throw adequate light on events and incidents. Characters reminiscences about the past by looking at old family pictures, and thus narrate the sweet and bitter memories of their lives. The past is therefore re-lived, and the present acquires new meaning. In this process, readers have a glimpse into the inner selves of the characters.

In "The Ottawa Valley", which closes the collection *Something I've Been Meaning to Tell You,* Munro uses the analogue of the photograph to comment on her work: "Now I look at what I have done and it is like a series of snapshots like the brownish snapshots with fancy borders that my parents' old camera used to take" (*Something*: 246).

The photograph, thus, becomes a means for reconciling the past, giving a new meaning to the present. Almost all other collections stem from photographic still-shots, or from old photographs of the by-gone days.

> Again, she says that her story "Privilege" in *Who Do You Think You Are?*...began...On a not very deep fictional level, just with the desire, an almost documentary desire.... There's a deeper level that you're not going to when you do that kind of writing, which doesn't mean it isn't valid. (Struthers: 21)

In Munro's fiction one observes that her paradoxical photographic vision, makes the familiar and prosaic appear unfamiliar, even threatening at times. In "The Ottawa Valley", the mother's sense of sickness and loss turns the most familiar presences—into something dark and remote.

> She went on as if she had not heard, her familiar bulk ahead of me turning stage, indifferent. She withdrew, she darkened in front of me, though all she did in fact was keep on walking along the path that she and Aunt Dodie had made when they were girls.... It was still there. (*Something*: 244)

Thus, photography assumes paramount significance in Munro's narrative art, as this form enables the artist to scan into the lives of the people in and around her. In addition, the writings convey more meaning than is apparently evident. Rose in "Royal Beatings" has summed this up when she says, "Pots can show malice, the patterns of linoleum can leer up at you, treachery is the other side of dailiness" (*Who*: 20).

In *Lives of Girls and Women,* Munro's use of photography in fiction writing is seen in its fullest form, where the final chapter is named "Epilogue: The Photographer". Here the artist attempts to present intricacies of life and the familiar and the grotesque through photographic imagery. Del, the protagonist, is in quest for the truth of life. In thinking of writing a novel on the town of Jubilee, she thinks of creating a town which would be "dull, simple amazing and unfathomable", where "every smell, pothole, pain, crack, delusion" will be "radiant, everlasting" (*Lives*: 253). Thus, like a photographer Del wants to capture life in its total hue and colour in fiction.

In *Something I've Been Meaning to Tell You,* Munro presents a coalition of the past and present through the analogue of photography. In the title story, Et, draws a comparison between the two profiles of her sister Char. The photograph reveals that in the past "Char was beautiful" (*Something*: 5). Now looking at Char scrubbing in the kitchen she recognizes "the same almost disdainful harmony as in the photograph" (*Something*: 6). Like Del's photographer, Et realizes that "the qualities of legend were real, that they surfaced where and when you least expected" (*Something*: 6).

In "Material", in the same collection, the narrator while browsing in a bookstore comes across a paperback collection of short stories with the photograph of her ex-husband on the cover-page:

> He looked, however, very much as I would have changed him.... Pouches under his eyes, a dragged-down look to the cheeks even when he is laughing. He is laughing into the camera. His teeth have gone from bad to worse. He hated dentists, said his father died of a heart attack in the dentist's chair. A lie, like so much else, or at least an exaggeration. He used to smile crookedly for photographs to hide the right top incisor.... (*Something*: 28)

The narrator then goes on to narrate the story of Hugo, her ex-husband, where much of the veiled truths of his life become known. The photograph thus, becomes a means, for exposing the past. However, much remains concealed. Thus, the past becomes juxtaposed to the present and the narrator presumes from the photograph that what Hugo is presenting is not the whole truth but only a distortion of reality. As a matter of fact, Hugo is only trying to present his credentials as a creative artist. Moreover his use of Dotty, whom the narrator and Hugo had once referred to as "harlot-in residence" (*Something*: 23) now forms the materials for his work, and seems to be only "Lovely tricks, honest tricks" (*Something*: 43), which the narrator cannot excuse. Towards the end of the story, she says: "This is not enough, Hugo. You think it is, but it isn't you are mistaken, Hugo" (*Something*: 44).

"Winter wind" is yet another story, where Munro uses the photograph as an analogue to her narrative art. Here the narrator tells the readers that there was a family photograph in the room, of her "grandmother and Aunt Madge, with their parents, and this sister who had died..." (*Something*: 194). But she had not heeded to it. Only with her grandmother's death, and Aunt Madge's admission to the nursing home, did she "salvage it..." (*Something*: 194). The photograph also spoke of her great-grandfather as "handsome still, bearded, hand-on knee, patriarchal...the sign and record of his achievement: respectability, moderate prosperity, mollified wife in a black silk dress, the well-turned-out tall daughters" (*Something*: 194). Thus, the photograph here serves as a link with the past and highlights the family heritage of the narrator.

In "The Ottawa Valley", again Munro shows life in terms of flux and change. The narrator glances through the "series of snapshots..." of "Aunt Dodie and Uncle James and even Aunt Lena, ever her children, come out clear enough". However, the image of her mother "is indistinct, her edges and flow" (*Something*: 246). Munro places this photographic imagery at the end of the collection, in order to exemplify the fact that life is a series of events. She tells Hancock: "There are just flashes of things we know and find out. I don't see life very much in terms of progress" (Hancock: 102). Susan Sontag too has described the photographic conception of the world as "series of unrelated, freestanding particles" (Sontag: 23).

In *Friend of My Youth,* Munro again resorts to photographic metaphors to enhance the dramatic effect of story. In "Menesteung", the author, at the outset mentions a book, *Offerings,* with photograph on the frontispiece, indicating its author 'Almeda Joynt Roth'. The story moves forward and the photographic imagery, which abounds throughout, contributes to the singular artistic effect of the story.

Photography again forms a vital part of narrative art in "Pictures of the Ice", where Austen shows Karin his housekeeper, a picture of Sheila Brothers, the woman he is to marry. It thus sets the groundwork on which the story unfolds itself. Similar patterns of revelation and confession through photograph, is evident in "Lichen". Here too, David shows Stella his ex-wife, a "Polaroid snapshot" (*Progress*: 41) of his latest girlfriend. The photograph gives an ironic twist to the story, as it mystifies relationships, and fails to explain unusual human predicaments. As Stella observes: "Whom does he want to be cruel to...Stella, Catherine, the girl, himself?" (*Progress*: 42).

In "The Turkey Season", the barn workers gather, at Christmas time and have their photograph taken by the foreman, Herb Abbot. Describing this picture years later, the narrator says:

> We still wore our working clothes: overalls and shirts.... I am stout and cheerful and comradely in the picture, transformed into someone I don't even remember being to or pretending to be. I look years older than fourteen. Irene...peers out from [her long red hair] with a meek, sluttish, inviting look, which would match her reputation but is not like any look of hers I remember. Yes, it must have been her camera; she is posting for it, with that look, more deliberately than anyone else is. Marjorie and Lily are smiling, true to form, but their smiles are sour and reckless.... We are all holding mugs or large, thick china cups, which contain not the usual tea but rye

> whiskey.... I don't need Herb in the picture to remember what he looked like. That is, if he looked like himself, as he did...all the times in my life when I saw him accept one. (*Something*: 72-73)

Here, the picture that the narrator looks into after many years, revives past memories, and seems to imply more than is expressed. Photographic imagery is also explicit in Munro's other stories. In "An Ounce of Cure", the narrator after consuming an over-dose of whisky, stares at "...the tiles, which lay together in such an admirable and logical pattern" on the bathroom floor (*Dance*: 81). In "Images", the narrator describes her father's boots with comic irony and a pictorial quality:

> His boots were to me as unique and familiar, as much an index to himself as his face was. When he had taken them off, they stood in a corner of the kitchen, giving off a complicated smell of manure, machine oil, caked black mud, and the ripe and disintegrating material that lined their soles. They were a part of himself, temporarily discarded, waiting. (*Dance*: 36)

When Geoff Hancock, talking to Munro suggested: "...the formal technical processes of using a camera are remarkably similar to the way you use your prose", and whether she tried to "render a scene as a photograph might"; Munro replied, "Well, I see the scene. I see it awfully clearly. And I want the reader to see it the way I see it" (Hancock: 107).

Munro has always wanted the story to be a pictorial one, which would "generate some other images and attract them like a magnet. Things stick to it. Anecdotes and details" (Hancock: 104). This pictorial representation of life in art is one of Munro's greatness as an artist. She says: "Even totally commonplace things...are.... Endlessly interesting in their physical reality.... They seem to mean something way beyond themselves" (Hancock: 101). For Munro, the surface reality exampled more than it revealed. In this context, Lorraine McMullen writes: "The use of surface details to reveal the essential (is) a central aspect of Munro's style. (McMullen: 147)

Munro's art of depicting the realities of life, with accuracy and perfection has evoked the admiration of critics. Her photographic sensibility forms an integral part of her narrative art. In her fiction, one finds a continual use and reference to photography. Her paradoxical vision of human life and its transience is singularly reflected in her art, which is presented beautifully through photographic metaphors. Munro firmly believed that human life is a juxtaposition of events and happenings, taking place in the life of an individual. In addition, this can be accurately depicted through photographic art. Moreover, as photography tries to provide an understanding between perception and reality, Munro has tried to manifest that through photography; one can unfold the past, re-live it, and in turn recreate a new present. Since photography conceals more than it reveals, it has made her work open-ended, complex and intriguing. Munro's success as an artist lies in her ability to draw the picture of life in its holistic form, and this has been rendered possible by the use of photographic imagery in narrative art. This forms her greatest forte.

Munro's interest in photography and photographic realism can be compared to the Conradian concept of the "truth disclosed in a moment of illusion" (*Lord Jim*: 232). It also reveals the fact that Munro sought to represent the unresolved mysteries of life through paradoxical metaphors. This could well be presented through photographs. Munro's narrative art has always had a defamiliarizing effect, so that the unfamiliar and strange may appear to be common and familiar. This she has accomplished through the use of photography in narrative art. For Munro, the surface reality is not the whole truth, but that it lies imbedded deep within. Thus, the synthesis between illusion and reality as well as between motion and stillness, is achieved through photographic representation in art. Munro's vision of life, as embodied in her writings. It is voiced through snapshots: the still moments of life.

Notes

1. To 'dechronologize' narratives is to reduce it to a series of dominating 'paradigmatic' functions. This has been outlined by various narrative theorists, such as Propp, Greimas and Levi-Strauss.

2. Plot is the chain of causation that dictates that story events, which are somehow linked and they are therefore to be depicted in relation to each other. "The 'plot' or, in Ricoeur's terms, derived from Aristotle, *muthos* or emplotment, drives the story events" (Cobley: 239).
3. Amongst other theorists, Shlomith Rimmon-Kenan's comprehensive definition of narrotology deserves mention. In his opinion it should have "double orientation" that allows it "to present a description of the system governing all fictional narratives", and "...to indicate a way in which individual narratives can be studied as unique realizations of the general system" (Rimmon-Kenan, 1983: 4).
4. In this context, Shklovsky argued that all of these constructions perform the same function; they splinter even apparently unified non-aesthetic material, distort and alter it, making it artistically perceptible. In most literary works, the devices of plot construction are motivated realistically, with the author providing valid reason for their presence. But in some texts the devices are 'laid bare' making the reader aware of their presence. For Shklovsky, the best example of 'laying bare' the device was Laurence Sterne's novel *Tristam Shandy* with its continuous interruptions of the actions, authorial digressions, displacement of chronology, transpositions of chapters and retardation. Shklovsky expressed a decided preference for unmotivated devices. He believed the writer should play with the expectations of the readers and deliberately destroy the illusion of reality (Ref. Makaryk: 55).
5. The 'skaz' was of two types, the 'narrating skaz' relying on jokes and puns and the 'reproducing skaz', which introduced elements of mimicry, gestures, comic articulations and phonetic puns. The first type was use by Nikolai Leskov in the colloquial idioms and folk etymology. The second type is seen in the works of Nikolai Gogol (Ref. Makaryk: 55).
6. 'Prague structuralists' were the successors to the formalists. They formulated an oriented theory to see the literary text as a structure of difference.
7. One of the Bakhtin literary key concepts is 'polyphony' literally meaning 'many voices'. Its origins are in *Problems of Dostoevsky's Poetics,* the text in which Bakhtin first began to draw his crucial, discriminatory distinction between 'monological' and 'polyphonic'/'dialogic' tendencies in literature and culture, with Dostoevsky's 'liberation' of multiple,

independent voices into his novels regarded as nothing short of revolutionary (Waugh: 224).

8. It has the ability to report or reproduce speech; parody different language uses and has within a narratolorial or author's voice. This narratorial voice at times overlaps with other voices in the text. Bakhtin uses the term 'dialogue' to define the signs that passes between human beings "When heteroglossia enters the novel", writes Bakhtin, "it is subject to an artistic reworking" (1981, 300). Dialogue is thus becomes indispensable at a theme in all narratives (Cobley: 233).
9. Saussure's main aim was to give substance to what he called the new 'science of linguistics'. This appeared in a publication of series of lectures that he delivered at University of Geneva between 1906 and 1911. The lecturers were published after his death as *Course in General Linguistics* (1916). He emphasized upon the use of language 'as the norm of all other manifestations of speech' (Waugh: 260).
10. In *Introduction to the Structural Analysis of Narratives* (1966), Barthes provided a study of prose narratives. Where he devised a deductive method for the structural analysis, following the example of generative linguistics of narratives at the discourse level. Drawing on the Todorov, Barthes emphasized the need to construct a 'functional syntax', capable of accounting for every type of narrative. He improved the Russian formalist model and that of Todorov and maintained that understanding of narratives does not merely follow the unfolding of narratives from beginning middle to end, but rather it is a vertical construction. He observed that there are three main levels in which a narrative Works: "the level of 'function', the level of 'action', and the level of 'narration' (Ref. Waugh: 270).
11. Hermeneutic code: Code in narrative identified by Roland Barthes in *S/*,(1974): The code has a dual function in relation to the establishment of narrative 'space' and 'time' because it (a) Pushes the narrative forward towards disclosure; and (b) simultaneously retards a narrative's progress "The code is manifested in narrative events by story features such as 'equivocation', 'snares' and 'false replies' Brooks (1982) refers to such events as *detours*." (Cobley: 233)
12. The second key figure in the development of post-structuralism in the late 1960s is the philosopher Jacques Derrida. Indeed, the starting point of post-structuralism may be taken as his

1966 lecture 'Structure, Sign and Play in the Discourse of the Human Sciences'.

13. 'Free Play': In his lecture Derrida embraces this decentred universe of 'free play' as liberating, just as Barthes in 'The Death of the Author' celebrates the demise of the author as ushering in an era of joyous freedom (Barry: 67).

14. Munro's first collection *Dance of the Happy Shad* was published in 1968. This collection consists of fifteen stories. Some of the stories were published in the various Journals & Magazine. These are:

    "Thanks for the Ride", *The Tamarak Review* 2, Winter 1957.

    "The Office", *The Montrealer,* May 1961.

    "The Time of Death", *The Canadian Forum* 36, June 1965.

    "Day of the Butterfly", *Chatelaine,* July 1956.

    "Boys and Girls", *The Montrealer,* December 1964.

    "Post Card", The Tamarak Review 47, Spring 1968.

    "Red Dress—1946", *The Montrealer,* May 1965.

    "Sunday Afternoon", *The Canadian Forum* 37, September 1957.

    "The Peace of Utrecht", *The Tamarak Review* 15, Spring 1960.

    "Dance of the Happy Shades", *The Montrealer,* February 1961 [Martin 208].

    Remaining stories incorporated in this collection:

    "Walker Brothers Cowboy"

    "The Shining Houses"

    "Images"

    "A Trip to The Coast"

    "An Ounce of Cure".

15. *Something I've Been Meaning to Tell You,* first published in 1974. Thirteen stories have been incorporated in this third compilation. Out of thirteen, two stories were published in two separate journals:

    "Material", *The Tamarack Review* 61, November 1973;

    "How I met my Husband", *McCall's,* February 1974 [Martin 209].

    Other stories compiled in this collection:

    "Some thing I've Been Meaning to Tell You"

"Walking on Water"
"Forgiveness in Families"
"Tell Me Yes or No"
"The Found Boat"
"Executioners"
"Marrakesh"
"The Spanish Lady"
"Winter Wind"
"Memorial"
"The Ottawa Valley"

16. *Who Do You Think You Are?* consists of ten stories, written in 1977 and 1978. Other then a few, all the stories have been published in different Journals and Magazine. These are:

    "Royal Beating", *The New Yorker,* 14 March 1977.

    "Privilge", *The Honeyman's Granddaughter* No. 4, October 1978.

    "Half a Grapefruit", *Redbook* 151, No. I May 1978.

    "Wild Swans", *Toronto Life,* April 1978.

    "The Beggar Maid", *The New Yorker,* 27 June 1977.

    "Mischief", *Viva* 6, April 1978.

    "Providence", *Redbook* 149, No. 4, August 1977.

    "Spelling", *Weekend* 28, 17 June 1978.

    Remaining stories incorporated in this collection are:

    Simon's Luck

    Who Do You Think You Are?

17. *The Moons of Jupiter*: this compilation consists of eleven stories, written from November 1978 to July 1982. Some of the stories were published previously in various Journals & Magazines.

    "Chaddeleys and Flemings": 1. Connection in *Chatelaine,* Nov. 1978.

    "Chaddeleys and Flemings": 2. *The Stone in the Field, Saturday Night,* April 1979.

    "Dulse", *The New Yorker,* 21 July 1980.

    "The Turkey Season", *The New Yorker,* 29 December 1980.

    "Accident", *Toronto Life,* November 1977.

    "Prue", *The New Yorker,* 30 March 1981.

"Labor Day Dinner", *The New Yorker,* 28 September 1981.

"Mrs. Cross and Mrs. Kidd", *The Tamarack Review,* winter, 1982.

"Visitors", *The Atlantic,* April 1982.

"The Moons and Jupiter", *The New Yorker,* 22 May 1978. [Martin 210].

Remaining stories are:

"Bardon Bus"

"Hard-Luck Stories"

18. Stories incorporated in *Progress of Love* (1986) were written in the year 1985 & 1986, and most of the stories were published in different Journals and Magazine.

"Progress of Love", *The New Yorker*, 7 October 1985.

"Lichen", *The New Yorker,* 25 July 1985.

"Monsieur Les Deux Chapeaux", *Grand Street* 4, No. 3, Spring 1985.

"Miles City, Montana", *The New Yorker,* 14 January 1985.

"Fits", *Grand Street* 5, No. 2, Winter 1986.

"The Moon in the Orange Street Skating Rink", *The New Yorker,* 31 March 1986.

"Jesse and Meribeth (Secrets between Friends)", *Mademoiselle,* November 1985.

"Eskimo", *Gentlemen's Quarterly* 55, No. 12, December 1985.

"A Queer Streak (Part I)" *Granta* 17, Autumn 1985.

"A Queer Streak (Part II)" *Granta* 18, Spring 1986.

"Circle of Prayer", *Paris Review 100,* Summer/Fall 1986.

"White Dump", *The New Yorker,* 28 July 1986.

19. *Friend of My Youth,* Published in 1990. This collection consists of ten stories.

Namely,

"Friend of My Youth"

"Five Points"

"Menseteung"

"Hold Me Fast, Don't Let Me Pass"

"Oranges and Apples"

"Pictures of the Ice"

"Goodness and Mercy"

"Oh, What Avails"
"Differently"
"Wigtim"

20. *Open Secrets,* Munro's seventh collection, published in 1994, which consists of eight stories. All stories were published in:
"Carried Away", *The New Yorker.*
"A Real Life", (Originally entitled "A Forum of Marriage") *The New Yorker.*
"The Albanian Virgin" (Originally entitled "Lottar"), *The New Yorker.*
"Open Secrets", *The New Yorker.*
"The Jack Randa Hotel", *The New Yorker.*
"A Wilderness Station", *The Paris Review.*
"Spaceships Have Landed", *The Paris Review.*
"Vandals", *The New Yorker.*
21. *The Love of a Good Woman,* Munro's eighth Collection, published in 1998. Some of the stories were originally published in the following:
"Love of a Good Woman", *The New Yorker.*
"Jakarta", *Saturday Night.*
"Cortes Island", *The New Yorker.*
"Save the Rapper", *The New Yorker.*
"The Children Stay", *The New Yorker.*
"Before the Change", *The New Yorker.*
Remaining two stories are:
"Ricb as Stink" &
"My Mother's Dream".
22. Gentry, Marshal Bruce, *Love of A Good Woman* by Alice Munro (review), 21.08.2006, <Yahoo.com.http://English.uindy.edu/reviews/woman.htm>.
23. qtd. in *The Other Side of Dailines,* York, p. 18.
24. Alice Munro, "An Open Letter", *Jubilee,* 1 (nd), p. 7.

Works Cited

Avistotle. *Poetics,* trans. Malcolm Heath, Harmondsworth: Penguin, 1996.

Barthes, Roland. *Image Music Text,* trans. Stephen Heath, London: Fontana Press, 1977.

Barry, Peter. *Beginning Theory: An Introduction to Literary and Cultural Theory*, Manchester and New York: Manchester University Press, 1995. First Indian rpt. Chennai, 1999.

Beran, Carol L. "The Luxury of Excellence: Alice Munro in the New Yorker", ed. Jack Berger, John, and Jean Mohar. *Another Way of Telling*. New York: Pantheon, 1982.

Bertens, Hans. *Literary Theory: The Basics*, London and New York: Routledge, 2001.

Bowerng, George. "Modernism Could Not Last Forever", *Canadian Fiction Magazine*, 32/33, 1979/80: 4-9.

Booth, C. Wayne. *The Rhetoric of Fiction*, Chicago: University of Chicago Press, 1961.

Burgin, Victor. ed. "Looking at Photographs", *Thinking Photography*, London: Macmillan, 1982.

CBC Radio. "Morningside". 1994.

Cobley, Paul. *Narrative*, London and New York: Routledge, 2001.

Coleman, A.D. *Light Readings: A Photography Critic's Writings, 1968-1978*, New York: Oxford UP, 1979.

Culler, Jonathan. *Barthes: A Very Short Introduction*, Oxford and New York: Oxford University Press, 2002.

David, et al. *Essays on Canadian Writing 66*, Alice Munro Issue, Winter 1998.

DeWiel, Alexa. "Mothers, Moons and Mafiosi" Broadside, May 1983: 11-13.

Eliot, T.S. *Collected Poem of T.S. Eliot 1909-1962*. New York: Harcourt, 1963.

Foy, Nathalie. "Darkness Collecting": Reading "Vandals" as a Code to Open Secrets, ed. Jack David, et al. *Essays on Canadian Writing 66*, Alice Munro Issue, Winter 1998.

Genette, Gerard. *Narrative Discourse*, trans. Jane E. Lewin, Oxford: Blackwell, 1980.

Gentry, Marshal Bruce. The Love of A Good Woman by Alice Munro (review), 21.08.2006, <Yahoo.com.http://English.uindy.edu/reviews/woman.htm>

Gibson, Graeme. Eleven Canadian Novelists (Interviewed by Graeme Gibson) Toronto: Anansi, 1972.

Gzowski, Peter. Interview with Alice Munro on "Morning Side", CBC National Radio Programme, 21 October, 1982.

Hancock, Geoff. "An Interview with Alice Munro", *Canadian Fiction Magazine,* 43, 1982.

——. "The Colonel's Hash Resettled" in *The Narrative Voice: Stories and Reflections by Canadian Authors,* ed. John Metcalf, Toronto, Mcgraw Hill: Ryerson, 1972.

——. "What Is Alice Munro". With Alan Twigg. *For Openers: Conversations with 24 Canadian Writers.* Madeira Park BC: Harbour, 1981.

Heble, Ajoy. *The Trumble of Reason: Alice Munro's Discourse of Absence,* Toronto, Buffalo, London: University of Toronto Press, 1994.

Howells, Coral Ann. *Alice Ann Munro,* ed. W.H. New, *Encyclopedia of Literature Canada.* Toronto: University of Toronto Press, 2002.

Krishnaswami, N., S.K. Verma, M. Nagarajan, eds. *Modern Applied Linguistics: An Introduction,* Macmillan India Limited, Madras, Macmillan India Press, 1992.

Lyotard, J.F. *The Post Modern Condition: A Report on Knowledge,* tans. G. Bennington and B. Massumi, Manchester: Manchester University Press, 1984.

McCulloch, Jeanne and Mona Simpson. "Alice Munro: The Art of Fiction cxxxvii." (Interview with Alice Munro), *Paris Review* 131 (1994): 226-64.

MacFarlane, David. "Writer in Residence." *Saturday Night,* Dec. 1986: 51-55.

Mackendrick, Louis K. ed. *Probable Fictions: Alice Munro's Narrative Acts.* Downsview Ontario: ECW Press. 1983.

Makaryk, Irena. R. ed. & Complied, *Encyclopedia of Contemporary Literary Theory.* Approaches, Scholars, Terms. Toronto, Buffalo, London: University of Toronto Press, 1995.

Mallinson, Jean. "Jon Robert Colombo: Documentary Poet as Visionary", *Essay on Canadian Writing* 5, 1976: 67-70.

Moss, John. *The Paradox of Meaning Cultural Poetics and Critical Fictions.* Winnipeg, Manitoba: Turstone Press, 1999.

Munro, Alice. *Dance of the Happy Shades,* Toronto: McGraw, 1968.

——. *Lives of Girls and Women,* Toronto: McGraw-Hill Ryerson, 1971.

——. *Something I've Been Meaning to Tell You: Thirteen Stories,* Toronto: McGraw-Hill Ryerson, 1974.

——. *Who Do You Think You Are?* Toronto: Macmillan of Canada, 1978.

——. *Women and Writing*, ed. Michele Barrett. New York: Harcourt Brace Jovanovich, 1980.

——. "Simon's Luck", *The Beggar Maid: Stories of Flo and Rose.* London: Penguin, 1980.

——. *The Moons of Jupiter*. Toronto: Macmillan of Canada, 1982.

——. *Progress of Love.* McClelland and Stewart, A Douglas Gibson Book, 1986.

——. *Friend of My Youth*. Toronto: McClelland & Stewart, 1990.

——. *"What is Real?" Making It New: Contemporary Canadian Stories,* ed. John Metcalf and (Tim) Struthers. Erin ON: Porcupine's Quill, 1993.

——. "The Real Material: An Interview with Alice Munro", with J.R. (Tim) Struhers. *Probable Fictions: Alice Munro's Narrative Acts,* ed., Louis K. Mac Kendrick. Downsview Toronto: ECW Press, 1983, pp. 5-36.

——. *Open Secrets*, Toronto: Knopf, 1994.

——. "Alice Munro: The Art of Fiction cxxxvii." Interview with Jeanne Mcculloch and Mona Simpson, *Paris Review,* 131 (1994): 226-64.

——. *Selected Stories*. Toronto: McClelland & Stewart, 1996.

——. *Hateship, Friendship, Courtship, Loveship, Marriage*. Toronto: McClelland & Stewart, 2001.

——. *The Love of a Good Woman*. Toronto: McClelland & Stewart, 1998.

——. *The Love of a Good Woman*. Toronto: 1998. rpr. Harvest/HBL edition. San Diego: Harcourt Brace Jovanorich Publishers, 1989.

——. "A Conversation with Alice Munro" with John Metcalf, *Journal of Canadian Fiction* 1.4, 1972.

Murch, Kem. "Name: Alice Munro. Occupation: Writer." *Chatelaine,* August 1974.

Newhall, Beaumont. *The History of Photography: From 1839 to the Present Day,* 1939. 4th ed., New York: Museum of the Modern Art, 1978. 22.

Nightingale, Dr. Barbra. *Alice Munro's Message* (Research Paper), ENC 1102, August 1, 2003.

Noonan, Gerald. "The Structure of Style in Alice Munro's Fiction", ed. Louis K. Mackendrick, *Probable Fictions,* (Downsview, Ontario: ECW Press, 1983.

Orange, John. "Alice Munro and a Maze of Time". *Probable Fictions: Alice Munro's Narrative Acts* ed. Louis K. Mackendrick. Downsview Ontario: ECW Press, 1983.

Osachoff, Gail Margaret "Treacheries of the Heart": Memoir, Confession, and Meditation in Stories of Alice Munro. *Probable Fictions. Alice Munro's Narrative Acts.* ed. Louis K. Mackendrick. Downsview Ontario: ECW Press, 1983.

Plato. *Republic, trans. Desmond* Lee, intro. Rachana Kamtekar, Harmondsworth: Penguin, 2003.

Prince, Gerald. *A Dictionary of Naratology,* Nilcoln & London: University of Nebraska Press, 1987.

Rasporich, Beverly J. *Dance of the Sexes: Art and Gender in the Fiction of Alice Munro.* Edmonton, Alberta: University of Alberta Press, Canada, 1990.

Reading Group Center, "A Conversation with Alice Munro", Vintage Books, dt.2/18/309:05PM <http://www.randomhouse.com/vintage/read/secrets/munro.html.>

Redekop, Magdalene. "Alice Munro and the Scottish Nostalgic Grotesque", ed. Jack David et al. *Essays on Canadian Writing 66,* Alice Munro Issue, Winter 1998.

Rimmori-Kenan, Shlomith. *Narrative Fiction: Contemporary Poetics,* London: Routledge, 1983.

Ross, Catherine Sheldrick. *Alice Munro: A Double Life.* Toronto: ECW Press, 1992.

Scobie, Stephen. "A Visit with Alice Munro", *Monday,* 19 Nov. 1982: 12-13.

Struthers, J.R. (Tim) "The Real Material": *Interview with Alice Munro. Narrative Acts.* ed. Louis K. Mackendrick Downs view Ontario: ECW Press, 1983.

Thacker, Robert. "Clear Jelly: Alice Munro's Narrative Dialectics" in *Probable Fiction: Alice Munro's Narrative Acts* Ed. Louis K. Mackendrick. Downs view, Ontario: ECW Press, 1983.

The Globe and Mail, Toronto, "Writing's Something I Did, Like the Ironing", 11 Dec. 1982.

Toye, William, ed. *The Concise Oxford Companion to Canadian Literature.* Oxford, New York: Oxford University Press, 2001.

Twigg, Alan. (Interview with Alice Munro) "What Is: Alice Munro", *For Openers: Conversations with 24 Canadian Writers*. Madeira Park BC: Harbour, 1981.

Twigg, Alan. *For Openers: Conversations with 24 Canadian Writers*. Madeira Park B.C.: Harbour Publishing, 1981.

Wachtel, Eleanor. "An Interview with Alice Munro". *Brick* 40 (1991): 48-53.

Waugh, Patricia, ed. *Literary Theory and Criticism*. New York: Oxford University Press, 2006.

Wake, Paul. "Narrative and Narratology", eds. Simon Malpas, and Paul Wake. *The Routledge Companion to Critical Theory*, London & New York: Routledge, 2006.

Webster, Frank. *The New Photography: Responsibility in Visual Communication*. London: John Calder, 1980.

White, Hayden. *Metahistory: The Historical Imagination in Nineteenth-Century Europe*, Baltimore and London: Johns Hopkins University Press, 1973.

York, Lorraine M. *The Others Side of Dailiness: Photography in the Works of Alice Munro, Timothy Findley, Michael Ondaatje, Margaret Laurence*. Toronto: ECW Press, 1988.

4

Reality or Fiction: Munro's Autobiographical Quest

Autobiography is most commonly defined as, "the biography of a person narrated by that person," or "the story of a person's life as told by him or herself" (Duran: Website citation par. 1). The word 'Autobiography' is derived from the Greek *auton,* or 'self', *bios,* 'life' and *graphein,* to 'write' (Wikipedia, *The Free Encyclopedia:* Website Citation par. 1). The origin of the genre may be traced to post-Homeric Greece and works by Hesiod, Empedocles, Plato (Epistle: 7) and Isocrates. It developed in the Roman world in Ovid's autobiographical poems, Cicero's *Brutus* and St. Augustine's *Confession.*[1]

The English word "autobiography" however, was first coined in the late eighteenth century, when the genre began to flourish in Europe and North America, notably in Rousseau's *Confessions* (1782), Benjamin Franklin's *Autobiography* (1784). Writers, such as John Henry Newman considered autobiographical narrative as an essential form of self-justification and called his autobiography '*Apologia pro vita sua*' (Wikipedia: Website Citation par. 2).

John Banyan's *Grace Abounding to the Chief of Sinners,* Goethe's *Dichtung und Wahrheit,* William Wordsworth's *The Prelude,* Walt Whitman's *Song of Myself* and Dickens' *David Copperfield* are some of the masterpieces of this genre.

An Autobiography differs from a biography as well as a memoir. While biography is based on documentary evidence such as letters, diaries, photographs and multiple viewpoints, autobiography concentrates on memory and imagination, with the help of which the writer is able to recall the past and recreate the present. Roy Pascal distinguished memoir from reminiscence—the former "concerns itself with public events" and the latter with "private relationships"—and both of these form autobiography proper, whose "attention is focused on the self, in the memoir or reminiscence on others" (Pascal: 5). Pascal also said that confession is like autobiography but focuses on the internal life of an individual. It started as a religious form of autobiography and in his *Confessions* St. Augustine created "the coherent history of his own soul" (Pascal: 22). When used as a literary form confession does not imply admission as in the religious form but rather a writer's self-justification. Jean Rousseau's *Confessions* becomes "a search for the true self, and a means to come to terms with it" (Osachoff: 82). Meditations are a form of devotional literature, the most famous example being the *Meditations* of Marcus Aurelius[2] "Meditations are reflections on moral and spiritual topics. They have no order, narrative, or consecutive arrangements. They are private soliloquies intended for no eyes but the writer's own..." (Osachoff: 82). As a subject of literary discourse, autobiography is primarily related to the artistic re-creation of the author's life. While recapitulating, the autobiographer makes a truthful and impartial observation of the past. In this context, James Olney observes: "Confessions of the past realizes as a work in the present: it effects as true creations of the self by the self" (Olney: 44).

The art therefore becomes an act of self-reflection, and a quest for the inner self. Human mind acts as a receptor, where a series of impressions and ideas are recorded. In an autobiographical art, the writer delves into the conscious self, and attempts to draw out the impressions stored in memory. While presenting the incidents and events of life, the author recaptures the past, assimilates and synchronizes those experiences and presents them before the reader from a new perspective. This process calls for an objective reflection of the subjective self. Emphasizing on the relevance of self in creative art, Wayne C. Booth observes:

> As he writes, he creates not simply an ideal, impersonal 'man in general' but an implied version of 'himself that is different from the implied authors we meet in other men's works. (Booth: 70)

Thus, a new self emerges, as the writer views the experiences of the past from a new perspective. Jean Starobinski is of the view that in autobiographical creations, the past "I" becomes different from the present "I". The narrator describes not only what happened to him at different moments of his life but above all how he became his present self.

The incident of the past that may have been insignificant at the time of occurrence now acquires new dimensions, as it is enlivened by the author's fictional art. This leads to an examination of the inner self. James Olney opines that autobiography is: "Self-portraiture...a synonym of self-knowledge" (Olney: 166). On the other hand, Rabindranath Tagore had emphasized on the uniqueness of self: "I am absolutely unique, I am I, I am incomparable" (Sadhana: 57). Autobiographical art or the re-telling of the story of one's own life therefore becomes a means for opening the pent-up emotions within. In this context, Bell Hooks opines:

> The longing to tell one's story and the process of telling is symbolically a gesture of longing to recover the past in such a way that one experiences both a sense of reunion and a sense of release. (Hooks: 1038)

Through this process the experiences of the author no longer remain singular and personal but acquires universal propensity. This self-preferentiality calls for a re-creation of personality and the inner self of the author. The autobiographical art therefore becomes the mirror which reflects the individual's his own image.

While writing about one's own self, the author not only interrelates the experiences to familial bonds and other relationships but also to the social contexts. The autobiography does not remain merely a chronicle of the author's life but a work of fiction, where the events are colored by the writer's emotion and imagination. According to A.O.J. Cockshut, writing of autobiography is an exercise in inner assimilation, which involves qualities like "articulateness, fidelity to experience, sensitiveness to small currents of feeling, and, above all curiosity" (Cockshut: 17). A comprehensive definition of the autobiographical art was given by James Olney, when he says that the art is "...a temporal, committed to a vertical thrust from consciousness down into the unconsciousness rather than to a horizontal thrust from the present into the past,..." (Onley: [qtd Benstock] 1040). As a work of art, autobiography is intrinsically expressive, for it perceives life and expresses it in its fullest.

Feminist critics, expressing their views on the genre, differentiate the autobiographies of women from their male counterparts. They point out that while writing, women are generally concerned with the question as to how to express their sensibilities as women, and their inner selves in social constructs. The telling of their stories becomes difficult, being characterized by the gaps and fissures of their lives. But at the same time the art gives them an opportunity to assert their thoughts and feelings. Their narratives, therefore becomes a quest for identity. A notable feature of women's autobiographies is that women generally talk about their familial bonds, kinships and also about their social setups. Moreover, as women's lives are characterized by fragmentariness and disruptions, so too are their narratives.

"Autobiography is ubiquitous in feminist literary criticism" (Warhol: 1033). This statement is a pointer to the fact that women's art of narrating the stories of their lives are rendered problematic by the presence of a "double or divided inner self (Warhol: 1033), one that exists for the outer world and the other—the inner true self. This results in their narratives being open-ended.

Virginia Woolf and Maxine Hong Kingston are the two distinguished women writers of this century. In her diaries, and fragments of memoir, Woolf has shown how a woman autobiographer can explore the unconscious through the genre. Her journals explore the fact that autobiographical writings can include '"everything that forms the background of perception and action" everything traditionally left out of autobiography' (Warhol: 1034). Woolf therefore becomes a model for feminist autobiographers. Maxine Hong Kingston's *The Warrior Woman: Memoirs of a Girlhood among Ghosts 1977*, 'intertwines stories of her own memories with legends, her mother told her, so that her "self gets represented within the context of her familial and cultural heritages"' (Warhol: 1035). In this reference Jane Tompkins is of the view that in the art of autobiography, she finds an oscillation, 'a split between two voices, that of an academic critic, and of "a person who wants to write about her feelings"' (Warhol: 1035). Thus, the art of the autobiography becomes a complex form of narrative, which requires of the author an impartial representation of the self. Bell Hooks terms the narrative as a kind of "hope chest",[3] which stores the events, experiences of life, and which when brought to light, from the unconscious to the conscious self, acts as a "means of self growth and change in a practical way" (Warhol: 1039).

In Canada, autobiographical writings have existed in the form of dairies and memoirs from early settlement. The pioneer narratives of Susanna Moodie's *Roughing It in The Bush* (1852) and *Life in the Clearings* (1853); and Catherine Parr Trail's letters published as *The Backwoods of Canada* (1836), *Canadian Settlers Guide* (1855), are records of early settlement. Anna Jameson's work *Winter Studies and Summer Rambles* (1838) is an autobiographical account of a dissatisfied wife's sojourn in an alien land. Emily Carr's autobiography *Growing Pains* (1946) is also distinguished for its literary qualities. In this work Carr recapitulates her past, recreates her self on the basis of her present. Other eminent autobiographies are: John Kenneth Galbraith's *A Life in Our Times* (1981) and Michael Ignatieffs *The Russian Album* (1987) and many more.[4]

Alice Munro's works of fiction are largely autobiographical, as her stories are mainly based on her personal experiences. Events of her life form the groundwork of her stories. However, in her interviews to critics and writers, Munro is reluctant to call her works purely autobiographical. She points out that there is an "emotional reality" in her stories ("A Conversation": 58). In reply to a question posed by John Metcalf: "How far is your work autobiographical?" Munro replied:

> I guess I have a standard answer to this.... In incident no...in emotion completely. In incident up to a point too, but of course, in *Lives of Girls and Women* which is a...I suppose it could be called an autobiographical novel... most of the incidents are changed version of real incidents. Some are completely invented, but the emotional reality, the girl's feeling for her mother, for men, for life is all...it's all solidly autobiographical. I would not disclaim this at all. (Metcalf: 58)

Munro further says "Sunday Afternoon" and "Boys and Girls" use autobiographical material and that "Peace of Utrecht" was her "first painful autobiography" (Martin: 39).

A close look at Munro's revelations implies that the incidents, narrated in her fiction are based on personal experiences, and its emotional contents are truly autobiographical. In her art, she has fictionalized reality. The stories are narrated by a first person narrator, 'I', who is not the author herself, but the protagonist, whose experiences are common to those of the creator. In other words, Munro through her narrators recounts her experiences, only by giving them a fictive touch. In this process, she fictionalizes the past and projects them through the narrator who becomes the projector "I". However, the events narrated have close bearing on her personal life. Like her protagonists, Munro too had grown up in the relatively poor rural town of South Western Ontario, during the years of the Great Depression. Like them she had undergone emotional upheavals as a child, adolescent, a young woman, housewife, mother and above all as a writer of fiction. She too had felt the pain of suffering, experienced by women in their old age, and had felt the sense of loss at death. All these incidents become an integral part of her literary creations. Fiction and reality therefore become intermingled in her art. Thus, Munro's fiction tends to have the essence of an autobiographical art. At the same time it offers a realistic picture of life and society of the early thirties and forties.

Margaret Gail Osachoff categorizes Munro's autobiographical art into three components. She points out that in Munro's fiction, distinction is discernable depending on "what the story is about, on the reason of telling, and on its resolution. The stories can be called memoirs, confessions, or meditations keeping in view Munro's use of voice and its relation to her concern with the proper use of autobiographical material in fiction" (Osachoff: 63). Thus, it is observed that while *Dance of the Happy Shades,* and *Lives of Girls and Women* are in the form of a memoir, *Something I've Been Meaning to Tell You,* is in the nature of confessions or meditations.

Speaking about her work, Munro says that *Dance of the Happy Shades* started on an anecdote that someone told her at a family dinner party, a story "done in the form of a memoir more or less as a matter of convenience" ("The Colonel Hash Resettled", 183).

However, she goes on:

> The 'I' of the story is a masquerade, she is a little middle-class girl, I never was, an attempt to see the story through the eyes of a relative who told it to me. ("The Colonel Hash Resettled", 183)

By calling her art a memoir, Munro drives home the fact that in this collection the narrators are adults who now looks back and recollects some memorable or traumatic childhood or adolescent experiences. The incidents therefore acquire new dimension with the passage of time. Thus, it is observed that "Boys and Girls", "Red Dress—1946", "Images" are all in the form of memoirs. However, in certain other stories, the narrator confides to the reader and speaks of "the treachery of my own heart" (*Dance,* 111). Here, the narrator tries to unburden and to free herself from her inner guilt. Stories such as "Day of the Butterfly", "An Ounce of Cure", "Forgiveness in Families", etc. are all written in the form of a confession, as the speaker tries to release her inner self through her stories. Again, in certain stories such as "Material", "Tell Me Yes or No", Munro's characters reflect on the past, frames letters in the mind, which they are unable to communicate. These stories take the shape of meditations or reflections.

We may therefore say that in her attempt to recapture the past Munro has explored the various forms of autobiographical art and has adhered to impartial observation, accurate representation, trying to capture the exact images and voices of the people in fiction.

An examination of the personal materials inherent in the stories reveal that the background is generally 'Huron County, Ontario', where she had grown up as a child, and where she had spent a considerable part of her life. "The area of Huron County around Wingham is known internationally as Alice Munro country" (Ross: 21). This small town of Wingham is variously named in her fiction as: 'Jubilee, Hanratty, and Dalgleish'. The art of highlighting her own region and projecting it as a manifestation of the universal is common features, which Munro shares with other fiction writers, viz., "Sara Jeannette Duncan's Elgin, Stephen Leacock's Mariposa, James Reaney's Stratford, and Robertson Davies's Deptford" (Ross: 21). Robert Thacker calls Munro's Huron County "a place remembered, recovered, revised, and, at times renounced" (Thacker: 214). In spite of its close proximity to London, Toronto, and the lake port town of Goderich, Wingham is somehow a remote area regarding which the narrator in 'The Peace of Utrecht' says "there is no easy way to get to Jubilee from anywhere on earth" (*Dance*: 196).

The people, figured in her fiction are generally from the middle-class society of Wingham, Ontario, whose life patterns were familiar to the author. As she tells Alan Twigg:

> We lived outside the whole social structure.... We lived in this kind of little ghetto where all the bootleggers and prostitutes and hangers-on lived. Those were the people

> I knew. It was a community of outcasts. I had that feeling about myself. (Twigg: 18)

This community is portrayed through the characters of Becky Tyde, Hat Nettleton and others in *Who Do You Think You Are?*

As for the geographical setting, Munro refers to the Maitland River, which flowed "past the foot of the Laidlaw property on its way from Wingham to Lake Huron at Goderich. Indians had called it 'Meneseteung' before it was renamed the Maitland" (*Double Life*: 24). In her story titled 'Meneseteung' (*Friend*), the river is fictionalized. For Munro, this river had a legendary quality, for she says:

> This little stretch of river will provide whatever myths you want, whatever adventures.... This ordinary place is sufficient, everything here touchable and mysterious. (Ross: 24)

The culture of Huron County is also picturized in her works. Munro has herself summed it up as:

> ...rural culture with strong Scots-Irish background.... That has become fairly stagnant. With a big sense of righteousness. But with big hustings—out and grotesque crime. And ferocious sexual humour and the habit of getting drunk and killing each other off on the roads.... I always think the country I was born and brought up in is full of event and emotions and amazing things going on all the time. (Hancock: 93)

Thus, it has been observed that Munro has in her art, fictionalized the geographical and the demographical setting of her early childhood.

In presenting her characters, Munro has drawn heavily on her family history and lineage. The Chaddeley cousins in "Connections", who were presented as ambitious, self-confident, and self-dramatizing, and who saw "life in terms of change and possibility" (*Moons*: 29) were based upon Munro's mother's family. Her father's family who were Presbyterian Scots, "against the English Church and the family Compact, Bishop Strachan, and saloons" ("Working": 15), are portrayed as the Fleming sisters in "The Stone in the Field". These women were "diligent, self-controlled, and self-denying, seeing life in terms of ritualized work for its sake" (Ross: 27). Aunt Elspeth is presented by Munro as sitting on the couch now, her feet close together in rough men's boots. Her hands, red and rough from all the scrubbing, were folded in her lap.... Her features were pleasant enough but held tightly, as was her whole body, in the tenseness, almost fear, of a wild animal" (*Moons*: 48-49).

In an interview to Ross, Munro says:

> That's the kind of women we saw around us. My father did have a family of cousins who were like that. They had a primitive lack of ability to communicate. They just sort of trembled with the horror of [our visit]. My father used to claim in his last years that this was a family characteristic. I have an extraordinary timidity, which I have mostly overcome. (Ross: 29)

Munro portrays these women repeatedly in her stories.

In Munro's art, mother-daughter relationship forms a composite part of story telling. The stories are based on the author's personal relationship with her mother, Anne Clarke Chamney, who was "brave, prim, energetic, and single-minded, with a forceful personality" (Ross: 30), and who serves as a model for Del's mother. A woman of strong determination with an independent mind, her influence on Del in her formative years, makes Del remark: "Her concern about my life, which I needed and took for granted, I could not bear to have expressed" (*Lives*: 193).

Talking about her mother, Munro says: "My mother was in some ways very conventional. She was full of self-assertion. But what she wanted really, was a place in society where you could live in a nice way and have people to tea. She valued material things that would make your life comfortable and would remove your life from all this physical mess that we always had to confront" (Ross: 33). This mother image is presented in "Oh What Avail" (*Friend*). Again, in the title story Munro draws the mother as "a young woman with a soft mischievous face and shiny, opaque silk stockings on her plump legs" (*Friend*: 40). Marietta, in *Progress of Love* is modeled on Anne's mother, who was a carriage-maker's daughter, coming from "that small-town kind of entrepreneurial class, which has more ambition and is less conservative, probably than the man she married, who was a very nice Irish Protestant farmer" (Ross: 30).

Munro's mother suffered from the dreaded Parkinson's disease. The pangs of suffering are drawn in her fiction. In the autobiographical story "The Ottawa Valley", the protagonist's mother too suffers from the same malady and the narrator first notices her mother's left hand and forearm trembling when they are on a visit to her mother's family in the Ottawa Valley. Embedded in this story is a description from a medical encyclopedia of the symptoms of the dreaded disease:

> The onset is slow...[The patient] shows slowly increasing bodily rigidity, associated with tremors of the head and limbs. There may be various tics, twitches, muscle spasms, and other involuntary movements...the face begin to lose its customary expressiveness..... No recoveries are recorded. (*Something:* 236-37)

Munro tells Eleanor Wachtel, that her mother's illness made her very self-protective, unable to afford any pity for her mother because she didn't want to get trapped:

> In families like ours it is the oldest daughter's job to stay home and look when they're in this situation, until they die. I, instead, got a scholarship and went to university. There is enormous guilt about doing that, but at the time you're so busy protecting yourself that you simply push it under, and then you suffer from it later on. (Wachtel: 50)

Like Munro, the narrator too in "Miles city Montana" suffers from a sense of guilt for having neglected her ailing mother. In "The Peace of Utrecht", Munro gives a painful account of her mother's death, following which she visits her grandmother home, where her mother's clothes were shown to her. This had a touching effect on her. Speaking on the matter, Munro says:

> I didn't really understand what writing was all about until I wrote that story. It turned me around. It gave me some idea of what writing could do, approaching that kind of material. (Connolly & others: 8)

However, the use of personal material in writing came about only with her mother's death. As she told Tausky:

> Until my mother died, though the relationship with her was a very painful, deep one, I wasn't able to look at it or think about it. And the same thing happened when my father died and wrote "Royal Beatings". These are stories that come out of life. You can't rush them. It's as if until a certain point I was much more an artist than a person. I was essentially fairly tight emotionally.... I was very self-protective.... I was going through the motions of being a regular person, but the writing was always first. (Tausky: Webcite citation. Par. 15)

Munro's mother image also appears in "Winter Wind" and "Friend of My Youth", where she appears as a young teacher. "As Alice the writer gets older, the mother in the stories goes from old age and paralysis to youth, until, in *Friend of My Youth*, a time is recovered from before her marriage when she is a hopeful young schoolteacher (Ross: 41).

Personal relations also figure in "Winter Wind" where Munro portrays her paternal grandmother and great—aunt who had come to stay at Wingham in 1944, to keep house and help the family when her mother had become an invalid. These two senior women were upholders of social traditions. Munro draws them as women who rigidly upheld their values:

> They urged conventionality to a degree that you couldn't deny...they tried desperately to turn me into the right kind of woman. Sewing was the chief thing they urged on me. And they made me embarrassed about the situations at home. (Ross: 42)

These two women reappear in many other stories as well. Del's two aunts in *Lives of Girls and Women* are representatives of these types.

In her fiction Munro picturizes the "Lower Town School", where she started her grade one in 1937. In "Privilege" (*Who Do You Think You Are?*), which Munro has called "an autobiographical piece, not fiction at all" ("Who" Gerson: 6). She describes Rose's schooling at a place very much like Lower Town School, with its outhouse smells, lunch pail robbing, and coat slashing:

> Her schooling seemed deplorable.... But she was not miserable.... Learning to survive, no matter with what cravenness and caution, what shocks and forebodings, is not the same as being miserable.... It is too interesting. (*Who*: 28)

Talking about her school Munro says:

> Life in that school was shaming, vulgar, unintelligible, and frightening, but it taught her to build up her defenses. She learned not to confide in people—"you'd be crushed and beaten down if you did". (Ross: 34)

A major autobiographical element in her stories is the picturization of the Great Depression. During this period the silver-fox industry was just opening up, and foxes were selectively bred for white hairs along the back and tail. Munro's father following the Depression took up this rearing of silver foxes. In "Boys and Girls", the protagonist's father is also a fox farmer, who raises silver foxes, and sells their pelts to the Hudson Bay Company or the Montreal Fur Traders.

Real life characters and events drawn from family relations abound Munro's fiction. Uncle Benny is modeled on the hired man that Alice's father had employed on his farm. 'Flo' in *Who Do You Think You Are?* is portrayed on 'Etta', whom Robert Laidlaw had married after the death of his wife. In addition, in *The Moons of Jupiter,* Munro gives a factual account of her father's death, her visit to the Planetarium highlighting on father-daughter relationship.

In *The Love of a Good Woman,* Munro has skillfully interwoven the narrative structure with memories of her past, bringing about a coalescing of fact and fiction. 'My Mother's Dream', presents a fictional representation of autobiographical facts. This story "shows Munro experimenting with female fictive autobiography where the story of a near-fatal battle between a mother and daughter is told from the baby's perspective" (Howells: 771). Here the narrator tell the circumstances of her birth, the first few following months, as well as the various incidents in the life of her mother in its minute detail. Significantly, enough, this story is based on Munro's personal experience. In August 1955, her second daughter, Catherine was born. Without functioning kidneys, she lived less than two days. The intense grief for this lost daughter surfaced later. The baby was buried in a shoebox, without ceremony, in an available open grave. Since then and until the birth of her next child Jenny, Munro was haunted by a recurring dream (Ross: 53). As she says:

> I was doing something and had the feeling I was forgetting something very, very, important. It was a baby. I had left it out in the rain. By the time I remembered what it was, the baby was dead. This dream stopped when Jenny was born. (Ross: 53)

This unfortunate incident in referred to in the story when the narrator telling of her mother's dream, says:

> Within her dream she awakened from a dream, to knowledge of her responsibility and mistake. She had left her baby out overnight, she had forgotten about it. Left it exposed somewhere as if it was a doll she tired of.... It would be dead, shriveled and brown, its head like a nut, and on its tiny shut-up face there would be an expression not of distress but of bereavement, an old patient grief. (*Love*: 341)

Another feature of Munro's autobiographical art that calls for attention is that, the stories reveal a double self of the narrator, one for the outer world and the other, the inner secret self. This bears resemblance to the author herself. From her early childhood she was aware of the existence of the two selves: "From the age of 11, art was my religion.... Nothing in my life seemed more important to me" (Ross: 67). This vocation was her secret, which she kept to herself. As she revealed to Eleanor Wachtel in 1990: "I very early on got the motion that my real life had hidden, had to be protected.... I just, I suppose, lived a very deceptive life" (Wachtel: 48).

Talking about her own life, she said that she had the inclination of using "the motifs of the spy story: deception, disguises, the role of the detached watcher, and the contrast between the life of appearance and the real, secret life" (Ross: 19). Again, she has revealed to Barbara Frum, in 1973 that she led "two completely different lives—the real and absolutely solitary life and the life of appearances" ("Great Dames": 38). This strategy of holding onto the two women, and leading parallel and separate lives becomes the leading feature of all Munro's fictional creations. In *Dance of the Happy Shades,* the young observant child', minutely watches the adult world and draws her own conclusions. This "watching is associated with shame, betrayal, and exposure, while in the later books the idea of a hidden identity appears as a fascination with the theme of adultery" (Ross: 21). A double life is especially created for a "married wife and mother, who is expected to live her life for other people. Instead, she can be living this secret, exploratory life" (Ross: 67).

Summing up, we observe that Munro's autobiographical art highlights the emotional upheavals of the author's life, and this forms the groundwork of her fiction. By recapitulating the past and presenting it through her characters, Munro has fictionalized reality. For her, art becomes "...very much grafted on from the female experience and its social, psychological and physical realities..." (Rasporich: 32).

Munro's autobiographical art becomes a means for releasing her emotions, as well as an attempt to re-live and re-construct the past through either a first or an a third person narrator. In most of her stories, Munro talks about familial bonds and relationships and family history. This throws adequate light on the social convention of the times, as presented by the grandmothers and aunts. It also shows how women have tried to liberate themselves from these bondages, and break away from all sets of rules and regulations.

A special feature of this mode of autobiographical art is that, the stories recounted, are not always first hand experience of the individual narrators. Rather they are stories that were narrated to them by their mothers, which the mother had at times collected from town gossips, documents, or photographs. Thus, the mother's story becomes interwoven with the author's fictive imagination, which is again re-created by the narrator. The narration therefore becomes photographic presentation of the reality. As has been observed, Munro's narrators seem to enter into a dialogue with self, as well as the reader. This process helps in the re-creation of an inner self, and also the self gets represented within the context of the familial and cultural heritage.

In her narratives, Munro has problematized the workings of female psyche and tried to delve deep into the innermost recess of a woman's heart. Woman's personality is made up of multiple selves and the inner voice of woman has always remained suppressed under the layers of subjugation. Through her autobiographical texts, Munro has intensively looked into lives of her characters. Her exploration has revealed that the female experience is universal and that the biographical setup is responsible for shaping the personality of the individual. Here, Munro has shown that genealogy is of great significance as one's self is rooted in the past, which cannot be ignored in life. By shuttling back and forth in time and space, Munro has tried to recapture the past, through the eyes of her narrator. The fictional art has therefore become a voyage of self-discovery.

Munro's autobiographical quest thus becomes an exploration of the split in women's subjective selves, and the hidden truth lying beneath the apparent calm exterior. The quest for identity through self-revelation becomes the vision of Munro's fictive imagination. The very open-ended nesses of the texts have revealed the suppressed inner voice of womanhood and their need for self-assertion. Munro's characters provide a wide psychological study of Canadian female sensibility in its realistic perspectives. The emotional autobiography becomes for the author, a medium of self-expression in art.

Notes

1. Augustine's *Confessions,* written between the years 397 and 400 AD, was a landmark in establishing the conversion of experience into narrative, that is, in an autobiography. It is conversion of life into textual self-representation.
2. *Meditations* by Marcus Aurelius were translated by A.S.L. Farquharson, and introduced by D.A. Rees. London: Dent 1961.
3. Bell Hooks's terms the narrative as "Hope Chest", *Feminisms,* p. 1039.
4. New, W.H. Ed. *Encyclopedia of Literature: Canada,* University or Toronto Press, Toronto, Buffalo: London 2002 (pp. 662-63).

Works Cited

Booth, Wayne C. *The Rhetoric of Fiction.* The University of Chicago Press, 1970.

Benstock, Shari. "Authorising the Autobiographical" *Feminism,* ed. Robyn R. Warhol and Diane Price Herndl, New Brunswick, New Jersey, Third Paperback Printing, Rutgers University Press, 1996.

Cockshut, A.O.J. *The Art of Autobiography in the 19th and 20th Century England,* New Haven, Yale University Press, 1984.

Duran, Isabel. "Autobiography (2000 *BCE*)", *The Literary Encyclopedia,* <dt.24/11/2006http://www.litencyc.com/php/stopics.php?rec=trueUID=1232, >

——. Gerson, Carole. "Who Do You Think You Are?" Review/Interview with Alice Munro" *Room of One's Own* 4 No. 4 (Winter, 1979): 2-7.

Hooks, Bell. "Writing Autobiography", from *Talking Back: Thinking Feminist, Thinking Black,* rpt. *Feminism: An Anthology of Literary Theory And Criticism,* ed. Robyn R. Warhol and Diane Price Herndl, Rutgers University Press, New Brunswick, New Jersey, Third Paperback Printing, 1996.

Langer, Susanne K. *Feeling and Form: The Theory of Art,* London: Routledge and Kegan Paul, 1967.

Martin, W.R. *Alice Munro Paradox and Parallel.* Edmonton, Alberta, Canada: The University of Alberta Press, 1987.

Munro, Alice. "A Conversation with Alice Munro" with John Metcalf, *Journal of Canadian Fiction* 1.4, 1972.

——. "The Colonel's Hash Resettled" in *The Narrative Voice: Stories and Reflections by Canadian Authors,* ed. John Metcalf, Toronto, Mcgraw Hill: Ryerson, 1972.

——. "What Is: Alice Munro". With Alan Twigg. *For Openers: Conversations with 24 Canadian Writers.* Madeira Park BC: Harbour, 1981.

——. "Everything Here Is Touchable and Mysterious", *Weekend Magazine* 11 May, 1974.

——. "An Interview with Alice Munro" with Geoff Hancock. *Canadian Fiction Magazine* 43, 1982.

——. "Interview: Alice Munro" with Kevin Connolly, Douglas Freake and Jason Sherman, *What,* Sept.-Oct. 1986.

——. *Friend of My Youth.*

——. "An Interview with Alice Munro" with Eleanor Wachtel, Brick 40, 1991.

——. "Working for a Living", Grand Street 1.1, 1981.

——. "Who Do You Think You Are?: Review-Interview with Alice Munro." With Carole Gerson, *Room of One's Own,* 4.4, 1979.

——. et al. "Great Dames." With Barbara Frum. Maclean's April. 1973.

New, W.H. ed. *Encyclopedia of Literature: Canada,* University or Toronto Press, Toronto, Buffalo: London, 2002.

Olney, James, ed. *Studies in Autobiography.* New York and Oxford: Oxford University Press, 1988.

Osachoff, Margaret Gail. "Treacheries of the Heart", ed. Louis K. Mackendrick, *Probable Fictions: Alice Munro's Narrative Acts,* ECW Press, Strong College, Downsview, Ontario: York University, 1982.

Pascal, Roy. *Design and Truth in Autobiography,* London: Routledge & Kegan Paul, 1960.

Reynolds, Susana Salter. "Alice Munro—The Author Talks About her Life and Work", *The Writing Life, Los Angels Time,* dt.05.01.2007 <http://www.calendarlive.com/books/book revreynolds5nov05,0,/5400682.htmlstory?Coll=cl-book review>

Ross, Catherine Sheldrick. *Alice Munro: A Double Life.* Toronto: ECW Press, 1992.

Smith, Sidonie. "Maxine Hong Kingston's Woman Warrior: Finality and Woman's Autobiographical Storytelling" [from a Poetics of Women's Autobiography], *Feminism: An Anthology of Literary Theory and Criticism*, ed. Robyn R. Warholand Diane Price Herndl, New Brunswick, New Jersey, Rutgers University Press, Third Paperback Printing, 1996.

Sodhi, Meena. *Indian English Writing: The Autobiographical Mode,* Creative New Literature's Series-35, Creative Books, New Delhi, ed. 1999, p. 38.

Starobinski, Jean. "The Style of Autobiography", *Autobiography: Essays Theoretical and Critical,* ed. James Olney. Princeton University Press, 1980.

Sturrock, John. ed. *The Oxford Guide to Contemporary Writing*, Oxford University Press, 1994.

Tagore, R.N. "The Problem of Self", *Sadhana,* Macmillan, 1988.

Tausky, Thomas E. "Alice Munro Biocritical Essay", *Canadian Literary Archives*, University of Calgary Library (Special Collection), 1986. <10/25/2006 http://www.ucalgarv.cal/libold/ specoll/monrobiochtm (1-12).

Timson, Judith. "Merciful Light: Alice Munro's New Stories are Luminous", *MacLean's*. 7 May 1990.

Warhol, Robyn R. and Diane Prince Herndl. Ed. *Feminisms: An Anthology of Literary Theory and Criticism.* New Jersey: Rutgers University Press, New Brunswick, 3rd Paperback Printing, 1996.

5

The Inner Voice: A Woman Speaks Out

One is not born, but rather becomes a woman.

(*The Second Sex*: 295)

I

Women's position in society is conditioned by social constructs, impositions and restrictions are the givens under which women have been living since early times. Patriarchal mindsets have always played a dominant role in outlining, "what is feminine" (Freedman: 14), and have defined the behavioral patterns of women in family as well in society.[1] Women have been constrained in their thought, expression and activities as society has appropriated gender roles as well as the norms, and conditions of their social life. A well-observed fact is that human civilizations down the ages have differentiated sex from gender, and have ordained a code of conduct for women, in conformity with socio-cultural patterns. One may be born a woman, but it is society that is responsible for defining role models for women as a wife, mother and as an individual. The voices of women have been stifled and they have remained unheard in social history, as patriarchal hierarchy has compelled them to remain a shadow of their inner selves.

> The oppression of woman is both a material reality, originating in material conditions, and a psychological phenomenon, a function of the way women and men

> perceive one another and themselves. But it is generally true that gender is constructed in patriarchy to save the interest of male supremacy. (Moi: 3)

History bears evidence to the fact that women could not possess property in their own names, engage in business, or gain the disposal of their children or even of their own persons; and this was sanctioned by law and religion as women were regarded inferior to men both physically and intellectually. Thus, feminist theorist while re-examining the social conditioning of women's lives, and discrimination on the ground of sex, argued that the biological as well as the social should not be treated as identical entities, and that both need proper attention and differentiation. In this context, Ann Oakley comments:

> Such a strategy only works because gender was invented to help explain Women's position: men neither wonder about their nor need to explain it. (Oakley: 1997:30)

Referring to this pre-conceived notion of sex and gender and subjection, Mary M. Talbot, opines that sex is "...a matter of genes, gonads, and hormones' and it is 'essentially binary as one is 'either male or female', while gender is 'socially constructed...'" (Talbot: 7).

Further, she views that it is the social culture, history and milieu, which causes "sex-exclusive and sex-preferential differentiations" (Talbot: 7).

A look at the movement for the cause of women reveals that the struggle against victimization and social oppressions had been a longstanding one, of nearly two centuries. However, it took an organized form from the last decade of the eighteenth century, and had its roots in the humanism of the 18th century and the Industrial Revolution. Forerunners such as Anne Hutchinson however, had voiced her concern during the English and French Revolutions, but only with the Seneca Falls did a corporate body of feminist thinkers emerge in the West. French feminism however dates back to Christine de Pisan (1364-1430), who was considered to have held modern feminist views. In this context, Joan Kelly observed:

> If Petrarch can be called the first modern man, then Christine de Pisan is the poet and author who introduced her countrymen to Petrarch and Boccaccio, to Parisian culture in the early 1400, is surely the first modern woman. (Kelly: 69)

The feminist thinkers of the 19th and early 20th centuries took up the burning issues of the day such as the attainment of basic political rights and liberty for women, the right for married women to own property, enter into contracts, the right to have women on juries, and the crucial right to vote. The result was that England won the voting right for women in 1918 and America in 1920. Mary Astell and others had earlier pleaded for a just social order for women, and the first feminist document was Mary Wollstonecraft's *Vindication of the Rights of Women* (1792). This was followed by Margaret Fuller's *Women in the Nineteenth Century* (1845), John Stuart Mill's *The Subjection of Women* (1869), Fredrich Engel's *The Origin of the Family* (1884) and Oliver Scheiner's *Women and Labour* (1911).

A landmark in feminist criticism was achieved by Virginia Woolf. In her classic work *Room of Ones Own* (1929), Woolf argued for the value of independence and privacy for any creative writer. She questioned the negligence, marginalization as well as the limitation of women's space in literary creations. Her essay *Professions for Women* was a protest against the patriarchal social set-up, which had pressurized women writers to the ideology of the angel-in-the house. It had also made women suffer economically and socio-culturally, thereby preventing them from articulating their innermost feelings. Woolf also pointed out that Dorothy Richardson's stream of consciousness novel *Pilgrimage* was the first attempt to probe into the psyche of women.

The post-war period saw the publication of Simone de Beauvoir's *The Second Sex* (1949), which evolved transformational changes in feminist thinking and movement. An unparalleled work, it probed into the socio-economic, cultural, as well as the political lives of women vis-a-vis the patriarchal social constructs. Beauvoir closely observed that:

> One wonders if women still exist, if they will always exist, whether or not it is desirable that they should, what place they occupy in this world, what their place should be. (Beauvoir: "Introduction": 13)

This observation undoubtedly highlighted the situation of women in male dominated society; the restrictions imposed upon them by male prejudices and biased social attitudes. The work continues to be a milestone in feminist thought as it draws attention to the difference of attitudes towards the female gender. Based on the existentialist philosophy of Sartre *The Second Sex* stands, five decades after its appearance, as the first landmark in the modern feminist upsurge that transformed perceptions of the social relationship between the two sexes.

Various other feminist theorists have also outlined the concepts of the movement and forwarded their viewpoints to provide a substantial definition of the term feminism. They have also tried to establish the role and position of women, their rights and status in society.

To Lisa Tuttle the term 'feminism', originating from the Latin word "femina" meant, "having the qualities of women" (Tuttle, 1986: 107). Toril Moi viewed that, "...the word 'feminist' and 'feminism' are political labels indicating support for the aims of the new movement which emerged in the late 1960s" (Moi, 1986: 204). But Simone de Beauvoir was most comprehensive, when she writes:

> The terms masculine and feminine are used symmetrically only as a matter of form. In actuality, the relation of the two sexes is not quite like that of two electrical poles, for man represents both the positive an the neutral, as is indicated by the common use of man to designate human beings in general; whereas woman represents only the negative, defined by limiting criteria, without reciprocity.... A man is in the right in being a man; it is the woman who is in the wrong. (Beauvoir: 15)

Beauvoir's observations thus became indispensable in paving the way towards feminist consciousness.

Feminist movement has encapsulated all the divergent approaches, and has sought to amend injustices towards woman in family and society. Its philosophy was to probe into the inherent cause of women's sufferings and provide suggestions for reform. The feminist movement, fore grounded the injustices towards women on grounds of sex, and called for equality of treatment and status—legal, social and economical. It also sought to assert the position of women in society, so that they may be treated at par with their male counterparts, and not be discriminated on grounds of their gender. The movement did not subscribe differentiation between men and women or only further women's causes but rather sought to create an environment of awareness against oppressions with a call for a humanistic approach to women's problems. Thus, we may say that feminism cannot be called a unitary concept, but a "...diverse and multifaceted grouping of ideas, and...actions" (Freedman: 1).

The late 1960s also saw the feminist movement reach its zenith with its sweeping across the world, and feminists voicing their cry against social injustices and oppression of women in every occupation. It was no longer confined to demonstrative protests on the streets but soon entered the academic circles and became an important subject of literary debate and discussion. Betty Friedan, in *The Feminine Mystique* (1963), gave a clarion call to all women when she questioned the impositions by the social patriarchal system, limiting women to the confines of domesticity and childcare. She asserted:

> For women, as for man, the need for self-fulfillment-autonomy, self-realization, independence, individuality, self-actualization—is as important as the sexual need. (Friedan: 282)

Others, who recorded similar thoughts, were Mary Ellman (*Thinking about Women,* 1968), Kate Millet (*Sexual Politics,* 1969), Shulamith Firestone (*The Dialectic of Sex,* 1972), and Toril Moi (*Sexual/Textual Politics: Feminist Literary Theory,* 1985). Elaine Showalter's *The New Feminist Criticism: Essays on Women, Literature and Theory* (1985), Sara Mills, and others, *Feminist Readings/Feminists Reading* (1989), Sandra

Gilbert and Susan Gubar's *The Madwomen in the Attic: The Woman Writer and the Nineteenth Century Imagination* (1979).

A study of these theories show that, all these critics and writers were very much conscious of the descending position of women in every walk of life, as well as in literary criticism. Women were being prejudiced because of their gender, and there was biasness in assessing and evaluating their writings. Highlighting this aspect of male devaluation, Mary Ellman in *Thinking about Women* (1968) pointed out that the social constructs had derogated the position of women. She also observed that women's writings were not judged objectively, but were viewed from the angle of their gender:

> Books by women are treated as though they themselves were women, and criticism embarks, at its happiest, upon an intellectual measuring of busts and hips. (Ellman: 29)

In this context, Abrams points out that woman were "...stereotypes in literature written by men..." (Abrams: 234). Similar sentiments were also expressed by Kate Millet.[2] In *Sexual Politics* (1970), she took a more polemical stand against male dominance. By using the term politics, she referred "to the mechanisms that express and enforce the relations of power in society" (Abrams: 234). She also observed that politics was the base for the relationship between the sexes. *The Myth of the Fall,* central myth of the Judeo-Christian belief centered on the fact that woman was the cause of human sufferings and sin. Eve had been created by God out of Adam's ribs, and was God's second mistake. This concept had an impact upon Western traditional thought, compelling men to: "...manipulate power so as to establish and perpetuate the dominance of men and subordination of women" (Abrams: 234).

Toril Moi too shared similar thoughts and viewed that "...the feminist critic can be seen as the product of a struggle mainly concerned with social and political change; her specific role within it becomes an attempt to extend such general political action to cultural domain" (Moi, 1985: 23).

It is to be noted here that social history reveals that women have been neglected, and even obliterated from literary criticism. In her essay *Towards a Feminist Poetics* (1979), Elaine Showalter, probed into literary history and unearthed the startling fact that women writers have been wiped away from the literary tradition, and that their works were considered insignificant, unfit to comply with the literary criterion. She questioned:

> How were women represented in men's literary texts? What was the relationship between the textual harassment of women and the oppression of women in society? Why were women absent from literary history? If literature, Roland Barthes had said, 'what gets taught', was women's writing, rarely taught, not 'literature'? Was there a tradition of women's writing, or an autonomous female aesthetics? And if one could talk about women's writing, was 'men's writing' also marked by gender? (Showalter, 1990: 179)

As an answer to these questions, the critic herself pointed out that female literary tradition does exist, and the task of the literary critics is to unearth and retrieve the lost or repressed women's writings. Here, she coined the term "gynocriticism"[3] (Showalter, 1990: 190) for the analysis and criticism of women's writings. According to her feminist criticism is of two major types: the first *feminist critique* is concerned with woman as reader. The second *gynocritic,* concerned with woman as writer, a producer of textual meaning. In her essay *Towards a Feminist Poetics* (1979), she expressed the view that:

> The first type is concerned with...woman as the consumer of male-produced literature, and with the way in which the hypothesis of a female reader changes our apprehension of a given text, awakening us to the significance of its textual codes.... Its subjects include images and stereotypes of women in literature, the omissions of and misconceptions about women in criticism, and the fissures in male constructed literary history. (Showalter, 1979: 128)

She also said that when feminist criticism focuses on the woman as writer it concerns itself:

> Woman as the producer of textual meaning, with history, genres and structures of literatures by women. Its subjects include the psychodynamics of female creativity; Linguistics and the problem of female languages; the trajectory of the individual or collective literary career; literary history; and of course, studies of particular writers and works. (Showalter, 1979: 128)

Moreover, Showalter questioned whether a distinct language for writing of women's sensibilities, feelings emotions, etc. existed and that literary creations should be a reflection of those sensibilities. In *A Literature of Their Own: British Women Novelists from Bronte to Lessing.* Princeton University Press (1977), she categorically described the stages in the history of women's literature. First comes an androgynist poetics. Next a feminist critique and female aesthetic, accompanied by gynocritics, and then the gynesic poststructuralist feminist criticism and gender theory. Summing up Showalter's study, Barry points out:

> ...feminine phase (1840-80) in which women writers imitated dominant male artistic norms and aesthetic standards; then a feminist phase (1880-1920), in which radical and often separatist positions are maintained, and finally a female phase (1920 onwards) which looked particularly at female writing and female experience. (Barry: 123)

Showalter's theory opened-up new avenues of feminist literary criticism. It questioned sexual difference and the exclusion of women from literary tradition. The late seventies were also marked by the call of other theorists for an enlarged space for women's creative excellence. Eminent among them was Ellen Moers, whose *Literary Women* (1976) was the result of a long. process of reflection on women and literature, a process that started in 1963, the year in which Betty Friedan's *The Feminine Mystique* was published. *Literary Women* received wide acclamation, as it was the first attempt to provide an outline of the literary history of women. The work proved to be a catalyst, which authoritatively establishes the scope, depth, and variety of literature written by women.

The age also saw another exemplar of feminist literary criticism, Sandra Gilbert and Susan Gubar. In *The Madwomen in the Attic: The Woman Writer and the Nineteenth Century Literary Imagination* (1979), these writers revealed: "...obsessive imagery of confinement...the ways in which female artists feel trapped and sickened both by suffocating alternatives and the culture that had created them" (Gilbert and Gubar, 1979: 64).

Both these critics showed that the female critics because of their personal experience of the workings of patriarchy are arguably better equipped to bring to light and analyze such typically female preoccupations. Gilbert and Gubar's research showed that artistic creativity was considered a male prerogative and as such, women writers were unable to focus on their true inner selves. They pointed out:

> Since both patriarchy and its texts subordinate and imprison women, before women can even attempt that pen which is so rigorously kept from them they must escape just those male texts which, defining as 'Cyphers', deny them the autonomy to formulate alternatives to the authority that has imprisoned them and kept them from attempting the pen. (Gilbet and Gubar: 13)

Since creativity was confined to males, it is obvious that women were, represented only from the male angle of vision in literary creations. Women were glorified in texts written by men, while in practical life they were relegated to the backyard. Virginia Woolf as has highlighted this:

> Imaginatively she is the highest importance; practically she is completely insignificant. She pervades poetry from cover, she is all but absent from history.... (*Room of Ones Own*: 44-45)

While emphasizing the situation of women under the patriarchal constraints Gilbert and Gubar argued that:

> ...in the nineteenth century the *'eternal feminine'* was assumed to be a vision of angelic beauty and sweetness: from Dante's *Beatrice* and Goethe's *Gretchen* and *Makarie* to Coventry Patmore's *'Angel in the House'*, the

> ideal women is seen as passive, docile and above all *selfless* creature. (Moi, 1985: 58)

Thus, the authors point out that female writers in their creations have worked against patriarchal modes of dominance, creating the true inner female voice.

The feminist movement now opened up vistas of thought and a search for new paradigms of creativity. The rubric of the feminist literary criticism was that, sexual difference has always existed in literary representation and that the female voice has been excluded from literary creativity, theory and criticism. Therefore, the prime need of the hour was to re-look into the writings of women with fresh insight and evaluation. Feminist thinkers now appealed for the rehabilitation of the lost female literary tradition and the formation of a literary canon for the proper assessment of women's creativity. To quote Jameela Begum:

> Feminist writers and critics have embarked upon an agenda that centers on the mapping of unexplored realms of female experience, which hitherto remained outside the documented scenario of human experience. Placing herself at the centre and redrawing the circle of existence around her, shifting the angles of vision at the periphery, the writer focuses on the unmapped wilderness of the female psyche. (Begum: 261)

Thus, recognition of the creative talents of women, ignored in literary history, began to take roots. Works by women were read with renewed interest and a literary canon was established to evaluate women's art. "Women critics now began to voice aloud what it means to 'think' and 'read as a woman" (Begum: 263). Lorraine Weir too argued that women's writing is an expression of their subjective selves and that all women texts are a reflection of a "...unwritten text namely the world of women, which binds them into an interpretative community" (Weir: 66). Living on the periphery, women have always wanted a space to express themselves, and to share with the readers their experiences and sensibilities. This has become possible through their creations. Louise Forsyth points out those texts circulated and remained open, like a friend's voice, creating new common spaces for women. Suzanne Lamy,[4] Brossard[5] in their criticisms, expressed similar thought. Feminist literary criticism therefore condemned the socio-cultural conventions that had been instrumental in repressing women's sensibilities.

Along with the Anglo-American feminist criticism, French feminists also made profound contribution to the feminist movement: "French feminists adopted and adapted a great deal of (mainly) post-structural and psychoanalytic criticism as the basis of much of their work" (Barry: 124). It was more radical in thought and expression, and postulated certain ideas which formed a strong base for future thinking. More theoretical in nature, it concentrated on the insights of the post-structuralists, especially on Lacan, Foucault and Derrida. Amongst these French critics, mention may be made of Julia Kristeva, Héléne Cixous and Luce Irigaray.

According to Héléne Cixous the existence of an *é criture feminine,* in women's language cannot be overruled. By this expression, she means that women's expressions differ from men's discourse. In her essay "The Laugh of the Medusa", Helene Cixous contends that because women's experience is mediated by a variety of social discourses, women must write through their bodies and that they must invent a language that will break down the differences not only in society but also in the language for literary construction.

The body thus becomes equivalent to a text which encoded women's sensibilities and emotions and became a manifestation of their inner voice. Summarizing Cixous's stance, Abrams says:

> ...in that stage of the mother-child relations before the child acquires the male-centered verbal language. Thereafter...this prelinguistic potentiality in the unconscious manifests itself in those written texts that, abolishing all repression...and "closure" opens out into a joyous free play of meaning. (Abrams: 338)

Further expressions of *é criture feminine* are found in the writings of Julia Kristeva. In her essay "The System and the Speaking Subject", she used the terms the *symbolic* and the *semiotic* to designate two different aspects of language. According to her, the *symbolic* aspect is associated with authority, order, fathers, repression and control, while the *semiotic* aspect of discourse is characterized not by logic and order, but by displacement slippage, condensation, which suggests, again a much looser, more randomized way of making connections, one which increases the available range of possibilities. The *semiotic* aspect of the language therefore opens up a variety of possibilities for the expression of women's sensibilities.

Another indispensable aspect of the feminist criticism, which requires attention, is its relationship with psychoanalysis. It had its beginning with Kate Millet's *Sexual Politics* in 1969. The feminists' activities condemned Freud, as he was a prime source of patriarchal attitudes.[6] Freud was later on defended by Juliet Millet and others.[7] In his study into the female psyche Freud viewed that the lack of external genitals is the principal cause of woman's feminine character. This causes a sense of inferiority in women, while for the male, it ignites a desire to master and subdue as well as to exert power. Moi puts it:

> Thus the female castration complex becomes still more of the same. Woman is not only the Other, as Simone de Beauvoir discovered, but is quite specifically *man's* Other: his negative or mirror-image. (Moi, 1985: 133)

This theory opened up controversial discussion and was the target of many debates. Freud's theory was later worked upon and modified by Jacques Lacan who based his theory on linguistic, structuralist and semiotic approach. According to Lacan, the "...*phallus* as the signifier...signifies patriarchal character".[8] As the child enters from the *Imaginary* world to the *Symbolic,* the language becomes one of acceptance of the social environment and cultural systems. It begins to be a symbol of the patriarchal setup and therefore signifies the sexual power of men. In patriarchal social structures, femininity or the voice of women therefore becomes repressed leading to the production of male centered texts.

From the 1980s, feminist movement underwent diverse change. It became more: "...eclectic in nature...drawing upon other critical approaches—Marxism, structuralism, linguistics and so on..." (Barry: 122).

Feminist literary criticism,[9] a product of the feminist movement, has initiated introspection into the consciousness of the role of women and their stance in literary theory. It has also taken a polemical stand in its contention of providing a proper space for women's writings and use of language in literary art. A vital question, now attended to, was the exposition of the biasness of socio-cultural mindset. This had perpetuated inequality of treatment amongst the sexes, down the centuries.

Thus, we may say that the feminist movement questioned the long-standing, phallocentric ideologies and patriarchal attitudes. It attacked male notions of value in literature and criticized male authors for their biased attitude, in their representation of women in literature. It further challenged traditional and accepted male notions about women's sensibilities and emotions, which presented only the male view points. The movement called for a re-look into the literary works by women so that their literary quality may be rightly assessed.

From the sixties onwards, the feminist movement has come a long way, and today the term connotes a wide variety of approaches. It has not only a single meaning, rather multiple interpretations with wide paradigms. Under the umbrella term 'feminism', it includes *Radical feminism, Socialist feminism, Liberal feminism, Marxist feminism, Black feminism, Lesbian feminism,* etc. Feminism now denotes women's inner freedom and awakening, and seeks to establish the interdependence between the sexes. It also heralds a new phase of feminist thought and invites attention with fresh insight and wider understanding to women's problems. It incorporates mutual respect. Moreover, the ideology emphasizes upon presenting the real life situations in the literature by women. In this context, we may agree with Ann Rosalind Jones when she says:

> Women writings will be more accessible to writers and readers alike if we recognize it as a conscious response to socio literary realities, rather than accept it as an overflow of one woman's unmediated communication with her body. (Jones: 367)

Concisely, feminism looks towards an egalitarian future, a humanistic approach to all women's problems, a liberal social set-up that promises a humane and just life for all.

II

The voice of women in Canada has always been a loud cry of protest against social structures and male hegemony. Marginalized, oppressed and victimized by social setups, the conditions of Canadian women were no better than in other countries across the globe. The quest for a private space and the assertion of the inner self was therefore a prime concern for Canadian women. While consciousness against subjugation had been a longstanding one, it took the form of an organized movement in 1929 with feminists voicing their demand for political rights, and the right to vote and elect representatives. The Suffrage movement was a positive step in the direction of giving women the right to voice their public opinion, and have a say in the constitutional formation of their government.[10]

A pertinent question often addressed by the feminist theorists was—why were women obliterated from literary history? Canadian women questioned their marginalization and the efforts by social constructs to repress their inner voice, and thereby silence them. Dorothy Smith argued that these institutions have always exerted control over women and have excluded them from the expression of their independent thought.

Thus, the second phase of the Canadian feminist movement from 1960 onwards, "...set out to formulate theories that linked political action with scholarly analysis, and feminism became a serious pursuit in academia" (Parameswaran: 54). Its aim and objective was to create a space for women, so that they may be able to articulate and express their inner selves in their writings thereby creating an aura of social awareness. The movement also sought to establish a literary canon for women, retrieve their lost and neglected works from literary history, and place them before the reading public.[11] Nevertheless, the questions that now surfaced both in English and in French speaking Canada were —how should one write as a woman? Should women's language be different from their male counterparts? Discussing the situation, eminent Canadian critic Barbara Godard pointed out that, Canadian women writers were engaged in exploring "...how to write that difference implicit in her sexuality into the literary text" (Godard, 1987: 2). These writers, while delving into the reasons for this qualitative differentiation, re-looked into their subjective realities, and concluded that, the difference is partly rooted in their biological formation. In this context, Shirin Kudchedkar provides explanation that is more realistic:

> A woman's sexual experience is at a level different from a man's, while her experience as a bearer of children sets her totally apart from him. How she lives these experiences, how she images and reconstitutes them, how she perceives the difference between what she knows them to be and the manner in which society represents them—these are among the factors that constitute her subjective reality. (Kudchedkar: 84)

The aim of the movement was therefore, to provide women writers "...new dimensions of space, to allow women freedom of movement, without hesitancy, or fear, or obstacle, through geographic and political spaces, but, more fundamentally, through cultural, conceptual, and imaginary spaces" (Godard, 1987: 2). This new ideology encouraged them to explore their own selves and write their experiences, in a language that singularly expressed their feelings and thought. In this context, Parameswaran writes:

> ...wordplay, search into the semantic sources, experimentation of words on page, sound effects of words, words in song, words dissected and reassembled...wave upon wave they came to revise the old canon. (Parameswaran: 55)

Moreover, this new form of creative art, when deconstructed revealed multiple voices of the experiences of women, and opened up many untold stories of female oppression. Salat relates this environment of social transformation in the following words:

> More and more women, therefore, took to writing as a profession or a vocation and their writings portrayed the aspirations and ambitions of the 'new woman' and her yearnings for independence and liberation from the limiting constraints of the convention-ridden society. (Salat: 62)

The quest for self and a humanistic approach to women's problems became a pervasive theme in almost all literary works. Shulamith Firestone expresses this attitude in the following words:

> The development of 'female' art...is progressive: an exploration of the strictly female reality is a necessary step to correct the wrap in a sexually biased culture. (Firestone: 167)

It may therefore be said that the movement "...acted as a catalyst to generate a greater awareness of the need for self-definition and self-assertion among Canadian women as it did elsewhere in the world" (Salat: 62).

Henceforth, Canadian women writers reflected in their works, the social setup as well as life patterns of women and realities of their existence. Literature thus became a forum for understanding women's problems as well a platform for raising social consciousness. In conformity with the situation, Cheri Register wrote that literary writings should:

> 1. Serve as a forum for women; 2. Help to achieve cultural androgyny; 3. Provide role models; 4. Promote sisterhood; and 5. Augment consciousness raising. (Register: 18-19)

Narrating the stories of the lives of women became an effective strategy for voicing their sensibilities in patriarchal setup. It helped to create a private space for women, where language became a metaphor for exerting their selves. This situation has been explained by Lorna Irvine in the following words:

> Thus although both male and female writers in Canada construct narrative patterns different from those that dominate American literature, women's narratives, often covertly, more commonly, stress gender issues...situate and celebrate a maternal domain that presents an alternative structuring to that of patriarchal systems.... Women writers find that subversive language powerfully connects their cultural and psychological situations their positions as Canadians and as women. (Irvine: 10)

What is also notable is that in a multicultural country like Canada, feminist literary criticism becomes pluralistic in its context, as the women's movement differed between French and English Canada. In Quebec, women's movement was more radical in its concepts; adhered to revolt in language and form of expression, and focused on issues raised by post-structuralists—Roland Barthes, Jacques Derida, and feminist thinkers like Luce Irigary and Helene Cixous. Leading feminist writers in French Canada were Nicole Brossard, Madeleine Gagnon and Denise Desautels, while English Canada too had famous women writers, viz., Sheila Watson, Margaret Laurence, Mavis Gallant, Margaret Atwood, Alice Munro and Audrey Thomas.

As for the progression of the feminist movement[12] in English Canada, it is observed that feminist critics "...embarked on their own programme to identify discrimination and advance the status of women writers" (Godard, 1987: 7). Consequently, the 'Royal Commission on the Status of Women' took the first step in mapping out the differences on grounds of sex. Sandra Gwyn's in her introduction to her report to that Commission, published as *Women in the Arts in Canada* (1971), outlined "...the material and psychological obstacles women must overcome if they are to be writers at all, handicapped as they are by their deeply ingrained conditioning to serve others, which deprives them of the ruthlessness to become major artists, and by their time-consuming roles as wives and mothers" (Godard, 1987: 7).

The lack of facilities and amenities was a prime cause for women's inability to exert their latent talents and Gwyn drew the attention to the prevailing situation of women's education in the country, which was responsible for meager literary productivity.

Susan Mann Trofimenkoff also highlighted gender issues when she argued that by ignoring the role of women in Canadian intellectual history, historians—mostly males—had seriously limited their understanding of nationalism. Yet she maintained, that the role of women in the development of nationalism is difficult because, "...until relatively recently women did not leave tracts for study, did not write, and therefore by implication did not think" (Trofimenkoff: 16). She was also of the view that history could have been written from a different perspective, if we could hear women's stories as well.

A glance at the literary history of the country reveals that women's writings dominated the literary scenario from the early days of settlement. Frances Brooke's *The History of Emily Montague* (1769), Anna Jameson's journals, the works by Catherine Parr Trail and Susanna Moodie had distinctively reflected their lives in the backwoods of Canada. Exploring the situation Howells comments: "...best known nineteenth century records of English women's pioneer experience...as they rewrite male pioneer myths from the woman's point of view" (Howells: 16). Fraser too observed that Canada had such a great proportion of distinguished women writers, that in many ways the Canadian literary domain has become "the dominion of women" (Fraser: xxi).

However, the situation of women in Canada is remarkably different from that of other countries of the world. Linda Hutcheon has highlighted this in conversation with Kathleen O'Grady:

> ...our social situation as women in Canada is different even from that of women in Britain or the U.S.—because of legal as well as cultural differences—and our intellectual context is, for historical reasons, perhaps more of a hybrid than most (though obviously related to

> that of post-colonial nations). Framed geographically and historically between two major Anglophone empires (past and present), Canada has experienced an odd amalgam of British and American influences and both have played their role in shaping our intellectual heritage. When you add the Quebec context, with its strong links to French feminism—the hybridity increases.

Thus, women in Canada feel that they have been doubly marginalized in their own land, one by the dominating traditional social system, and the other by the strong cultural forces of other neighboring nations. This sense of marginalization leads them to re-define themselves in a language that subverts the master narratives, "...through ironic strategies of exaggeration, understatement, or literalization."[13] The works of women writers therefore, show an inclination for postmodern techniques of expression as it offers greater scope for parodying their situations. Kroetsch puts it: "...modern literature closed the boundaries; what is needed is a breaking across these boundaries, a post-modern literature" (Hutcheon, 1988: 4).

Women writings were therefore, marked by a shifting of generic boundaries, blurring of distinctions between reality and fiction, regional representations and the rewriting of history.[14] Many of these women writers stressed upon the use of local colour in their fiction. As Kroetsch observes: "Canadian writing treats the city as an invisible presence. The stories are written for urban audiences: the metaphorical base is adamantly rural or small-town" (Kroetsch, 1989: 67). In addition, Linda Hutcheon observes: "Canada can in some ways be defined as a country whose articulation of its national identity has sprung from regionalist impulses: the eccentric forces of Quebec, the Maritimes in the west" (Hutcheon, 1988: 4).

Canada is made up of different regions, The Maritimes, Quebec, Ontario and British Columbia. All these regions have their own distinctive cultural identities, which are explored and presented by writers in their texts. In this context W.J. Keith observes: "Every Canadian may be said to possess at least two loyalties that are not always easily reconcilable: one to the country, one to the local region which is not necessarily a province" (Keith, 1985: 8). In addition, Robert Wilson echoes similar thoughts when he says, "Canadians tend to think of themselves in obsessions and also think of themselves as, primarily regional..." (Wilson, 1990: 49). This regional representation is often seen in the writings of Laurence, Atwood and Munro. These writers have highlighted the region as a miniature of the universe. Thus, we may say that Canadian feminist writings were characterized by postmodern narrative strategies[15] and had strong inclination towards the local colour story.

The early seventies ushered in a period of new awareness in feminist thinking. Writings projected social injustices towards women and sought to create consciousness towards victimization. Accomplished writers such as, Margaret Laurence, Margaret Atwood, Alice Munro and others were deeply concerned by the social realities. Their works drew attention on women's deprivations in patriarchal hegemony.

Margaret Laurence was a staunch supporter of the women's cause and upheld stringent feministic views in her writing. She problematized women's struggle to survive, and in the process seek her identity, Margaret Atwood too took up the issues of gender-politics, patriarchal power dominance and hegemony. Like Laurence, Atwood too strongly believed in the social responsibilities of the creative writer. Both the writers were concerned with the creation of a woman's space in patriarchal constructs and the desire to evolve their distinctive self-identities. *Power Politics* (1971) is a singular feministic work, where Atwood questions relationships, stating that love is only a power game: language, the fist/proclaims by squeezing is for the weak only" (Atwood: 31).

Atwood's writings are therefore an attempt to focus on women discourse, the quest for identity for women, as well as of the nation within the feminist epistemology. In Linda Hutcheon's opinion:

> In all her writings, Atwood shows herself to be the tireless explorer and exposer of cultural cliches and

> stereotypes, in particular of those that effect women. (Hutcheon, 1969: 313).

Thus, Atwood's works are characterized by a strong sense of feminist consciousness, gender politics and a desire to transform the social structures that hinders women's progress.

III

The concept of feminism as outlined in the fiction of Alice Munro is widely different from her contemporaries in its interpretation and applications. As an ideology for social reformation and redressal of injustices towards women, Munro does not take any polemical stance, but rather offers a narrative of women's social conditioning, the compulsions under which they lead their lives, and their hopes for future changes. Her concern at women's situations, and their possible reform echoes in the voice of Del's mother when she prophecies:

> There is a change coming I think in the lives of girls and women. Yes. But it is up to us to make it come. All women have had up till now has been their connection with men. All we have had. No more lives of our own, really than domestic animals. (*Lives*: 146)

What Munro seeks to assert is that art is not simply a medium for upholding feminist agenda, but a means for creating social awareness of the basic problems of women in all its perspectives. Her fiction visualizes the lives of women in its entirety. It becomes the voice of every woman speaking out about universal problems in male-dominated society. In her writings Munro presents the convention ridden society from the early forties to the present times cutting across all barriers of time and space. Her texts open-up the world of women and examine the bond that binds their community lives.

Women down the ages have been unable to articulate their sensibilities, and Munro in her fiction takes up these sensitive issues, as she problematizes the prominent binaries that mark patriarchal discourses. Munro cannot be called a feminist writer as Atwood and Laurence are. Nor can her writing be called a didactic manifestation of the feminist movement. It is rather a presentation of an integrated vision of life, which promises equal treatment to both the sexes in society. In this context, Redekop observes: "Munro has no overt feminist agenda and yet no writer is more devastatingly effective at dismantling the operations of our patriarchal structures" (Redekop: xii).

Acutely conscious of the diverse problems of the lives of women, Munro focuses her art on their marginalized lives, gender constraints and male hegemony in social constructs. Each work is an interpretation of life and is an invaluable document of human relationships, as well as female experience under social values and expectations. In her work, Munro explores women's role in different situation of life—as a young girl, a career woman, a lover, wife or mother. In each of these roles, women are placed in conflicting situations, and are faced with alternatives selves, one for the public and the other for the inner private self. Through her art, Munro probed into the female psyche and laid bare the subtle sensibilities of a woman's heart. This art of representing women's feelings and emotions in fiction was a pioneering attempt, as it reflected the lives of woman in its entirety from the early adolescence, to maturity and old age. It gave a new paradigm to literary creativity, as for the first time, Canadian women found a reflection of their selves mirrored in Munro's chronicle of women's social history down the decades. A visionary writer, Munro's concern is for women, their subjugation and the repression of their inner voice. The aim of her art is to probe into the sensitive areas of human heart and create an environment of consciousness for social change.

As a writer, Munro's focus is on her birthplace in the small rural town of Wingham in south-western Ontario, which she mythologizes as Huron or Wawanash County in most of her stories. This interest in small-town settings invites comparison to American writers of the rural South, such as Faulkner and Flannery O'Connor. Munro concentrates upon the lives of women in those regions in its minutest detail and day-to-day existence. She records her observations as well as her response as an artist, to the rural Canadian society to which she primarily belonged. Rasporich has clearly summed up Munro's fascination for the regional, the locale. As she puts it:

> ...place is very much identity and despite the houses and social conventions which trapped these female characters in the past, they are nostalgic and loyal to their small towns, Jubilee and Hanratty and Dalgleish, because such places are woven into selfness. Theirs is a country of the mind which holds the psyche together in the desperate relativism and unpredictability of modern city life which begins to unfold in Munro's fiction. (Rasporich: 123)

Acknowledging her attachment to her roots, that of small town Ontario, which is repeatedly depicted in her art she observes: "I write about myself because I am the only truth I know" (Rasporich: xix).

Munro thus, universalizes the small township Ontario, and it becomes a macrocosm of the world. The quest for identity as sought by Canadians in general and addressed by Northrop Frye, "Where is here?" (Frye: 220) finds its answer in the fiction of Munro. This focusing on a particular region, is part of the Canadian feminist agenda for voicing protest against dominant cultural hegemony. This presentation of an accurate detail of the locale, is seen in words of Del Jordan, when she says, "People's lives in Jubilee, as elsewhere...were dull, simple, amazing and unfathomable" (Lives: 277). The word "elsewhere" according to W.J. Keith is an essential part of the insight, in Munro "...where the universal is always incarnate in the local and the particular" (Keith: 161-62).

Another aspect of Munro's art is the attempt to fictionalize and re-write history. In most of her stories, Munro draws upon the Great Depression of the 1930s, as a structural base. This evoking of the aftereffects of this historical event is explained by Linda Hutcheon when she says that it is seeing "...history as a construction...a process of selecting, ordering, and narrating...while at the same time offering a variety of historical perspectives" (Hutcheon, 1988: 15). Thus, we see that in "Walker Brothers Cowboy" Helen Louise's father, during the depression when prices fall, is unable to continue with his fox farming, and is compelled to become "...a pedlar knocking at backwoods kitchens" (*Dance*: 4). This story telling of the past is a feministic attempt to re-create history, and the quest of one's self against the backdrop of a particular historical event. Coral Ann Howells puts it:

> Their story-telling represents the imaginative effort to write oneself into one's inheritance by re-creating it from personal memory combined with the local history and legends of that community. (Howells: 35)

A notable feature of Munro's art is that it voices the concerns of women, who have not received proper representation in male texts and are glorified from the male viewpoint or have been placed in a minimum role in life. Her fiction draws and interprets the life of women in its reality and presents a silent protest against male-dominated society. She says: "I don't generalize. I don't see beyond."

However, in her art one finds that she has moved beyond the superficial and reflected on the universal problems of women. As a literary artist, she "...filters and refracts society through the prism of her own imagination" (Rasporich: xii). The aim of her writing is to portray women from the early forties and fifties, as they were in their social and familial situations. Her art makes one realize that they were victimized by male oriented social conventions. As Lorna Irvine puts it: "Her female characters are not new women: they represent past and present and dramatically act out old plots of female desire, masochistic and apparently victimized" (Irvine: 93). Simone de Beauvoir has analyzed this victimization on grounds of sex and the notion of pre-fixed role of two sexes in society from ancient civilization:

> The Golden Age of Woman is only a myth. To say that woman was the *other* is to say that there did not exist between the sexes a reciprocal relation: Earth, Mother, Goddess—she was no fellow creature in man's eyes; it was beyond the human realm that her power was affirmed, and she was therefore outside of that realm. Society has always been male; political power has always been in the hands of men. (Beauvoir: 70)

Moreover, most of her women characters are seen to lead a confined life performing their domestic chores and fulfilling their duties as daughters, wives and mothers. In *Lives of Girls and Women,* Del's Aunt Elspeth and Auntie Grace, spend their lives looking after her Uncle Craig, who works as a clerk in the local township. Del tells us, these women, "...respected men's work beyond anything; they also laughed at it.... And they would never meddle with it; between men's work and women's work was the clearest line drawn" (*Lives*: 27).

The works of the womenfolk of the day is also highlighted here, which consisted of:

> ...morning marathons of floor scrubbing, cucumber hoeing, potato digging, bean and tomato picking, canning, pickling, washing, starching, sprinkling, ironing, waxing, baking. They were not idle sitting there; their laps full of work—cherries to be stored, peas to be shelled, apples to be cored. (*Lives*: 36)

However, not all women were content with this way of living. Del's mother was revolutionary in spirit and sought to bring radical changes is the social system. She would drive a car; sell encyclopedias, discussed books such as *Antigone, Hamlet, The Republic and Das Capital.* She opposed compulsory religious education in schools, and asserted that: "God was made by man, not the other way around" (*Lives*: 89). Through the portrayal of Mrs. Jordan, Munro sought to focus on the need for social reform, thus creating a consciousness of the victimization of women. By re-telling the many untold stories of women's marginalization, because of gender biasness, Munro's seems to be driving home the fundamental realities of a woman's life. Her stories shed light on the dark places of women's existence. "By turning women's lives into narrative, Munro denies women the secrecy that has traditionally kept them mysterious and articulates the problems they encounter as desiring subjects" (Irvine: 95).

Society has always looked at woman as the other and objects for sexual gratification, and Munro's protagonists who are in their either adolescence, or adulthood try to combat life, in quest of their inner selves. Thus, the voice of the individual female seeking identity becomes the focal point in Munrovian fiction. In her attempt to establish her true self, the protagonist has at times, to "...shake free of conventional sexual roles in order to achieve independence and maturity in a modern, urban context" (Rasporich: xii).

The reconstruction of an inner space and position for women, against the traditional gender patterns and social impositions, therefore becomes the prime concern of Munro. In her presentation of women's problems, Munro seemed to be considerably influenced by the Anglo American feminist Elaine Showalter, who asserted that the female phase of the feminist movement from 1920 to the present day "...is a phase of self-discovery, a search for identity" (Showalter, 1977: 13). This quest for selfhood becomes a recurring concern for all Munro's heroines, as they face the challenges of life. Thus, we see that many of them move from the small rural town of Ontario to the sophisticated city life of Vancouver, and other places in quest of their inner voices.

Both Del Jordan and Rose, Munro's masterly creations try to break free from all social bindings and obligations. This becomes the guiding force that propels and motivates the young protagonists to move forward in life. The female quest for identity is seen to assume paramount significance in *Lives of Girls and Women.* Here Munro draws her characters from the common middle class, who throw adequate light on the social position of women and their living conditions. Del, the young protagonist, is the voice of the author trying to establish her individual self, in a setup that is at times hostile and defiant. Written in the classic manner of the Bildungsroman, Del's story marks the different stages of growing up—from adolescence to maturity. The trying experiences of the onset of puberty, initiation into adulthood, the first experiences of love, sex and finally Del's decision to become a writer are all realistically presented. In projecting Del's story, Munro here takes into consideration the social attitudes, moral and ethical conventions towards sex, virginity and marriage, that prevailed in the 1930s and 1940s. Thus, we see that while Del's mother warns her about the pitfalls of infatuations and sexual adventures: "Use your brains. Don't be distracted, over a man; your life will never be your own. You will get the burden; a woman always does" (*Lives*: 193).

Del, however points out that birth control measures are a common matter these days. That the burden of sexual responsibility actually rests on the girl is also asserted by Naomi, when quoting her mother she says:

> It's the girl who is responsible because our sex organs are on the inside and their's are on the outside and we can control our urges better than they can. A boy can't help himself. (*Lives*: 147)

A great difference therefore exists between the strong-willed Del, conscious of herself, and her friend Naomi, an embodiment of the up-to-date girls working in the Creamery. Munro points out that these girls, '...were firmly set towards marriage, whether they were perfect old maids or discreet adventuresses, like Fern...' (*Lives*: 199).

Del however, disliked the normal lives of these girls which:

> ...was showers, linen and pots and pans and silverware, that complicated feminine order; then turning it over, it was the life the Gay-la Dance Hall, driving drunk at night along black roads, listening to men's jokes, putting up with and warily fighting with men and getting hold of them, getting hold—One side of that life could not exist without the other, and by undertaking and getting used to them both a girl was putting herself on the road to marriage. (*Lives*: 212)

She hated being such female stereotypes and was adverse to any compromise in life. She was determined to find her own existence, and be as defiant as any man would be. As she firmly asserts: "And I was not going to be able to do it" (*Lives*: 212). To her, life was full of promises and it was one's privilege to lead it with a strong sense of individuality. Del's quest for the truth of life leads her to certain conclusions about love, sex and religion. For her sex seemed all surrender—not the woman's but the person's to the body, an act of pure faith and freedom in humility.

Yet when Garnet talked of baptizing her after ardent lovemaking, she vehemently resists and is unwilling to surrender herself, or even lose herself under domination. As she observes:

> I was too amazed to be angry. I forgot to be frightened, it seemed to me impossible that he should not understand that all the granted him were in play, that I meant to keep him sewed up in his golden lover's skin forever, even if five minutes before I had talked about marrying him. (*Lives*: 261)

Del's protest against co-ersion and the male tendency to overpower the other is different from her mother's, who in spite of her radical ideas is not able to establish the female voice, and is looked upon as queer and eccentric. Del's story, marked by startling revelations, sexual awakening, the daze of sex, and bodily desires of adolescence is also a form of the silent but firm protest against the social order. Through her art of narration, Munro draws attention to the universal problems of women's lives. Her narrator Del becomes a true observer of life. Over and above, Del's ambition to be a writer, voices her ambition to probe into the living conditions of women and project the realities of life through the prism of art.

Like Del, Munro's other protagonists too are placed in similar situations in life but are never thwarted, and do not take a pessimistic view of life. In *Something I've Been Meaning to Tell You,* we see that women are in their matured stage of life, and are economically self-reliant. Although they are liberated, yet they are forced to compromise with a world order that is inhumane, cruel and unjust. Thus, their condition is not an improvement upon that of Del's aunts, but one of sufferings, repression, unfulfilled desires, and a sense of isolation. However, being an embodiment of their creator with a spirit to fight domination, social injustices and victimization, they emerge in the end as individual with strong integrity and personality. Here the feminist quest for identity becomes a persisting force, though their situations remain many a time unresolved. This collection also explores intense sexual relationships and conflicts, which are repeatedly fraught with, betrayal, conceit and hatred. In "The Executioners", Helena contemplates revenge, when Howard Troy taunts her in class:

> Punishments. I thought of walking on Howard Troy's eyes. Driving spikes into his eyes. The spikes would be on he soles of my shoes, they would be long and sharp. His eyeballs would bulge out, unprotected, as big as overturned basins, and I would walk on them, puncturing, flattening bloodying, at a calm pace.... I would have liked his head torn from his body, flesh pulpy and dripping like watermelon, limbs wrenched aways; axes, saws, knives and hammers applied to him. (*Something*: 120)

Marriage, separation divorce and endless waiting for lovers, all come here under the artist's preview. Even the language tones and attitudes towards sex take on a liberated outlook. However, underlying theme of the victimization of women in social, familial life remains inherent. Moreover, this volume deals with women of the urban middle class of the late sixties, who were independent and updated, yet they too fall a prey to social victimization, impositions, abuse and male domination are the themes round which these stories revolve. Narrated either in the first person or third, they express the collective voice of female experiences, gender biasness and social attitudes towards women, where self-assertion becomes a perpetual occurrence.

Dance of the Happy Shades, Munro's first collection however looks into human psychology in its developing stage. Here the female quest is slightly different from that of other collections. The mark of the individuality and a strong sense of self are evident here, as the young protagonists experience psychological and emotional upheavals in trying to accommodate themselves to their environment.

This is evident in "Walker Brother's Cowboy", where Munro concentrates upon the questing mind and introspective nature of the child as she curiously observes the adult world of her father and his unconsummated love. Significantly, this story forms the literal base for all the later chronicles of female experience that follow.

"Red Dress-1946", addresses the adolescence stage where Munro's protagonist is on the threshold of adulthood and is about to go for her first dance in a new red velvet dress in which the "...new stiff brassiere, jutted out surprisingly, with mature authority, under the childish frills of the collar" (*Dance*: 155). The young girl is about to leave behind the safe, "boundaries of childhood" (*Dance*: 154), and step into the adult world with its varied hopes and failures. The story thus narrates the child's first experience of stepping into womanhood and her attempt to come to terms with life and the social set up.

In another story of this collection "The Office", Munro problematizes the concept of society's inability to accept a woman as writer, and the woman's struggle to establish herself. The story is an exposition of the male prejudice against women artists, as writing was generally considered as a male prerogative.

Nevertheless, the feminist quest is most explicit in "Boys and Girls", where Munro uncovers the social and familial attitudes towards the two sexes. The story focuses on the social norms and conditions, which govern a young girl from her early formative stage. The protagonist is a young girl growing up in a fox farm, where she watches her father pelting foxes for skin trade. The narrator proudly helps her father in feeding the foxes, bringing water and clearing the dishes. The feminist quest for her inner self begins at this early stage when she thinks of herself as equal to her brother Laird and the other male coworkers in the farm. She dislikes the female world of her mother but rather imitates her father, feels immense pride when she is compared with the male workers, and tries to exercise strong masculine qualities. At night, under the covers, she tells her brother stories of heroism, boldness and self-sacrifice that were essentially considered as male qualities. Yet, towards the end of the story when her father prepares to shoot the horse *Flora,* she lets the horse free. However, the horse is eventually caught and butchered. The final statement by the girl's father, "She's only a girl" (*Dance*: 130), when he comes to learn from Laird that she had done the deed, sums up the male voice of resignation and contempt. Thus, the notion of setting Flora free symbolizes the young narrator's desire for independence. Blodgett explains:

> To be only a girl is rejection of a radical kind, for in the world of the rural Ontario farm in the late thirties and early forties aspirations that went beyond those of sexual stereotypes were not simply wrong, they were taboo. They are not corrected by anger, but by a more powerful method, by "good humour". The implication is that to be a girl is a destiny that carries with it a certain stupidity that cannot be corrected. (Blodgett: 33)

Thus, *Dance of the Happy Shades* is marked by female spirit of revolt against social authority, and the dictates of male dominance. It initiates the voices of female concern and protest, which Munro will take up repeatedly in the later works that follow.

Who Do You Think You Are?, Munro's fourth collection again takes up female quest for identity, though the levels of consciousness and context is different. Here the canvas of the artist is the larger world of poverty-stricken West Hanratty. Rose, the protagonist, is a victim of social injustice and has to pay the penalty for being a woman. Throughout her life, she encounters the crude and harsh realities of existence, in its rudimental form but never loses her individual identity. Like Munro, Rose too leaves her small town of West Hanratty, for the West Coast, where she changes her rural accent, marries into a higher class, and then enters into world of glamour and popularity. However, in the end she returns to the place of her origin, with newer insights.

Sensitive issues such as, sexual abuse, victimization, child beatings, etc., all prevail in this text as the author lays bare the layer of injustices meted on the girl-child and women.

In the opening chapter "Royal Beatings", Rose's father, at the instigation of her stepmother Flo, flogs the young Rose. This primitive act of barbarity is looked upon by Rose both as a participant and a third person observer. She remains emotionless, playing a role in the scheme of things. Munro points out that this entire happening is escaped by Brian,

Rose's younger brother who flees, "...out the woodshed door, to do as he likes. Being a boy, free to help or not, involve himself or not. Not committed to the house hold struggle" (*Who*: 15).

As a matter of fact black humor was a part of life in that region where people were of "limited intellectual and economic resource making their own savage and exciting entertainment, by the melancholy understanding that in the end, old age and death make all, men and women alike, victims" (Rasporich: 60). This human predicament is pointed by the artist, through the characterization of Hat Nettleton, the horsewhipper, who had once been a terror in his youth, and is now mellowed with age. Munro reflects male desire and the resultant sexual assaults, in the form of physical abuse of the half-witted Franny by boys, including her own brother. Rose too becomes a victim of lust, when she travels to Toronto in a train alone, for the first time, in her life. A man, disguised as a United Church minister, tries to satisfy his passion by trying to molest her, on the pretexts of reading his newspaper. "It made her feel uncomfortable, resentful, slightly disgusted, trapped and wary" (*Who*: 75).

Rose's outlook changes as she matures and becomes the author's first independent career woman. Undergoing many trying situations of life, she learns to fight back and survive. She becomes conscious of the capacity to attract men, and mobilize them for her own needs. She falls in love with Patrick, breaks up the engagement, and then agrees to marry him. This satisfies her ego, and gives her a feeling of power. As she says: "It was really vanity, it was vanity pure and simple, to resurrect him, to bring back his happiness. To see if she could do that. She could resist such a test of power" (*Who*: 97).

The eventual break-up of her marriage, her affair with Clifford all point to the fact that she had let things happen, as she had wanted them to be. However, she is disturbed by the fragmentariness of life, which is highlighted by her deep love for Simon, his sudden disappearance, and her coming to learn of his death. This experience dawns in her the realization of the fragility of all human lives.

In drawing the character of Rose, Munro seems to elucidate women's attempt to voice themselves against male hierarchy and establish the viewpoint that women are not inferior to men. Thus, women's persistent quest for identity becomes a pervasive factor in this fiction. Rose is troubled by the question 'who do you think you are?', and her inner self tries to work out this puzzle, as she plays different roles in life, as—child, wife, lover, actress and as a mother. Performing these multiple roles, she realizes in the end that there is no unified self, and that a women's inner self is made up of a multiplicity of identities. In her return to Hanratty, she realizes her true self.

In her next two collections, *The Moons of Jupiter* and *Progress of Love,* Munro shifts her perspective to another phase of female experience, that of menopause and aging. This period, like the onset of puberty is another trying phase, as the female body now undergoes emotional, psychological, and physical change. However, the quest for identity continues, though the situation now is quite different. Munro examines in depth, the female consciousness at this juncture of life—desires, attitudes towards sex and men, as well as their position in family and society. Belonging either to the poor rural or to the middle class society, these women's lives are conditioned by their declining physical strengths, social norms and conventions. The quest for identity still remains a vital force as these women in spite of their declining physical abilities remain cheerful and accept the challenges of life. Rasporich puts it:

> Despite the anxiety and even suppressed hysteria of their recognitions, however, the cumulative emotional stance here is one of composure, endurance and maturity; these women ultimately brave their new physical frontiers and changing sexuality with interested recognition. (Rasporich: 70)

Munro records the entire genealogy of female voice, consisting of old maids, aunts, mothers, grandmothers, and cousins who have recognized their positions and have accepted with calm composure their changing conditions.

Here, Munro also draws our attention to the opposite sex and says that men however are indifferent and even contemptuous towards women at this stage of life. In "Bardon Bus", we see that the narrator, "an old maid" (*Moons*: 110), has a short affair with X, an anthropologist, who has had numerous affairs in his life, as revealed by his friend Dennis. Later on Dennis tells the narrator that he has a new theory about the life of women:

> The way they have to live, compared to men. Compared to aging. Think of the way your life should be, if you were a man. The choices you would have. I mean sexual choices. You could start all over. Men do. It's in all the novels and its in life too. Men fall in love with younger women. Men can get younger women. The new marriage, new babies, new families. (*Moons:* 121)

The narrator, however remains unperturbed at this observation and calmly replies: "Its only by natural renunciation and by accepting deprivation, that we prepare for death and therefore that we get any happiness..." (*Moons*: 121).

Disinterestedness, disgust and even hatred towards women who have lost their sexual appeal because of their approaching middle age is a part of male psyche, and Munro presents this aspect of life from the women's viewpoint. "In Labor Day Dinner", George tells Roberta:

> "Your armpits are flabby". To which she replies, "Are they? I'll put on something with sleeves"... 'A harsh satisfaction of airing disgust. He is disgusted by her aging body'. Finally, she resolves: 'She must get away, live alone, wear sleeves'. (*Moons*: 137)

Similar attitudes are observed in "Lichen", where Stella, is in her middle age, and "...the sort of women who has to come bursting out of the female envelope at this age, flaunting fat or an indecent scrawniness, sprouting warts and facial hair, refusing to cover pasty veined legs, almost gleeful about it, as if this was what she'd wanted to do all along" (*Progress*: 33).

Stella had been married to David for twenty-one years, and separated for eight (*Progress*: 34). Now after a long gap, David comes to visit Stella along with his latest love, Catherine. What may be observed here is that, while the ravages of time has taken its toll on Stella, it has failed to affect David who carries on his affairs with young women and girls. To David, Stella is a woman who has lost her beauty, and prime, and whose appearance creates repulsion:

> The outline of the breast has disappeared. You would never know that the legs were legs. The black has turned to grey, to the soft, dry color of a plant mysteriously nourished on the rocks. (*Progress*: 55)

Yet women such as Stella, Roberta and others have not lost their jest for life, and have all the pleasures of life. Reviewing the progress of love at this juncture of a woman's life, Munro shows that for females "...sex is not one thing...for women, sexual relations and sexuality can filter into many aspects of lived experience" (Rasporich: 77). Women, by their inherent nature are vulnerable to men during the period of sexual initiation as well as sexual decline. Referring to Munro's representation of middle-aged women, Martin argues that, Munro is demonstrating the social convention that values women according to their youth and beauty. By emphasizing on the importance of "positive representations" (Martin: 92) of middle age, Munro is only highlighting that, aging process death and loss are as much a part of life as youth and beauty.

However, the artist is not content to picture women in their prime only. In "Pictures of Ice", Munro looks at aging men too. Her representation of Austin Cobbet, whose inability to accept the realities of life, makes him end his life by drowning. Munro tells us at the very opening of the story:

> Three weeks before he died-drowned in a boating accident in a lake whose name nobody had heard him mention—Austin Cobbett stood deep in a three-way mirror in Crawford's Men's Wear.... (*Friend*: 137)

Here the salesman tells him, "There's no old men's clothes, no old ladies' clothes anymore. Style applies to everybody" (*Friend*: 137).

Desire for youth and vitality, is a part of human nature, and Austin is no exception. As the narrator of the story tells us, after the death of his wife, Austin, "...had lost weight, his muscles had shrunk, he was getting the pot-bellied caved-in shape of an old man. His neck was corded and his nose lengthened and his cheeks drooping (*Friend*: 137-38). Yet, in his attempt to conceal loneliness, avoid the sympathy and consideration of all, he circulates the news that he would retire to Hawaii sea resort, marry a young widow, spend a fulfilling life, read and play golf.

Again, in this collection Munro shows that femininity and motherhood are inherent in female nature. Motherhood receives prime significance in "Mile City Montana", where the narrator, when her child slips into a pool, cries out in desperation "Where are the children?" (*Progress*: 104). This incident brings out basic female sensibility that qualifies a woman.

Munro in her art, also looks at life from another angle of vision, that of aging, senility and death. In "Winter Wind", Aunt Madge, who is in the nursing home, "...lives on and on, unrecognizable, unrecognizing, completely divested of herself, dried up like a little monkey, past all memory and past bewilderment, free" (*Something*: 194).

"Spelling" gives a vivid picture of the helpless state of human life in old age and advancing death. Here Munro draws women who are in the County Home, where, "Bodies were fed and wiped, taken up and tied in chairs, untied and put to bed. Taking in oxygen, giving out carbon dioxide, they continued to participate in the life of the world" (*Who*: 226). What Munro wants us to understand is that, life has its own challenges, and one has to accept it as a part of life.

Munro takes up another aspect of women's sensibility in her fiction when she takes up the issues of deserted women, left alone to fend their way in life. "Circle of Prayer" (*Progress*), shows Trudy deserted by her husband Dan, for a young woman, but she remains nonchalant at his going. She shows no interest when he returns, as she has become used to the ways of her husband. Trudy's will power and fortitude, enables her to resist servile male subjugation. Dan's mother too undergoes similar situations in life, but unlike her daughter-in-law, she confines herself to her situation. Trudy thus symbolizes the feminist impulse of fighting against male domination, her sympathy for Dan's mother reflects the spirit of unity, companionship, and sisterhood prevalent amongst women, a feature highlighted upon by feminist ideology.

In her other two collections, *Open Secrets* (1994), *Love of a Good Woman* (1998), Munro combines phases of young age, and maturity in a woman's life. Male dominance, injustices, social inequities are all present as Munro repeatedly explores women's experiences in various situations of life. The quest for self-entity remains an inevitable force, which propels the protagonists to face the realities of life. Deceit, pretensions, false hopes and promises, unfulfilled desires and longings, male chauvinism and expectations repeatedly frustrated, are some of the facts of existence, taken up by the author in these collections.

In "Carried Away", we see that the theme is more or less a repetition of "How I Met My Husband" where Louisa, "went on expecting a letter everyday, and nothing came" (*Something*: 39). Betrayal and false maneuverings by men dominate the text and the story ends with Louisa's self-realization. She understands that the man had been fooling with her all along: "Oh, what a kind of trick was being played on her, or what kind of trick was she playing on herself! She would not have it" ("Carried Away": *Open Secrets*: 55). In "The Jack Randa Hotel" in *Open Secrets,* the female assertion assumes a different texture as Gail the protagonist, having been forsaken by her lover Will, decides to follow him to Australia, in disguise, where he now resides with his new love Sandy. Gail constructs a new identity for herself, writes letters to Will in pseudonym and exercises her power to mobilize him. Being unperturbed by Will's betrayal of trust, she undertakes this reckless adventure, only to prove that women are not weak or frail, but are capable of taking up any challenge of life. The story closes with the following:

> Now it's up to you to follow me. (*Open Secrets*: 221)

In *Love of a Good Woman,* women issues becomes the central point of the writer's concern. Insight into life, its predicaments and disaster are all delved into. Sex, crime, abortion all figure in this collection. As Marshall Bruce Gentry in his review of *Love of a Good Woman* observes: "Much of Munro's feminism is in the sadness we are led to feel over the maneuvers her women have had to teach themselves for achieving any sort of power" (Gentry, Website citation: par. 3). The critic also opines that in this collection, people are brought together by "...weakness, silence, and denial rather than by sweet and open communication" (Gentry, Website citation: par. 4). In "Before the Change" male exploitation and social restrictions imposed on women are revealed, as Munro shows that the protagonist is compelled by her lover to think of aborting her child, as pregnancy before marriage would hamper his position as Minister of the Theological College. Side by side, Munro presents ironically, the protagonist's father who is a doctor, performs abortions himself, but suffers a severe heart attack that ultimately takes his life, when he learns the truth about his daughter. She speculates:

> Change the law, change the person. Yet we don't want everything—not the whole story—to be dictated from outside. We don't want what we are, all we are to be concocted that way. (*Love*: 332)

Concern of aging and entry into middle age also figures in this collection as in "Jakarta" the characters are aware that "...the progression got dimmer and it was hard to sure just when you had arrived at where ever it was you were going" (*Love*: 94).

In all her works Munro, points out that in spite of the adversaries of life, her protagonists do not give up their individuality, the spirit to resist the forces that try to subjugate them. Over and above, they accept and face the challenges of life with stoic endurance and composure. The quest for self-identity persistently motivates them throughout their lives.

One important feature that feminist literary critics have pointed out is that, women writers have time and again portrayed deranged women in order to voice their protest against patriarchal order and dominance. Munro too takes up the question of female insanity in her art, and we come across Violet, in "A Queer Streak" (*Progress*), who suffers from senile dementia in her old age. Violet's life too was one of sacrifice for her sister, Dawn Rose, who had shown signs of mental derangement at the age of fourteen, for which Violet's own engagement had been broken off. Towards the end of the story, we see that when the young feminists visit her, she tells them the story of her family history. Later on, they send her a letter sympathizing on her cause:

> Thank you a million, million times for your help and openness. You have given us a wonderful story. It is a classic story of anti-patriarchal rage. Your gift to us, can we give it to others? What is called Female Craziness is nothing but centuries of Frustration and Oppression. The part about the creek is wonderful just by itself and how many women can identify! (*Progress*: 248)

Thus, Munro has addressed a very sensitive issue here when she problematizes women's deprivation, which leads to madness. Showalter had asserted: "...the mad women have become an emblematic figure of freedom and struggle" (Showalter, 1985: 4). Munro is conscious of the fact that, "...because women feel and are forced to confront their physical wreckage, theirs would seem to be a more difficult struggle for sanity, particularly at puberty and menopause" (Rasporich: 83).

A singular concern of Munro's fiction is her interest in exploring the concept of femininity in the socio-cultural milieu, an area widely argued upon by feminist thinking. Simone de Beauvoir observes:

> The weight of patriarchal tradition educates woman into nothingness, assigning to her the non-I, the emotions, the emotions the body principle, nature, which, must be overcome by Man-the-as he undertakes the work of civilization, creating languages and cultures. (Beavour: 714)

Munro, through her characters questions the social conventions and protests against the concepts of femininity, as well as feminine behavioral patterns, expected of women in social setups. In "Boys and Girls", we see that although the grandmother of the young protagonist urges her to follow social norms, she revolts at it and says: "I continued to slam the doors and sit as awkwardly as possible, thinking that by such measures I kept myself free" (*Dance*: 122).

However, Munro's characters are not divested of their femininity. They too have love and sex, enter into relationship with men, but at the same time retain their individuality. Thus, the intricate workings of the heart become a primordial area of concern for Munro. In her personal life, Munro too had experienced the transformational changes in the Canadian society from the early forties. Like her protagonist Rose, Munro too moved through education from rural Ontario to Vancouver, marriage, motherhood and eventually divorce and remarriage. She too had experienced economic deprivation and had pulled through every crisis in life, but had at the same time established herself as the female-artist. This stoic acceptance of the challenges of life is also ingrained in her characters. Like Munro, they too protest against set rules in silent revolution. As Virginia Woolf had asserted that the female authors' task is a "...uphill battle of resisting the conventional female role, which is obviously and historically determined..." (Woolf, 1980: 17). Simone de Beauvoir sums up the situation thus: "Precisely because the concept of femininity is artificially shaped by custom and fashion, it is imposed on women from without" (*The Second Sex*: 683).

Munro's art thus, voices the female concern for upliftment of the status and dignity of women, as well as their freedom from all social restraints. Del voicing her creator's concern says:

> I felt that it was not so different from all other advice handed out to women, to girls, advice that assumed being female made you damageable, that a certain amount of carelessness and solemn fuss and self-protection were called for, whereas men were supposed to be able to go out and take on all kinds of experience

and shuck off what they didn't want and come back proud. (*Lives*: 147)

Significantly enough all Munro's characters are bonded in sisterhood. Familial ties too form a strong base for the stories. In her fiction one comes across aunts, cousins, grandmothers, and sisters, who are interdependent and share and care for each other. Thus, in the opening story "Connection" (*The Moons of Jupiter*), we come across the narrator's mother's four maiden cousins, who in spite of their being spinsters enjoy life in every aspect. Commenting on the work Lorna Irvine says: "The narrator remembers their cigarettes, their chocolates, their fondness for American coffee and for liquor. Their sensuality depends on their independence. They make fun of love, jokingly singing "The Indian Love Call" and "Woman Are Fickle", song that underline their rejection of marriage. Without men, they have pleasure and maintain their own voices" (Irvine: 97). In sharp contrast to them are the cousins on the narrator's father. These women are thin and bent, and "...their faces were pale, eyebrows thick and furry, eyes deep set" (*Moons*: 25). Their lives were confined to endless toils, cleaning, ironing, and cooking, without any connection with the outer world. As the narrator says that she would no longer believe that "...people's secrets are defined and communicable, or their feelings full-blown and easy to recognize" (*Moons*: 35). Munro here sets before us female characters that are on the one hand independent, and enjoy every ounce of life, while on the other, those who are generally confined, silent, and timid women with repressed emotions. Women, belonging to the first category are dismissed by men for "...being too loud, too vulgar to be taken seriously" (Irvine: 98).

As a woman writer probing into their lives, Munro examines the mother-daughter relationship that features as groundwork for most of her stories. Feminist literary critics have well argued that the favored relationship among women is a subject for literary criticism. Critics such as Adrienne Rich and Nancy Chodorow have expressed similar viewpoints. In this context, Godard is of the view:

> Unlike the male, the female has a more complex development to make, one which involves the recognition of identity as well as of difference.... In order for women to grow into authentic individuals, they must explore their relationship with their mothers, and by extension, their place in the matrilineal literary tradition. (Godard, 1987: 12)

Munro was herself strongly influenced by her mother, who died of Parkinson's disease, and she acknowledged during a conversation with Geoff Hancock that: "...the whole mother-daughter relationship interests me a great deal. It probably obsesses me" (Hancock, 1982: 215).

This obsession becomes a creative force in her works, and we find that Munro's protagonists are greatly motivated by the overwhelming presence of their mothers. Redekop maintains that Munro's stories are:

> Peopled with stepmothers, foster mothers, adoptive mothers, child mothers, nurses, old maids mothering their parents, lovers mothering each other and numerous women and men behaving in ways that could be described as maternal. (Redekop: 4)

Munro has also showed that women are not always cowed down by male domination. They too have their individual say in every familial matter and at times exert their personality. In this context, Redekop observes:

> The women in her stories are robust presences, and they exercise power in more obvious ways: they tell stories; they read books; they have and voice opinion. (Redekop: 231)

Munro's mother had a domineering personality, and it is obvious that in her texts, Munro drew her women characters on her mother's image. Here, reference may be made of Del's mother who made a tremendous impact on her daughter, and was a constant source of embarrassment, as well as pride for young girl.

Feminist criticism is an exploration of women's writings, which are characterized by an intense reflection on the female body as a subject of discourse. These thinkers have forwarded the theory, that while writing about their inner selves, women have concentrated on the female bodily experiences, feelings, etc., which are very different from the male experience. For them, the female body becomes the prime concern from which all writing proceeds.

For Munro too, female experience is of major interest, and the corpus of her writings cover the entire range of emotions, desires and pleasures of the female body. In her writings one comes across singular female experience such as menstruating, love-making and even childbirth, which is used as a metaphor in *Who Do You Think You Are?* In *Progress of Love* the metamorphosis of the female body is taken up, and Munro dwells on the menopausal, as well as the aging of women. In 'Meneseteung', Munro again refers to the female body and Almeda's menstrual flow becomes a reflection of the flowering of her creativity. This is symbolized by:

> The grape pulp and juice...stained the swollen cloth a dark purple. Plop, pulp, into the basin beneath. ("Meneseteung": 68)

Dermot McCarthy observes: "Grape juice, menstrual blood, words—all flow into the image of the river, the Meneseteung, which Meda sees as the symbol and subject of the poem she needs to write (8). This flow of blood may also be interpreted as a signal of the absence of conception as well as the realization of her creative self. Munro here tries to "write[s] from within a woman's body without trapping that body inside old symbols" (Redekop: 222).

In addition, her menstruating may be taken as a sign of her continuing fertility, her potentiality for future creation. Munro's text thus valorizes the form of '*ecriture feminine*' and the '*female jouissance*'. Thus, we may agree with Linda Hutcheon, that in order to assert their inner selves, women, "...must define their subjectivity before they can question it: they must first assert the selfhood they have been denied by the dominant culture before they can contest it" (Hutcheon: 6).

In the story "Meneseteung" (*Friend of My Youth*) Munro, by retrieving the lost nineteenth century poetess, Almeda Joynt

Roth, from literary history, rehabilitates her for evaluation and recognition. Also for Munro, female's bodily experiences, becomes a subject of discourse as highlighted by French feminists such as Helene Cixous and others.

IV

Women's movement in Canada has been one of the greatest social movements of the country. Both the first and second wave had its tremendous impact on the socio-cultural and political life of women in Canada. It brought about social reforms, by providing legal protection to women from injustices and oppressions. In the literary field, it expanded the horizon of creative mind, and provided a space for women. A pertinent question that came to be addressed by the feminist thinkers was the need for a language that would adequately express women's sensibilities and emotions. In French Canada, these writers were—Barbara Godard, Nicole Brossard, amongst others. In English Canada too, many women writers such as, Margaret Laurence, Margaret Atwood and Alice Munro, voiced their deep concern for women. Their writings exposed the plight of women in Canada, and sought to improve their living conditions. Moreover, their writings centered on their native regions, which in its turn became a projection of the universal.

Against this backdrop of socio-cultural transformations and reforms, Munro's writings added new contours to feminist research and thought. It drew attention to the multidimensional aspects of the problems, faced by women in personal and social life. Munro's short stories therefore become the voice of multitudes of women, who found a reflection of their inner selves in Munro's art. Her stories become the stories of their heart. It was an overflow of their feelings pent up within. Women now felt a strong sense of affinity with Munro, as she had spoken for them in a language that was singularly their own.

Although Munro cannot be termed as a feminist writer in the sense of Margaret Laurence and Margaret Atwood are, she is at heart an artist deeply concerned for women. Her works are aimed to rouse social consciousness, so that women's conditions may be improved upon, and they may not be subjected to victimization. Truly, Munro's fiction, spells out the inner voice of women, their unheard cry against injustices within the familial and the social framework. Women's stories voice the silent protest and hopes for change in the patriarchal mindset, dominating the socio-cultural norms and conventions. Society has subjected them to harassment, on grounds of gender constructs. Munro's plea is one of humanitarian consideration of women's problems. Through her narratives, Munro has painstakingly delved into the innermost recess of a woman's heart, its psychological implications, and has put into words, the layers of untold stories of pain and sufferings. No other writer in Canada has ever talked of the problems of women in such a manner, exposing the finer sensibilities of women's emotions, covering the entire span of a woman's life from childhood to decay and death. Herein lays her greatest achievement as a creative writer. Indeed, she is a woman, thinking for women, and writing about women, an arena she understands best.

Notes

1. Freedman in *Feminism* adopts a refreshing approach by focusing on issues rather than on thought. Focusing on the perennial question of equality and difference, the critic examines the ways in which this has been played out in different areas of feminist social and political theory. [Freedman Jane, *Feminism.* Viva Books Private Limited. Open University Press, New Delhi, Mumbai, Chennai, Kolkata: 2002, p. 14]
2. From the Hebrew Bible and Greek philosophy to the present day women have been relegated to the position of the other, while their male counterpart was considered as having the human norm. In her book, Millet also attacked the male bias in Freud psychoanalytical theory and analyzed selected passages by D.H. Lawrence.
3. One concern of 'gynocritics' is to identify what are taken to be the distinctively feminine subject matters in literature written by women—the world of domesticity and giving birth, nurturing, or the mother-daughter, and woman-to-woman

relations. Another concern is to uncover in literary history a female tradition. The third is to show that there is a distinctive feminine mode of experience, or subjectivity in thinking, feeling, valuing, and perceiving oneself and the outer world. Related to this is the attempt to specify a distinctively female style of narratology.

4. Suzanne Lamy illustrated the active process of writing as an interdependent activity that combines the process of critical and creative thinking.
5. Nicole Brossard emerged as a writer and critic in Quebec in 1970, and did not disassociate the creative from the critical process. Her contribution to literary theory is the perfect synchronization of the woman writer and the woman critic in the mental space of 'desiring' and 'thinking', the writing.
6. Feminists of the second wave popularly known as the 'bra-burning' period condemned Freud's theory, as it was a pointer to male dominance. Prominent amongst them were Kate Millet, Betty Frieda, Germaine Greer, et al. However, critics such as Juliet Mitchell, Nancy J. Chodorow were liberal in their attitude [Kanwar Dinesh Singh, p. 7].
7. Freud was defended by Juliet Mitchell and Jane Gallop.
8. The term *phallocentric,* which is of feminist origin and denotes the (false) assumption that maleness is the natural and in fact only source of authority and power" (Bertens: 161).
9. Feminist studies enabled many female authors to be highlighted. Among them were Aphra Behn, Lady Mary, Wortley Montagu, Jonna Baille, Kate Chopin, Charlotte Perkins Giliman, and a number of African-American writers such as Zora Neale Hutston (Abrams, 237).
10. The women's movement has been one of the most significant and successful movement in Canada. In the first wave, it challenged images of women and of femininity: the sexual division of labour in the home and the workplace; outdated laws and inadequate social service; the organization and delivery of health care to women; and the reproduction of stereotypic choices for girls and women within the education system. It has uncovered and named violence against women-sexual harassment, incest, rape, and wife abuse, etc. In 1988, the Supreme Court ruled that the federal abortion law, which had seriously restricted women's access to abortion services, was unconstitutional. In 1986, the federal government passed

Bill C-62, dealing with affirmative action for women, visible minorities such as native Canadians, and the disabled; in 1985 the Manitoba government passed equal-value legislation. In 1981, the Ontario Human Rights Code was amended to include protection against sexual harassment; also in 1981, women's right to equality was inscribed in Section 28 of the new Canadian constitution. ["Entering the World of the Women's Movement". *Feminist Organizing for Change: The Contemporary Women's Movement in Canada*—Nancy Adamson et al., 1988, p. 5.]

11. The phase was also marked by the publication of magazines where women were able to express their creativity. Examples of which are *Lip,* one of the innovative radical magazines that were produced in Vancouver by a Collective that included Angela Hrynuik, Daphne Marlatt, and Besty Warland and others. This collection was interested in a feminist transformation of language. Like Nicole Brossard in the east, these west coast writers indulged in extensive word-play, semantics, and study of words, diction and meanings. The title *lip* had many feminist interpretations, and had flip up pages like a note pad. Unfortunately, it did not last more than five years (1987-92), but it was an excellent example of feminist literary pursuit. (Parameswaran 55).

12. In 1965, there were few women's organizations in Canada, no women's Bookstores (because there were almost no books about women), and no women's studies courses in schools and universities. In contrast, today almost all large urban centres, as well as many small towns and rural communities have, rape crisis centres, shelters for battered wives, self-defenses courses, women's bookstores/music events/art galleries; all galleries; all universities have women's studies courses (and many have extensive degree-granting programs in women's studies) as well as women's centres...[*Feminist Organizing for Change: The Contemporary Women's Movement in Canada.* Nancy Adamson et al., 1988, p. 5.]

13. Linda Hutcheon (1997). A Conversation with Kathleen O' Grady. Has expressed clearly the Canadian situation. Voice of the Shuttle has republished this Interview from Rampike, special issue environments (1), 9 (No. 2; 1998): 20-22.

14. According to Patrica Waugh *ecriture feminine* is a "uniquely feminine style of writing, characterized by disruption in the text; gaps, silences, puns, rhythms, and new images all signal

ecriture feminine. It is eccentric, incomprehensible, and inconsistent and if such writing is difficult or frustrating to read, it is because the feminine voice has been repressed for so long, and can only speak in a borrowed language, that is unfamiliar when it is heard (Waugh: 335). Women have especially sought for a language that would express women's sensibilities effectively.

15. Feminist post structuralists have looked for the place of the mother in producing the *jouissance* that for critic Roland Barthes to Jacques Derrida in turn produces and disseminates meaning, desire and language (*Feminisms*: 59).

Works Cited

Abrams, M.H. *A Glossary of Literary Terms.* Ed. Sixth Prism Books Pvt. Ltd. Bangalore India, 1993.

Adamson, Nancy; Briskin, Linda; Me Hail. "Entering the World of the Movement", *Feminist Organizing for Change: The Contemporary Women's Movement in Canada.* Toronto: Oxford University Press, 1988.

Atwood, Margaret. *Power Politics.* Toronto: House of Anansi, 1972.

Barry, Peter. *Beginning Theory.* Manchester and New York: Manchester University Press, 1999.

Beauvoir de Simone, *The Second Sex,* translated and Ed. H.M. Parshley: UK Vintage, 1997.

Begum, Jameela. *"Gynocriticism, Gynesis, Syncrones: Centering Women's Texts" Literary Theory (Re) Reading Culture and Aesthetics.* Eds Jameela Begum and B. Hariharan. Delhi: Pencraft International, 1997.

Bertens, Hans. *Literary Theory The Basics.* London: Routledge, 2001.

Blodgett, E.D. *Alice Munro.* Boston: Twayne Publishers, 1988.

Cixous, Helene, "The Laugh of the Medusa", trans. Keith Cohen and Paula Cohen *New French Feminisms: An Anthology,* eds. Elaine Marks and Isabel de. Courtivron. New York: Harvester, Wheatsheaf, 1981.

Ellman, Mary. *Thinking about Women.* New York: Harcourt Brace Jovanovich, 1968.

Firestone, Shulamith. *Dialectic of Sex: The Case for Feminist Revolution, rev.* ed. New York: Bantam, 1971.

Fraser, Wayne. *The Dominion of Women.* Westport, Connecticut: Greenwood Press, 1991.

Freedman, Jane. *Feminism*. New Delhi. Mumbai. Chennai. Kolkata: Viva Books Private Limited Open University Press, 2002.

Friedan, Betty. *The Feminine Mystique,* Harmondsworth: Penguin. (1963) rpt. 1971.

Frye, Northrop. *The Bush Garden: Essays on the Canadian Imagination.* Toronto: Anansi, 1971.

Gentry, Marshall Bruce. The Love of a Good Woman by Alice Munro. Dt. 21-08-06. <yahoo.com http://English.uindy.edu/reviews/woman.htm>.

Gilbert, Sandra & Gubar, Susan. *The Madwoman in the Attic: The Woman Writer and the Nineteenth Century Imagination.* New Haven and London: Yale University Press, 1979.

Godard, Barbara, ed. *Gynocritics: Feminist Approaches to Canadian and Quebec Women's Writing.* Toronto: ECW Press, 1987.

Greene, Gayle and Coppelia Khan. *Making a Difference: Feminist Literary Criticism.* London: Metheun, 1986.

Hancock, Geoff. "An Interview with Alice Munro", *Canadian Fiction Magazine* 43, 1982.

Howells, Coral Ann. *Private and Fictional Words: Canadian Women Novelists of the 1970s and 1980s.* London: Methuen, 1987.

Hutcheon, Linda. *The Canadian Postmodern: A Study of Contemporary English Canadian Fiction.* Toronto: Oxford University Press, 1988.

Irvine, Lorna. *Sub/Version: Canadian Fictions by Women.* Toronto: ECW, 1986. Internet Sources: Yahoo.com <http://www.nvcc.edu/home/nleslie/feminist self. dt. 22-08-06.<http://www.english.uindy.edu/reviews/woman,htm, dt 21-08-06 Yahoo.com

Jackson, David. *Unmasking Masculinity: A Critical Autobiography.* London: Unwin Hyman, 1990.

Jones, Rosalind Ann. "*Writing the Body: Towards an Understanding of L'Ecriture Fe'minine*" (1981) *Feminisms: an anthology of literary theory and criticism* Ed. Robyn, R. Warhol and Diane Prince Herndl. New Brunswick, New Jersey: Rutgers University Press, 1996.

Keith, W.J. *The Canadian Literature in English.* London and New York: Longman Group Ltd., 1985.

Kelly, Joan. *Women, History, Theory: The Essays of Joan Kelly.* Chicago: University of Chicago Press, 1984.

Kroetsch, Roberts. *The Lovely Treachery of Words: Essays Selected New,* Toronto: Oxford University Press, 1989.

Kudcheedkar, Shirin. "Prisoned by Whom? Some Reflections on Gendered Imprisonment in Two Poems by Claire Harris" *Gender Text and Context Canadian & Indian Writing.* Ed., N. Ramachandran Nair M Snehapraba. New Delhi: Creative Books. 2000.

Marks, Elaine & De Courtivron Isabelle. Eds. *New French Feminisms.* Brighton: Harvester, 1981.

Martin, W.R. *Alice Munro Paradox and Parallel. Edmonton,* Alberta, Canada: The University of Alberta Press, 1987.

McCarthy, Dermot. "*The Woman Out Back: Alice Munro's 'Meneseteung'*" SCL/E/LC Vol. 19, Number 1: University of New Brunswick, 1994.

Millet, Kate. *Sexual Politics.* New York: Doubleday, 1970.

——. *Sexual/Textual Politics.* London: Methuen, 1985.

Moers, Ellen. *Literary Women: The Great Writers.* 1976. New York: Doubleday. London: The Women's Press. rpr. (1977).

Moi, Toril. "Feminist Literary Criticism", *Modern Literary Theory.* Eds. Ann Jefferson & David Robey. London: B.T. Batsford. Ltd., 1986.

Munro, Alice. *Dance of the Happy Shades,* Toronto: McGraw, 1968.

——. *Lives of Girls and Women,* Penguin Canada ed., 1996.

——. *Something I've Been Meaning to Tell You: Thirteen Stories,* Toronto: McGraw-Hill Ryerson, 1974.

——. *Who Do You Think You Are?,* Toronto: Macmillan of Canada, 1978.

——. *The Moons of Jupiter,* Toronto: Macmillan of Canada, 1982.

——. *Progress of Love,* McClelland and Stewart, A Douglas Gibson Book, 1986.

——. *Friend of My Youth.* Toronto: McClelland & Stewart, 1990.

——. *Open Secrets,* Toronto: Knopf, 1994.

——. *Love of a Good Woman.* Toronto: McClelland & Stewart, 1998.

Oakley, Ann. *Sex Gender and Society.* London: Temple Smith, 1972.

Parameswaran, Uma. "Canadian Women Think Aloud on their Life and Feminism". *Gender Text and Context. Canadian & Indian*

Writing. Eds. N. Ramachandran Nair and M. Snehaprabha. New Delhi: Creative Books, 2000.

Rasporich, J. Beverly. *Dance of the Sexes: Art and Gender in the Fiction of Alice Munro*. University of Alberta Press, 1990.

Redecop, Magdalene. *Mothers and Other Clowns: The Stories of Alice Munro*. London and New York: Routledge, 1992.

Register, Cheri. "American Feminist Literary Criticism: A Bibliographical Introduction", *Feminist Literary Criticism. Exploration in Theory,* Ed. Josephine Donovan Lexington: University of Kentucky Press, 1975.

Salat, F.M. *The Canadian Novel: A Search for Identity*. New Delhi: B.R. Publishing Corporation, 1993.

Showalter, Elaine. "Feminism and Literature", *Literary Theory Today*. Eds. Peter Collier and Helga Greye-Ryan. Ithaka, New York: Cornell University Press, 1990.

——. *The Female Malady: Women, Madness and English Culture, 1830-1980*, New York: Penguin, 1985.

Singh, Frank Birbal. *Novels and the Nation: Essays in Canadian Literature*. Toronto, Oxford: TSAR, 1995.

Singh, Kanwar Dinesh. *Feminism and Post Feminism: The Context of Modern Indian Women Poets Writing in English*, Sarup & Sons, New Delhi, 2004.

Singh, Sushila. *Feminism: Theory, Criticism, Analysis*. Delhi. Pencraft International, 1997.

Talbot, Mary M. *Language and Gender: An Introduction*, Cambridge: Polity Press, 1998.

Trofimenkoff, Mann Susan. "Nationalism, Feminism and Canadian Intellectual History", *Canadian Literature* 83, Winter 1969.8., (qtd. Wayne Fraser. *The Dominion of Women*. Westport, Connecticut: Greenwood Press, 1991, p. xvii (Introduction).

Tuttle, Lisa. *Encyclopedia of Feminism*. New York: Facts on File Publication, 1986.

Wallace, Browen. "Women's Lives: Alice Munro", *The Human Elements: Critical Essays,* Ed. David Helwig. Ottawa, Oberon Press, 1978.

Waugh, Patricia. Ed. *Literary Theory and Criticism (An Oxford Guide)*, International Student Edition, First Indian ed. Oxford University Press, New Delhi, 2006.

Weir, Lorraine. "Towards a Feminist Hermeneutics: Joy Macpherson's Welcoming Disaster". *Gynocritics: Feminist Approaches in Canadian and Quebec Women's Writing.* Toronto: ECW Press, 1987.

Wilson, Robert. "National Frontiers and International Movement: Postmodernism in Canadian Literature", O.P. Juneja and Chandra Mohan. Eds. *Ambivalence: Studies in Canadian Literature,* 1990.

Wollstonecraft, Mary, *Vindication of the Rights of Women,* rpt. Penguin Classics, London: Penguin Books Ltd., 1985.

Woolf, Virginia. *A Room of One's Own.* Ed. Jenifer Smith, (Series Editor: Judith Baxter), CUP, Published in South Asia by, Foundation Books, New Delhi: First South Indian ed. 1998. Reprinted Harvest/HBL edition. San Diego: Harcourt Brace Jovanorich Publishers, 1999.

——. *Women and Writing,* ed. Michele Barrett. New York: Harcourt Brace Jovanovich, 1980.

6

Conclusion

Alice Munro, the greatest short story writer of Canada today, has won worldwide acclamation for her versatile creative talent. Through her art, she has opened up new possibilities of the genre, and her outstanding contribution has set a tradition to Canadian Literary History. Compared rightly to the Great Russian master Anton Chekhov, Munro's stories concentrate on small events and happenings, that give sudden twist to human lives; leading at times to epiphanies or moments of revelation.

Based mostly on the small town of Huron County, Ontario, which had shaped Munro's life, the stories look into the lives of common people, especially women, who inhabit the region. Munro was greatly intrigued by the mysteries of life and in her writings, she has explored the sordid realities of existence. The longings of heart, joys, dreams, desires, promises and the deep sorrows, loneliness, diseases and death, that contour life, proliferates her canvas. Munro believed that life is made up of multiple layers of hidden mysteries, which are incomprehensive, remain unresolved, and defy understanding. In her fiction, Munro has tried to implicate these intricacies, which lie imbedded deep, underneath the apparent translucent surface.

Munro was obsessed by the passage of time, and the tiny moments of life, appalled her. It's fleeting away, left human beings lonely and isolated. Caught in the claustrophobia, Munro has shown that women in particular, accept the challenges of life, with girt and determination. They strive, in their search for the inner voice.

As has been observed, the short story in Canada has a long-standing tradition. From early settlement, Canadian writers of short fiction, most of whom were women, recorded their experiences of settlement in an environment that was alien to them. The harsh weather conditions, the unfamiliar surroundings, made survival a dominant concern. The journal and diaries of these women writers were documentary in nature, where description was more important than event. This was followed by the sketches and animals stories, which gained wide spread popularity in Canada and abroad. From 1920 onwards, the Canadian short story established itself as an independent literary genre.

What is remarkable about Canadian short fiction is that, it is largely dominated by women writers. These writers made outstanding contribution to its popularity and development. The genre provided a platform for women to structure their lives and inner voices. A new trend is therefore noticed in Canadian literature, which differentiates it from others.

What sets Alice Munro apart from her contemporaries is that she is truly a writer of short stories. A nonconformist, she has maneuvered the genre to examine the different stages of a woman's life, in an unconventional manner. As a trendsetter, Munro has scaled new heights with her enormous outputs. Through her art, Canadian short story has reached its zenith.

Munro's narrative art that forms her greatest forte is characterized by verisimilitude. As a realist, her narratives are in the nature of rambles, without any overt moralizations. In a revealing moment, she told Geoff Hancock, "Ahhhh! No lessons, No lessons ever" (Hancock: 222-23). Similar responses are found in her other interviews. To Alan Twiggs she agreed that there is "no preaching for any particular morality or politics" (Twigg: 15). Munro conspicuously avoided being didactic, as she believed that the purpose of art is to provide aesthetic pleasure.

A singular feature of her short fiction is that, the narrative is marked by horizontal progression. The sequences of her stories are at times disrupted with overlappings, followed by dramatic shifts and turns. Being a realist, she wanted to portray life in its minute detail. However, she does not document the everyday detail, but rather mirrors the realities of life. This projection is not merely a perception of the surface level, but an exposure of what remains unfathomable and deep.

Munro's stories are in the form of an imagist, where the plots are non-chronological and moods of atmosphere dictates the story-structure. She has accomplished this picturesque presentation of life in all its variety, through photographic imagery. This drawing of scenes and characters, by the use of photographs and paintings highlights her aesthetic sense of beauty. In addition, photographs help to present the paradoxical, comic and the unnatural in life.

Although Munro's works are not strictly autobiographical, they do echo her experiences of life. The environment in which she had grown up, the milieu, customs and traditions that the women of the times were accustomed to, all find a place in her fiction. This gives her work an emotional reality. Through the eyes of her fictitious narrators, Munro re-looks at the past in order to shape the present. Nevertheless, what characterizes her autobiographical narratives is that, they are not simply a narration of the past, but a reflection of the inner self. This deconstructive process gives a new attitude to the writing of autobiographical fiction.

As we have observed, theoretically, some of the stories of Munro can be called autobiographical. Stories, such as "Sunday Afternoon", "Time of Death", and "Winter Wind" all have overtones of personal material. It becomes most implicit in "The Peace of Utrecht" which was Munro's "first really painful autobiographical story" (Metcalf: 58) one that tore her up.

As for the women, who adorn her fictional world, it has been observed that Munro's protagonists tend to be women of her own generation, who find themselves caught between traditional gender roles, and new possibilities in the wake of the "sexual revolution" (Contemporary Literary Criticism: Website Citation). Enclosed within the social setup, most of her women battle against the situational realities and their conventional relationalships with men. In their endeavour to break away from all kinds of subjugation, they tend to locate their selves within their restrictive domain. This leads to conflicting emotions, one within them and the other in relation to the outer world. However, not all Munro's women are independent. Some repress their voices, remain silent, while others are powerful, self-sufficient, and speak out against domination.

Besides, it has been observed that Munro has held up to light the various experiences that dominate a woman's life. The voices of women have long remained repressed in social history, and Munro's women retaliate in silent opposition. Thus, silence speaks more than words do. Munro's attitude towards women's problem generates a new spark in feminist thinking. This sets her apart from all her contemporaries. While Atwood's writings are concerned with the politics of gender, Laurence too, took up the causes of the women's liberation. For Munro "the feminist quest includes the search for freedom of imagination and expression through the medium of art" (Rasporich: 32). Thus, the vision of Munro's art focuses on women's problems and unravels the inner voice of women—repressed, silenced and subjected to male gratification.

For the purpose, Munro has used the form of the short story, as a vehicle to expose the unjust social system. The choice of the genre is an appropriate one, as the protean and open-ended nature of the short story, has helped Munro tremendously in exploring women's lives which is itself characterized by discontinuities. Women have not been able to articulate their inner thoughts, and therefore the stories which structure their lives are filled with gaps and silences. Moreover, Munro has shown that human emotions can never be fully expressed. Many a time Munro's women think of saying things which they can only partially express, or not express at all. Thus their stories remain untold deep within them. Again, Munro has shown that human lives are made up of fragmentary events, with happenings intertwining each other. All these she skillfully presented through a form which could be adjusted to the very demand of the situation. Thus, Munro has subverted the very form of the short story to present women's problems from a new angle of vision. Herein lies her distinction as a short story writer.

This project has investigated over forty years of Munro's literary creations. It summarizes the fact that, Munro's art has undergone a gradual stage of spiral transition from simple narration to complex narratives. While *Dance of the Happy Shades, Lives of Girls and Women* and earlier collections, have a strong sense of regional focus being set in Huron County, the theme examines the dilemmas of adolescent girls coming to terms with family and small town. Here the art is more of the nature of introspection and speculation. In her later works such as *The Moons of Jupiter, Progress of Love, Friend of My Youth, Open Secrets,* and *Love of a Good Women,* the location shifts to Vancouver, Columbia and even to Australia. Art too becomes complicated with the interlining of multiple narrative strands, digressions, and the existence of parallel stories within the main story. Moreover, the narratives become open-ended leading to epiphanic discoveries.

A substantial amount of Munro's popularity as an artist lies in her use of language. Lucid and precise, it has a beauty and enchantment that elevates her work above the ordinary. Her prose style is one, which establishes precision through oxymoron, a startling juxtaposition of words with apparently contradictory meaning. The reader is lead through a maze of happenings, to jolting surprises at the end. Helen Hoy describes Munro's language as a "matter of fact, union of incompatible tendencies" and her sense of reality as "in heavenly contradictory" (Hoy: 103-07).

By piecing together small fragmentary moments of life, Munro gives us a holistic view of its complexities, which we can never fully comprehend. Her protagonists have an optimist viewpoint and accept, as well as enjoy life for what it is. In spite of life's adversaries and misfortunes, the ambivalent cultural and social attitudes, they try to overcome all its challenges. Munro reveals through her fiction that women, in spite of their apparent frailty, have inner strength and a sense of independence. They have in them the ability to reconstruct the social setup into a well-knit organic whole.

Munro's fiction makes us recognize ours inner selves; that the inner voice has fortitude to overcome whatever turmoil comes our way. For this purpose, the author reverts to her past, and dwells on her own experiences, which are common to ours. Women have at one point or other in life, made mistakes, wrong choices, been betrayed, deceived, yet in the end they discover their inner strength. Munro has opened up the world of girls and women, not through confessions or revelation but through shared experiences in reconciliation. For this reason she has been acclaimed worldwide as a great writer of short stories.

Within this patriarchal space. Munro's women, and women in general continue to survive, looking for new frontiers, braving all odds in quest for their "inner voice".

Works Cited

Contemporary Literary Criticism. Munro, Alice (Vol. 95) Dec. 15, 2006 <http://www.enotes.com/contemporary-literary-criticism/munro-alice-vol-95/introduction?print=1/17-12-2006>

Hancock, Geoff. "An Interview with Alice Munro", *Canadian Fiction Magazine* 43, 1982, pp. 222-23.

Hoy, Helen. "'Dull, Simple, Amazing and Unfathomable': Paradox and Double Vision in Alice Munro's Fiction." *Studies in Canadian Literature* 5. No. 1, Spring, 1989, pp. 100-25.

Metcalf, John. "A Conversation with Alice Munro" with *Journal of Canadian Fiction* 1.4, 1972.

Rasporich, Beverly J. *Dance of the Sexes: Art and Gender in the Fiction of Alice Munro*. Edmonton, Alberta: University of Alberta Press, Canada, 1990.

Twigg, Alan. "What Is: Alice Munro". With *For Openers: Conversations with 24 Canadian Writers*. Madeira Park BC: Harbour, 1981.

Bibliography

Primary Source

Munro, Alice. *Dance of the Happy Shades.* Toronto. McGraw, 1968. (rpt. Penguin Books, 1997).

———. *Lives of Girls and Women.* Toronto: McGraw-Hill Ryerson, 1971. (rpt. Penguin Books, 1997).

———. *Something I've Been Meaning to Tell You: Thirteen Stories.* Toronto: McGraw-Hill Ryerson, 1974 (rpt. Penguin Books, 1990).

———. *Who Do You Think You Are?* Toronto: Macmillan of Canada, 1978. (rpt. Penguin Books, 1991).

———. *The Moons of Jupiter.* Toronto: Macmillan of Canada, 1982. (rpt. Penguin Books, 1983).

———. *Progress of Love.* McClelland and Stewart. A Douglas Gibson Book, 1986. (rpt. Vintage, 1997).

———. *Friend of My Youth.* Toronto: McCelland and Stewart. 1990. (rpt. Penguin Books, 1991).

———. *Open Secrets.* Toronto: Knopf, 1994. (rpt. Penguin Books, 1995).

———. *Selected Stories.* Toronto: McClelland and Stewart, 1996.

———. *Love of a Good Woman.* Toronto: McClelland and Stewart, 1998. (rpt. Penguin Books, 1999).

———. *Hateship, Friendship, Courtship, Loveship, Marriage.* Toronto: McClelland & Stewart, 2001.

Alice Munro Papers. Department of Rare Books and Special Collection, University of Calgary Library, Calgary, Alberta.

———. The Alice Munro Papers: First Accession (1950-79. Comp. Jean, M. Moore and Jean F. Tener. Calgary: University Press, 1986.

———. The Alice Munro Papers: Second Accession (1973-82) Comp. Jean, M. Moore and Jean F. Tener. Calgary: University of Calgary Press, 1986.

Interviews

CBC Radio. Interview with Morley Callagan 16 September, 1983.

———. "Sunday Morning" 21 August 1983.

———. "Morningside", 1994.

Connell, Kelvin, Douglas Freake and Jason Sherman. Interview with Alice Munro What Sept-Oct. 1986: 8-10.

Frum, Barbara, et al. "Great Dames" Interview with Barbara Frum, Maclean's April 1973: 32, 38.

Gerson, Carole. "Who Do You Think You Are? Review/ Interview with Alice Munro" *Room of One's Own* 4, No. 4 (Winter, 1979): 2-7.

Gibson, Graeme. "Alice Munro" Eleven Canadian Novelists Interviewed by Graeme Gibson. Toronto: Anansi, 1973, 237-64.

Gzowski, Peter. "Interview with Alice Munro Morning Side", CBC National Radio Programme, 21 Oct. 1982.

Hancock, Geoff. "An Interview with Alice Munro". *Canadian Fiction Magazine* 43, (1982): 75-114.

Horwood, Harold. "Interview with Alice Munro Papers From Waterloo Conf. *The Art of Alice Munro: Saying the Unsayable* ed Judith Miller. Waterloo: University of Waterloo Press, 1984. 123-35.

Kroll, Jeri. "Interview with Alice Munro". *Literature North Queensland*. 8.1 (1980) 47-55.

McCulloch, Jeanne and Mona Simpon. "Alice Munro: The Art of Fiction cxxxvii". (Interview with Alice Munro), *Paris Review* 131(1994): 226-64.

Metcalf, John. "A Conversation with Alice Munro", *Journal of Canadian Fiction* 1.4, 1972.

———. "What is Real?" Making it New: *Contemporary Canadian Studies,* ed. John Metcalf. Toronto, Methuen, 1982. 223-26.

Murch, Kem. "Name: Alice Munro; Occupation Writer" (Interview) *Chatelaine,* August 1975:43, 69-72.

Ozick, Cynthia. "A. Conversation With Alice Munro", *Reading Group Center,* Vintage Books, Internet, 05.01.2007. <http://www.randomhouse.com/vintage/read/secrets/munro. html. d2/18/30. 9:05PM>.

Rasporich, Beverly J. "An interview with Alice Munro", February 15, 1981.

Ross, Catherine Sheldrick "An interview with Alice Munro", *Canadian Children's Literature* 53 (1989): 15-24.

Stainsby, Mari. "Alice Munro talks with Stainsby, Mari" *British Columbia Library Quarterly,* July 1971, 27-31.

Struthers, J.R. Tim. "The Real Material: An interview with Alice Munro", *Probable Fictions: Alice Munro's Narrative Acts.* ed. Lious K. Mackendrick. Downsview. Ontario: ECW, 1983. 5-36.

Tausky, Thomas E. "Interview with Alice Munro", 20 July 1984.

Twigg, Alan. "What Is: Alice Munro" Interview with Alice Munro, *For Openers: Conversation with 24 Canadian Writers.* Madeira Park, BC: Harbour Publishing, 1981.

Wachtel, Eleanor. "An Interview with Alice Munro". *Brick 40* (1991): 48-53.

Secondary Source

Abrams, M.H. *A Glossary of Literary Terms.* 6th ed., Bangalore: Prism Books Pvt. Ltd. India, 1993.

Adamson, Nancy; Linda Briskin, Margaret McPhail. "Entering the World of the Women's Movement", *Feminist Organizing for Change: The Contemporary Women's Movement in Canada.* Toronto: Oxford University Press, 1988.

Agee, James and Walker Evans. *Let Us Now Praise Famous Men: Three Tenant Families.* 1941. Boston: Houghton, 1960.

Aristotle. *Poetics*, trans. Malcom Heath, Harmondsworth: Penguin, 1996.

Atwood, Margaret. *Power Politics.* Toronto: House of Anansi, 1972.

———. *Survival: A Thematic Guide to Canadian Literature.* Toronto: Anansi, 1972.

———. *True Stories,* London: Cape, 1982.

Austin, Gayle. *Feminist Theories for Dramatic Criticism.* Ann Arbor: The University of Michigan Press, 1990.

Baily, Tom. Ed. *On Writing Short Stories.* New York: Oxford University Press, 2000.

———. H. Fenson and H. Kritzer. *Reading Understanding and Writing about Short Stories.* New York: The Free Press, 1966.

Bakhtin, Mikhail. *Rabelais and His World.* Trans. H. Iswolsky. Cambridge, MA; MIT, 1986.

———. *Problems of Dostoevsky's Poetics,* trans. Caryl Emerson, Minneapolis: University of Minnesota Press, 1984.

———. *The Dialogic Imagination: Four Essays* by M.M. Bakhtin, ed. Michael. Holquist, trans. Caryl Emerson and Michael. Holquist, Austin, Tex: University of Texas Press, 1981.

Banks, Russell. Appreciation of Alice Munro, ed. Lisa Dickler Awano. *The Virginia Quarterly Review,* Summer 2006.

Barry, Peter. *Beginning Theory: An Introduction to Literary and Cultural Theory.* Manchester and New York: Manchester

University Press, First Indian Reprint Edition, Chennai, 1999.

Barthes, Roland. *Image Music Text,* trans. Sthephen Heath. New York: Hill and Wang, 1977.

———. *The Pleasure of the Text* trans. Richard Miller. Oxford: Blackwell, 1975.

———. *Roland Barthes* by *Roland Barthes,* trans. Richard Howard, New York: Hill and Wang, 1977.

———. S/Z tras. Richard Miller. Oxford: Blackwell, 1990.

———. *Mythologies,* trans. Annette Lavers, London: Vintage, 1993.

Basu. Aparna. Ed. *Imperialism, Nationalism and Regionalism in Canadian and Modern Indian History.* New Delhi, 1989.

Beauvoir, Simone de. *The Second Sex,* translated and Ed. H.M. Parshley. UK: Vintage, 1997.

Begum, Jameela. ed. *Post-colonial Preoccupations in Canadian and Indian: English Fiction.* India: Kerala University Press, 1989.

———. ed. *Canadian Literature: Perspectives.* Macmillan India Ltd., 1994.

———. *Postmodern as Feminist Text: A Reading of the Short Text of Canadian Women Writers, Postmodernism and Feminism: Canadian Context* ed. Shirin Kudchedkar. Delhi: Pencraft International, 1995.

Begum, Tameela and B. Hariharan, eds. *Literary Theory: (Re) Reading Culture and Aesthetics.* Delhi: Pencraft International, 1997.

———. *Canadian Diaspora: Asia Pacific Immigration.* New Delhi: Creative Books, 2001.

———. ed. *Canadian Literature: Perspectives.* Macmillan India Ltd, 1994.

———. eds. "Gynocriticism, Gynesis, Syncrones: Centering Women's Texts", *Literary Theory (Re) Reading Culture and Aesthetics.* Delhi: Pencraft International, 1997.

Beran, Carol L. "Images of Women's Power in Contemporary Canadian Fiction by Women", *Studies in Canadian Literature* 15.2 (1990): 55-76.

Berger, John, and Jean Mohar. *Another Way of Telling.* New York: Pantheon, 1982.

Bertens, Hans. *Literary Theory: The Basics,* London and New York: Routledge, 2001.

Besner, Neil. *Introducing Alice Munro's Lives of Girls and Women.* Toronto: ECW Press, 1990.

Blodgett, E.D. *Alice Munro.* Boston: Twayne Publishers, 1988.

——. "Alice Munro": Biography, <http://tceplus. com/index, cfm ?PgNm=TCE&Params=AIARTA0005522.17-11-2006.

Booth, C. Wayne. *Distance and Point-of-View an Essay in Classification, Theory of the Novel.* Philip Stevick, New York London: The Free Press Collier-Macmillan Limited. 1967.

———. *The Rhetoric of Fiction,* Chicago: University of Chicago Press, 1961.

Bowen, Deborah. "In Camera: The Developed Photographs of Margaret Lawrence and Alice Munro", *Studies in Canadian Literature* 13.1 (1988): 20-33.

Bowen, Elizabeth. *Afterthoughts.* London: Longmans Green and Co., 1962.

Bowering George. "Modernism Could Not Last Forever", *Canadian Fiction Magazine*, 32/33, (1979/80): 4-9.

Brownmiller, Susan. *Feminity.* New York: Fawcett Columbine, 1984.

Bryant, Mangum. "Ernest-Hemingway", *Critical Survey of Short Fiction,* Ed. Frank Magill. Salem Press, 1982.

Burgin, Victor. Ed. "Looking at Photographs", *Thinking Photography,* London: Macmillan, 1982.

Carrington, Ildiko de Papp. *Controlling the Uncontrollable: The Fiction of Alice Munro.* De Kalb: Northern Illinois University Press, 1989.

———. "What's in a Title: Alice Munro's 'Carried Away'". *Studies in Short Fiction* 30.4 (Sept 1993): 555-64.

Carscallen, James. "The Shining House: A Group of Stories, Papers from Waterloo Conference". The Art of Alice Munro: Saying the Unsayable. Ed. Judith Miller. Waterloo: University of Waterloo Press, 1984. 85-101.

———. "Three Jokers: The Shape of Alice Munro's Stories." *Centre and Labyrinth Essays in Honour of Northrop Frye.* Eds. Eleanor Cook et al. Toronto: University of Toronto Press, 1983. 128-46.

———. "Alice Munro", *Profiles in Canadian Literature* 2. Jeffrey m. Heath. Ed. Toronto: Dundurn, 1980. 73-80.

Chatterjee, Krishna. *Modern English Short Story: A Critical Introduction.* Minerva, India 1991.

Chellapan, K. and Shankar, R. Eds. *Canadian Literature and Society.* Delhi: Pencraft International, 1996.

Childs, Peter. *Modernism: The New Critical Idiom.* London and New York: Routledge, 2002.

Cixous, Helene, "The Laugh of the Medusa" trans. Keith Cohen and Paula Cohen. *New French Feminisms: An Anthology,* eds Elaine Marks and Isabel de Courtivron. New York: Harvester, Wheatsheaf, 1981.

Cobley, Paul. *Narrative,* New York: Routledge, 2001.

Cockshut, A.O.J. *The Art of Autobiography in the 19th and 20th Century England,* New Haven: Yale University Press, 1984.

Coleman, A.D. *Light Readings: A Photography Critic's Writings, 1968-1978.* New York: Oxford University Press, 1979.

Connor, O' Frank. *The Lonely Voice: A Study of the Short Story.* London: Macmillan, 1965.

Culler, Jonathan. *Barthes: A Very Short Introduction.* OUP. 2002.

———. *Structuralist Poetics: Structuralism, Linguistics and the Study of Literature,* London: Routledge and Kegan Paul. 1975.

———. *Saussure,* London: Fontana Modern Masters, 1976.

———. *On Deconstruction,* London: Routledge, 1983.

———. *Barthes.: A Very Short Introduction.* New York: OUP: 2002.

Cunningham, Michael. *Appreciation of Alice Munro* ed. Lisa Dickler Awano, The Virginia Quarterly Review, Summer 2006.

Dahlie, Hallvard. *The Fiction of Alice Munro,* Ploughshares 4, No. 3, Summer 1978.

———. *Alice Munro and Her Works.* Toronto: ECW Press, 1984.

David, et al. *Essays on Canadian Writing* 66, Alice Munro Issue, Winter 1998.

Davidson, E. Arnold. *Studies on Canadian Literature: Introductory and Essays.* The Modern Language Association of America. New York, 1990.

———. ed. *Fiction in Canada: Introductory & Critical Essays, The Modern Language Association of America. Studies on Canadian Literature.* New York, 1990.

Derrida, Zacques, *Writing and Difference,* trans. Alan Bass. London: Routledge, 1978.

———. *Of Grammatology,* trans. Gayatri Chakraborty Spivak, Baltimore, MD: John Hopkins University Press, 1997.

Desmond, Morton. *A Short History of Canada.* Edmonton: Hurtig Publisher Limited. 1983.

DeWiel, Alexa. "Mothers, Moons and Mafiosi", *Broadside,* May 1983: 11-13.

Dhawan, R.K. Ed. *Canadian Literature Today.* New Delhi: Prestige Books, 1994.

Eichenbaum, B.M. "The Theory of the Formal Method", *Readings in Russian Poetics: Formalist and Structuralist Views,* eds. Ladislaw Matejka and Krystyna Pomorska, Cambridge, Mass: MIT Press, 1971.

Eldredge, L.M. "A Sense of Ending in Lives of Girls and Women", *Studies in Canadian Literature*. 9.1 (1984): 110-15.

Eliot, T.S. *Collected Poem of T.S. Eliot 1909-1962*. New York: Harcourt, 1963.

Ellman, Mary. *Thinking about Women*. New York: Harcourt Brace Jovanovich, 1968.

Faolain, Sean O'. *The Short Story*. London: Collins, St. James' Place, 1948.

Fenson, H. and H. Krittzer. eds. *Reading Understanding and Writing about Short Stories,* New York: The Free Press, 1996.

Firestone, Shulamith. *Dialectic of Sex: The Case for Feminist Revolution, rev.* ed. New York: Bantam, 1971.

Fitzpatrick, Margaret Anne. "Projection in Alice Munro's Something I've Been Meaning to Tell You; Papers from Waterloo Conference", *The Art of Alice Munro: Saying the Unsayable* ed. Judith Miller. Waterloo: University of Waterloo Press, 1984. 15-20.

Fowler, Rowena. "The Art of Alice Munro: The Beggar Maid and Lives of girls and Women", *Critique: Studies in Contemporary Fiction* 25.4 (June 1984): 189-98.

Foy, Nathalie. "Darkness Collecting": Reading "Vandals" as a Code to Open Secrets, Ed. Jack David, et al. *Essays on Canadian Writing 66,* Alice Munro Issue, Winter 1998.

Fraser, Wayne. *The Dominion of Women*. Westport, Connecticut: Greenwood Press, 1991.

Freedman, Jane. *Feminism*. New Delhi, Mumbai, Chennai, Kolkata: Viva Books Private Limited Open University Press, 2002.

Freud, Sigmund. *The Interpretation of Dreams,* trans. James A. Strachey, Harmondsworth: Penguin, 1991.

Friedan, Betty. *The Feminine Mystique,* Harmondsworth: Penguin. (1963) rpt. 1971.

Frye, Northrop. *The Bush Garden: Essays on the Canadian Imagination*. Canada: Anans Press, 1971.

———. Anatomy of Criticism: Four Essays, Oxford: Princeton University Press, 1990.

Gadpaille, Michalle. *The Canadian Short Story*. Toronto: Oxford University Press, 1988.

Garson, Marjorie. "Synecdoche and the Munrovian Sublime: Parts and Wholes in Lives of Girls and Women". *English Studies in Canada* 20.4 (Dec. 1994), 413-29.

Genette, Gerard. *Narrative Discourse*, trans. Jane E. Lewin, Oxford: Blackwell, 1980.

Gentry, Marshal Bruce. *Love of a Good Woman* by Alice Munro (review), 21.08. 2006, <Yahoo.com.http:// english.uindy.edu/reviews/woman. htm>

Gibadi, Joseph. *MLA Hand Book for Writers of Research Papers,* 6th ed. New Delhi: Affiliated to East-West Press Pvt. Ltd., 2004.

Gibson, Graeme. *Eleven Canadian Novelists,* Interviewed by Graeme Gibson. Anansi, 1973.

Gilbert, Sandra & Gubar, Susan. *The Madwoman in the Attic: The Woman Writer and the Nineteenth Century Imagination.* New Haven and London: Yale University Press, 1979.

Gill, M.C. ed. *The Pioneer Women: A Canadian Character Type.* Montreal and Kingston London. Buffalos: Queen's University Press, 1991.

Godard, Barbara. ed. *Gynocritics: Feminist Approaches to Canadian and Quebec Women's Writing.* Toronto: ECW Press, 1987.

———. "'Heirs of the Living Body': Alice Munro and the Question of a Female Aesthetic"; Papers from Waterloo Conference. *The Art of Alice Munro: Saying the Unsayable.* Judith Miller. Waterloo: University of Waterloo Press, 1984.

Goldman, Marlene. "Penning in the Bodies: The Construction of Gendered Subjects in Alice Munro's Boys and Girls", *Studies in Canadian Literature* 25.1 (1990): 62-75.

Grabes, Herbert. "Creating to Dissect: Strategies of Character Portrayal and Evaluation in Short Stories by Margaret Laurence, Alice Munro and Mavis Gallant", *Modes of Narrative: Approaches to American, Canadian and British Fiction,* eds. Reingard M. Nischik and Korte Barbara. Wurzburg: Konigshuasen & Neumann, 1990. 110-18.

Greene, Gayle and Coppelia Khan. *Making A Difference: Feminist Literary* Criticism. London: Metheun, 1986.

Guerin, Wilfred L., Earle Labor, Lee Morgan, Jeanne C. Reesman, and John R. Willingham. *A Hand Book of Critical Approaches to Literature,* 51 ed. New York: OUP, 2005.

Gupta, S.D. *Indian Canada Relations,* Jaipur: Jaipur Publishing House, India, 1990.

Hancock, Geoff. "The Colonel's Hash Resettled" in *The Narrative Voice: Stories and Reflections by Canadian Authors.* Ed. John Metcalf, Toronto, Mcgraw Hill: Ryerson, 1972.

———. "What Is: Alice Munro". With Alan Twigg. *For Openers: Conversations with 24 Canadian Writers.* Madeira Park BC: Harbour, 1981.

———. "Everything Here Is Touchable and Mysterious", *Weekend Magazine* 11 May 1974.

Hanly, Charles. "Autobiography and Creativity: Alice Munro's Story 'Fits'" Reflections: Autobiobraphy and Canadian Literature. ed. K.P. Stich. Ottawa Press, 1998. 163-74.

Harris, Margaret. "Authors and Authority in Lives of Girls and Women". *Sydney Studies in English.* 12 (1987): 101-13.

Hebel, Ajoy. *The Tumble of Reason: Alice Munro's Discourse of Absence,* Toronto, Buffalo, London University of Toronto Press, 1994.

Horwood, H. *Interview with Alice Munro: In the Art of Alice Munro: Saying the Unswayable,* ed. J. Miller. Waterloo: University of Waterloo Press, 1984.

Houston, Pam. "A Hopeful Sign: The Making of Metonymic Meaning in Munro's 'Meneseteung'." *The Kenyon Review* 14.4 (Sept 1992): 79-92.

Howells, Coral Ann. *Private and Fictional Words: Canadian Women Novelists of the 1970s and 1980s,* London and New York: Methuen, 1987.

———. *Narrative Strategies in Canadian Literature. Feminism Hunter Lynettee and Post colonialism.* Philadelphia: OUP, Milton Keynes, 1991.

———. Alice Ann Munro, ed. W.H. New, *Encyclopedia of Literature Canada,* Toronto University of Toronto Press, 2002.

Hoy, Helen. "'Dull, Simple, Amazing and Unfathomable': Paradox and Double Vision in Alice Munro's Fiction." *Studies in Canadian Literature* 5. no. 1, Spring, 1989, pp. 100-25.

———. "'Rose and Janet': Alice Munro's Metafiction", *Canadian Literature* 121 (June 1989): 59-83.

———. "Alice Munro: 'Unforgettable, Indigestable Messages'" *Journal of Canadian Studies* 26.1 (Mar. 1991): 5-21.

Hutcheon, Linda. *The Canadian Postmodern: A Study of Contemporary English—Canadian Fiction.* Toronto: OUP, 1988.

Indira, C.T. and Shivram Meenakshi. *Post-Coloniality: Reading Literature,* New Delhi: Vikash Publishing House Pvt. Ltd., 1999.

Ingran, Forrest L. *Representative Short Story Cycle of the Twentieth Century: Studies in a Literary Genre.* The Hague: Moutol, 1971.

Irvine, Lorna. *Subversion: Canadian Fiction by Women.* Toronto: ECW Press, 1986.

———. "Questioning Authority: Alice Munro's Fiction", *CEA Critic: An Official Journal of the College English Association* 50.1 (Sept. 1987): 57-66.

———. "Women's Desire/Women's Power The Moons of Jupiter" in Sub/Version, Downs view, Ontario: ECW Press, 1986.

Jackson, David. *Unmasking Masculinity: A Critical Autobiography*. London: Unwin Hyman, 1990.

James, Henry. *The Art of the Novel: Critical Prefaces.* New York: Charles Scribner's Sons, 1953.

James, Jancy. "Canadian Paradigms of Postmodern Feminism", *Postmodernism and Feminism Canadian Context,* ed. Shirin Kudchedkar. Delhi: Pencraft International, 1995.

John, Hills and U.B. Bhoite, ed. *The Tropical Maple Leaf: Indian Perspectives in Canadian Studies.* New Delhi: Manohar Book Service, 1989.

Jones, Rosalind Ann. "Writing the Body: Towards an Understanding of L'Ecriture Fe'minine" (1981) *Feminisms: An Anthology of Literary Theory and Criticism,* ed. Robyn, R. Warhol and Diane Prince Herndl. New Brunswick, New Jersey: Rutgers University Press, 1996.

Joyce, James. *Dubliners.* New York: The Modern Library, 1954.

Juneja, O.P. and Chandra Mohan. Ed. *Ambivalence: Studies in Canadian Literature*. New Delhi: Allied Publishers, 1990.

———. & Others, eds. *Indian Journal for Canadian Studies,* vol. 1, IACS Publication Baroda, 1992.

———. & Others, eds. *Indian Journal for Canadian Studies,* vol. 11, IACS Publication Baroda, 1993.

K. Balachandran. ed. *Critical Responses to Canadian Literature.* New Delhi: Sarup & Sons, 2004.

Kapoor, R.C. et al., eds. *Indian Journal for Canadian Studies,* Vol. VII, IACS Creative Books, New Delhi, 1998.

Keith, W.J. *Canadian Literature in English,* London and New York: Longman Group Ltd., 1985.

Kelly, Joan. *Women, History, Theory: The Essays of Joan Kelly.* Chicago: University of Chicago Press, 1984.

Khan, A.G. *Canadian Literature and Indian Literature: New Perspectives,* Creative Books, New Delhi, 1995.

Knelman, Martin. The Past the Present, and Alice Munro. *Saturday-Night*, November 1971.

Krishnaswamy, N., S.K.M. Nagarajan, eds. *Modern Applied Linguistics: An Introduction*, Madras: Macmillan India Press, 1992.

Kristeva, Julia. *Revolution in Poetic Language,* New York: Columbia University Press, 1974.

Kroetsch, Roberts. *The Lovely Treachery of Words: Essays Selected New*. Toronto: OUP, 1989.

Kudchedkar, Shirin. Ed. *Post Modernism and Feminism, Canadian Context,* 1st ed. New Delhi: Pencraft International, 1995.

———. "Prisoned by Whom? Some Reflections on Gendered Imprisonment in Two Poems by Claire Harris" *Gender Text and Context Canadian & Indian Writing*. Eds., N. Ramachandran Nair and M. Snehapraba. New Delhi: Creative Books, 2000.

Kudchedkar, Shirin, Begum Jameela A., ed. *Canadian Voices*. Delhi: Pencraft International, 1996.

Lacan, Jacques Seminar 7: *The Ethics of Psychoanalysis,* ed. Jacques-Alain Miller, trans. Dennis Porter, London: Tavistock/Routledge.

Langer, Susanne K. *Feeling and Form: The Theory of Art*. London: Routledge and Kegan Paul, 1967.

Lorraine, M. York. *The Other Sides of Dailiness: Photography in the Works of Alice Munro, Timothy Findley, Michael Ondaatje, and Margaret Lawrence*. Toronto: ECW Press, 1988.

Lubbock, Percy. *The Craft of Fiction*. Great Britain: John Dickens & Co Ltd, 1963.

Lyotard, J.F. *The Post Modern Condition: A Report on Knowledge,* tans. G. Bennington and B. Massumi, Manchester: Manchester University Press, 1984.

Mabbott, Thomas Ollive. ed. *The Selected Poetry and Prose of Edgar Allan Poe.* New York: The Modern Library, 1951.

———. ed. *Collected Works of Edgar Allan Poe. Tales and Sketches,* vol. 11, 1831-1842. The Belknap Press of Harvard University, Cambridge, Massachusetts London, England, 1978.

MacFarlane, David. "Writer in Residence", *Saturday Night,* Dec. 1986: 51-55.

MacKendrick, Louis K. Ed. *Probable Fictions: Alice Munro's Narrative Acts.* Toronto: ECW Press, 1983.

———. *Some Other Reality: Alice Munro's Something I've Been Meaning to Tell You.* Toronto: ECW Press, 1993.

Makaryk, Irena. R. Ed. & Complied, *Encyclopedia of Contemporary Literary Theory.* Approaches, Scholars, Terms. Toronto, Buffalo, London: University of Toronto Press, 1995.

Magmun, Bryant, *Ernest Hemmingway: Critical Survey of Short Fiction.* Salem Press, 1982.

Malpas, Simonm and Wake Paul, *The Routledge Companion to Critical Theory.* London & New York: Routledge, 2006.

Mallinson, Jean. "Jon Robert Colombo: Documentary Poet as Visionary", *Essay on Canadian Writing* 5, 1976.

Marks, Elaine & De Courtivron Isabelle. eds. *New French Feminisms.* Brighton: Harvester, 1981.

Martin, W.R. *Alice Munro Paradox and Parallel.* Edmonton, Alberta, Canada: The University of Alberta Press, 1987.

———. "Family Relations in Alice Munro's Fiction", *New Quarterly: New Directions in Canadian Writing* 7.1/2 (Mar. 1987): 247-54.

———. "The Strange and Familiar in Alice Munro", *Studies in Canadian Literature* 7.2 (1982): 214-66.

Marudanayagam, P. *Decolonisation And After: Studies in Indian and Canadian Writings.* New Delhi: Creative Books.

Mathews, Lawrence. "Who Do You Think You Are? Alice Munro's Art of Disarrangement." *Probable Fictions: Alice Munro's Narrative Acts.* Ed. Louis K. MacKendrick. Downsview, Ont.: ECW, 1983.

Maugham, Somerset. *Points of View.* London: Heinemann, 1960.

———. "Alice Munro and James Joyce", *Journal of Canadian Fiction,* 1979.

McCarthy, Dermot. "The Woman Out Back: Alice Munro's 'Meneseteung'" SCL/ELX Vol. 19 Number 1; University of Brunswick, 1994.

McMullen, Lorraine. "'Shameless, Marvellous, Shattering Absurdity': The Humour of Paradox in Alice Munro", *Probable Fictions: Alice Munro's Narrative Acts.* ed. Louis K. Mackendrick. Downsview, Ont: ECW, 1983. 144-62.

Metcalf, John. ed. *The Narrative Voice: Stories and Reflections by Canadian Authors,* Toronto, Megraw Hill: Ryerson, 1972.

———. "*What is Real?" Making It New: Contemporary Canadian Stories.* Ed. John Metcalf and (Tim) Struthers. Erin ON: Porcupine's Quill, 1993.

Miller, Judith. *Our Feeling Exactly: The Writing of Alice Munro, In the Art of Alice Munro: Saying the Unsayable,* ed. Joseph Gold. Waterloo, Ontario: University of Waterloo Press, 1984.

———. ed. *The Art of Alice Munro: Saying the Unsayable;* Papers from Waterloo Conference. Waterloo: University of Waterloo Press, 1984.

Millet, Kate. *Sexual Politics.* New York: Doubleday, 1970.

Moers, Ellen. *Literary Women: The Great Writers.* 1976. New York: Doubleday. Reprinted (1977) London: The Women's Press.

Mohan, Chandra. ed. *Regionalism in Canada: A Multi-dimensional Approach.* New Delhi: Allied Publishers, 1996.

Moi, Toril. "Feminist Literary Criticism", *Modern Literary Theory*. eds. Ann Jefferson & David Robey. London: B.T. Batsford. Ltd., 1986.

———. *Sexual/Textual Politics*. London: Methuen, 1985.

Moss, John. *The Canadian Novel Here and Now: A Critical Anthology*, ed. John Moss, Toronto, NC Press, 1978.

———. *The Paradox of Meaning: Cultural Poetics and Critical Fictions*. Winnipeg, Manitoba: Turstone Press, 1999.

———. *A Reader's Guide to the Canadian Novel*. Toronto: McClelland and Stewart, 1981.

———. "The Real Material: An Interview with Alice Munro", with J.R. (Tim) Struhers. *Probable Fictions: Alice Munro's Narrative Acts,* ed., Louis K. Mac Kendrick. Downsview Toronto: ECW Press, 1983. 5-36.

———. *Women and Writing,* ed. Michele Barrett. New York: Harcourt Brace Jovanovich, 1980.

Murch, Kem. "Name: Alice Munro Ocupation: Writer." *Chatelaine,* August 1974, 42-57.

Myles, Anita. *Feminism and the Post-Modern Indian Women Novelists in English,* 1st ed. New Delhi: Sarup & Sons, 2006.

Munro, Alice. "Appreciation" Room of One's Own 9.2 (June 1984): 32-33.

———. "Simon's Luck", *The Beggar Maid: Stories of Flo and Rose*. London: Penguin, 1980.

———. "Working for a Living", Grand Street 1, No. 1 Autumn 1981.

Nair, N. Ramachandran. ed. *Canadian Studies: New Perspectives*. New Delhi: Creative Books, 1998.

Nair, N. Ramachandran, and Snehaprabha M. eds. *Gender Text and Context. Canadian and Indian Writing*. New Delhi: Creative Books, 2000.

Narang, A.S. Morama Trikhil, S.S. Sharma, Usha Pathania, Nalini Thampi. eds *Indian Journal of Canadian Studies,* Vol. VII, 1999.

Neuman, S. and S. Kanboureli. Eds. *Edmontion: long spoon,* Newest Press, 1986.

New, W.H. ed. *Canadian Short Story from Myth to Modern.* University of British Columbia, 1986.

———. ed. *Encyclopedia of Literature in Canada.* Toronto, Buffalo, London: University of Toronto Press, 2002.

———. *Canadian Short Fiction. From Myth to Modern,* Ed. Vancouver: University of British Columbia Press, 1986.

———. *Dreams of Speech and Violence: The Art of the Short Story in Canada and New Zealand.* Toronto: University of Toronto Press, 1987.

———. "Tense/Present/Narrative: Reflections on English Language Short Fiction in Canada". Ed. E. Arnold Davidson. Ed. *Introductory & Critical Essays: Studies on Canadian Literature,* The Modern Language Association of America, New York, 1990.

———. *A History of Canadian Literature.* 2nd ed. Montreal & Kingston. Ithaca: Mc Grill-Queen's University Press, London, 2003.

Newhall, Beaumont. *The History of Photography: From 1839 to the Present Day, 1939.* 4th ed. New York: Museum of Modern Art, 1978.

Nightingale, Dr. Barbra. *Alice Munro's Message* (Research Paper), ENC 1102, August 1, 2003.

Noonan, Gerrald. *The Structure of Style in Alice Munro Fiction "In Probable Fiction. Alice Munro's Narrative Acts".* ed. Lorn is K. Mackendrick Downsview. Ontasis: ECW Press, 1983.

Oakley, Ann. *Sex Gender and Society.* London: Temple Smith, 1972.

O'Connor, Frank. *The Lonely Voice: A Study of the Short Story.* London: Macmillan, 1965.

O'Faolian, Sean. *The Short Story.* London: Collins, St. James' Place, 1984.

Olney, Jame. ed. *Autobiography: Essays Theoritical and Critical,* Princeton University Press, 1980.

Orange, John. "Alice Munro and a Maze of Time". *Probable Fictions: Alice Munro's Narrative Acts.* Ed. Louis K. Mackendrick. Downsview Ontario: ECW Press, 1983.

Osachoff, Gail Margaret. "Treacheries of the Heart": Memoir, Confession, and Meditation in Stories of Alice Munro. *Probable Fictions. Alice Munro's Narrative Acts.* Ed. Louis K. Mackendrick. Downsview Ontario: ECW Press, 1983.

Pandey, Sudhakar, ed. *Perspectives on Canadian Fiction.* New Delhi: Prestige Books, 1993.

Parameswaran, Uma. "Canadian Women Think Aloud on their Life and Feminism". *Gender Text and Context. Canadian & Indian Writing.* Eds. N. Ramachandran Nair and M. Snehaprabha. New Delhi: Creative Books, 2000.

Parikh, J.P. and Dhawan, Vimal. *Indian in Canadian Literature.* New Delhi: Creative Books, 1999.

Plato. *Republic,* trans. Desmond Lee, intro Penguin, 2003.

Poe, Edgar Allan, review of Nathaniel Hawthorne's http://ban2. uibk.ac.at /sg/poe/works/critics/twice-tohtml.02-08-06.

———. *Collected Works: Tales and Sketches,* (vol.) 1831-1842. ed. Thomas Ollive Mabbott, Cambridge: Harvard University Press, 1978.

Porter John. *The Measure of Canadian Society Education Equality and Opportunity.* Ottawa: Carleton University Press, Canada, 1987.

Prince, Gerald. *A Dictionary of Narratology.* Nilcoln & London: University Press, 1987.

Rahman, Anisur. *New Literatures in English.* New Delhi: Creative Books, 1996.

Ramamurti. K. Chellappan and R. Shankar Eds. *Canadian Literature and Society.* Delhi: Pencraft International, 1996.

———. *Indian Journal of Canadian Studies.* vol. v, IACS Publications, Trichirapalli, 1996.

Rasporich, Beverly J. *Dance of the Sexes: Art and Gender in the Fiction of Alice Munro.* Edmonton, Alberta: University of Alberta Press Canada, 1990.

Reading Group Center, "A Conversation with Alice Munro," Bintage Books, http://www.randomhouse.com/vintage/read/secrets/munro.html.

Redekop, Magdalene. "Alice Munro and the Scottish Nostalgic Grotesque", Ed. Jack David et al. *Essays on Canadian Writing* 66, Alice Munro Issue, Winter 1998.

———. *Mothers and Other Clowns: The Stories of Alice Munro.* London and New York: Routledge, 1992.

Register, Cheri. "American Feminist Literary Criticism: A Bibliographical Introduction", *Feminist Literary Criticism. Exploration in Theory,* Ed. Josephine Donovan. Lexington: University of Kentucky Press, 1975.

Remnick, David, ed. The New Yorker, From Wikipedia, the free encyclopaedia <http://en.wikipedia.org/wiki/Alice Munro>

Rimmon-Kenan, Shlomith. *Narrative Fiction: Contemporary Poetics*, London: Routledge (n.dp).

Rivkin, Julie and Ryma, Michael. Ed. *Literary Theory: An Anthology*, Blackwell Publishers Inc. first Indian Reprint, 2002.

Robyn, R. Warhol and Diane Price Herndl. Ed. *Feminisms: An Anthology of Literary Theory and Criticism.* New Jersey: Rutgers University Press, New Brunswick, 3rd Paperback Printing, 1996.

Robson, Nora. "Alice Munro and the While American South: The Quest; Papers from Waterloo Conference". *The Art of Alice Munro: Saying the Unsayable.* Ed. Judith Miller. Waterloo: University of Waterloo Press, 73-81.

Rooke, Constance. "Fear of the Open Heart". *A Mazing Space: Writing Canadian Women Writing.* Eds. Shirley Neuman and Smaro Kamboureli. Edmonton: Longspoon, 1986, 256-69.

Ross, Catherine Sheldrick. *Alice Munro: A Double Life.* Toronto: ECW Press, 1992.

———. "At Least Part Legend: The Fiction of Alice Munro" *Probable Fictions: Alice Munro's Narrative Acts.* Ed. Louis K. Mackendrick. Downsview Ontario: ECW Press, 1983.

———. "Sense of Place in Alice Munro's Fiction", *The Literary Criterion.* 19.3/4 (1984): 138-46.

Salat, M.F. *The Canadian Novel: A Search for Identity.* New Delhi: B.R. Publishing Corporation, 1993.

Saussure, Ferdinand de. *Course in General Linguistics,* trans. Wadebaskin, London: Fontana, 1974.

Scobie, Stephen. "A Visit with Alice Munro". *Monday,* 19 November, 1982: 12-13.

———. *Alice Munro and the Scottish Nostalgar Grotesque. Essays on Canadian Writing* Number 66 Winter 1998 Ed(s) Jack David Robert Lecker. Toronto Ontario: ECW Press.

Sean, O'Faolain. *The Short Story.* London: Collins, St James Place, 1948.

Sen, Krishna and Gupta, Tapati. ed. *Tagore and Modernity.* Kolkata: Das Gupta & Co. Pvt. Ltd., 2006.

Shahani, Roshan G. *Family in Fiction: Three Canadian Voices.* Bombay: SNDT Women's University, 1994.

Sharma, K.K. *The Litterateur as Theorist: Some Approaches to Art.* New Delhi: Sarup and Sons, 2003.

Showalter, Elaine. *Feminism and Literature Literary Theory Today.* Eds. Peter Collier and Helga Greyer-Ryan. Ithaka. New York: Cornell University Press, 1990.

———. *The Female Malady: Women Madness and English Criticism,* ed. New York: Penguin, 1985.

———. "Towards a Feminist Poetics". *The New Feminist Criticism,* ed. New York: Pantheon, 1979.

———. A Literature of their Own: British Women Novelists from Bronte to Lessing. London: Virago, 1987.

Singh, Frank Birbal. *Novels and the Nation Essays in Canadian Literature*. Toronto Oxford: TSAR, 1995.

Singh, Kanwar Dinesh. *Feminism and Post Feminism: The Context of Modern Indian Women Poets Writing in English*. New Delhi: Sarup & Sons, 2004.

Singh, M.P. and Mohan, Chandra. Eds. *Regionalism and National Identity: Canada and India: Interdisciplinary Perspectives*. Delhi: Pragati Publications, 1994.

Singh, Sushila. *Feminism: Theroy, Criticism Analysis*. Delhi: Pencraft Internation, 1977.

Sodhi, Meena. *Indian English Writing: The Autobiographical Mode*. New Delhi: Creative Books, 1999.

Sontag, Susan. *On Photography, 1973*. New York: Delta Books, 1977.

Smythe, Karen E. *Figuring Grief: Gallant, Munro and the Poetics of Elegy*. Montreal, Kingston, London and Buffalo: McGill-Queen's University Press, 1992.

Spivak, Gayatri Charkraborty. *In Other World: Essays in Cultural Politics*, London: Routledge, 1988.

Stainsby, Mari. *Alice Munro Talks with Mari Stainsby*, British Columbia Library Quarterly 35, 1971.

Steele Apollonia, Tener F. Jean Eds. The Alice Munro Papers. First Accession. The University of Calgary Press, 1986.

Stich, K.P. "The Cather Connection in Alice Munro's 'Dulse'", *Modern Language Studies* 19.4 (Sept. 1989): 102-11.

Stouck, David. *Major Canadian Authors*, 2nd ed. Lincoln & London: University of Nebraska Press, 1988.

Struthers, J.R. (Tim) "The Real Material": *Interview with Alice Munro. Narrative Acts*. Ed. Louis K. Mackendrick Downsview Ontario: ECW Press, 1983.

———. "Some Highly Subversive Activities: A Brief Polemic and Checklist of Works on Alice Munro". *Studies in Canadian Literature*, 1981.

Stubbs, Andrew. "Fictional Landscape: Mythology and Dialectic in the Fiction of Alice Munro". *World Literature Written in English* 23.1 (Dec. 1984): 53-62.

Sullivan, Rosemary, ed. *Stories by Canadian Women,* Toronto: Oxford University Press, 1984.

Talbot, Mary M. *Language and Gender: An Introduction.* Cambridge: Polity Press, 1998.

Tausky, Thomas E. *Alice Munro Biocritical Essay*, Canadian Literary Archives, University of Calgray Library (Special Collection) 1986, Internet: 10/25/2006.

———. 'What Happened to Marion?' Art and Realitiy in *Lives of Girls and Women" Studies in Canadian Literature* 11.1 (Mar. 1986) 52-76.

Taylor, Michael. *The Unimaginable Vancouver's Alice Munro's Narrative Acts,* Ed. Louis K. Mackendrick. Downsview, Ontario: ECW Press, 1983.

Thacker, Robert. *Clear Jelly: Alice Munro's Narrative Dialecties in Probable Fiction: Alice Munro's Narrative acts* Ed. Louis K. Mackendrick. Downsview, Ontario: ECW Press, 1983.

———. "Alice Munro: An Annotated Bibliography". *An Annotated Bibliography of Canada's Major Authors.* Robert Lecker, and Jack David Downsview, Ontario: ECW Press, 1983.

Thomas, Sue. "Reading Female Sexual Desire in Alice Munro's Lives of Girls and Women", *Critique: Studies in Contemporary Fiction* 36.2 (Dec. 1995): 107-20.

Todorov, Tzvetan. *The Poetics of Prose,* trans. Richard Howard, Oxford: Backwell, 1977.

Toye, William. ed. *The Concise Oxford Companion to Canadian Literature.* Oxford New York: Oxford University Press, 2001.

Trikha, Manorama. ed. *Canadian Short Stories.* New Delhi: Pencraft International, 1999.

———. ed. *Canadian Literature: Recent Essays.* New Delhi: Pencraft International, 1994.

Tuttle, Lisa. *Encyclopedia of Feminism.* New York: Facts on File Publication, 1986.

Twigg, Alan. *For Openers: Conversations with 24 Canadian Writers.* Madeira Park B.C.: Harbour Publishing, 1981.

———. "What Is: Alice Munro". Interview with Alan Twigg. *For Openers: Conversations with 24 Canadian Writers.* Madeira park BC: Harbour, 1981.

Trikha, Manorma. ed. *The Journal of Word Literature* (Special Issue on Canadian Literature) Vol. 1, No. 1 Dept. of English, Ch Charan Singh University, Meerut, 2000.

Trofimenkoff, Mann Susan. "Nationalism, Feminism and Canadian Intellectual History", *Canadian Literature* 83 Winter 1969.

Ventura, Heliane. "Alice Munro's 'Boys and Girls': Mapping Out Boundaries". *Commonwealth Essays and Studies.* 15.1 (1992): 80-87.

Vevaina, S. Coomi and Barbar Godard. Eds. *Intersexions: Issues of Race and Gender in Canadian Women's Writing.* New Delhi: Creative Books, 1996.

Wake, Paul. "Narrative and Narratology", Eds. Simon Malpas, and Paul Wake. *The Routledge Companion to Critical Theory,* London & New York: Routledge, 2006.

Wallace, B. "Women's Lives: Alive Munro, In The Human Elements", *Critical Essays,* ed. D. Helwig. Ottawa: Oberon Press, 1978.

Warhol, Robyn R. and Diane Price Herndl. ed. *Feminism: An Anthology of Literary Theory and Criticism.* New Jersey: Rutgers University Press, New Brunswick, 3rd Paperback Printing, 1996.

Waugh, Patricia. Ed. *Literary Theory and Criticism.* New York: Oxford University Press, 2006.

———. Metafiction: *The Theory and Practice of Self Conscious Fiction,* London: Routledge, 1984.

Webster, Frank. *The New Photograhy: Responsibility in Visual Communication.* London: John Calder, 1980.

Weinhouse, Linda, "Alice Munro: Hard Luck Stories or There is No Sexual Relation". *Critique: Studies in Contemporary Fiction* 36.2 (Dec. 1995): 121-29.

Webster, Frank. *The New Photography: Responsibility in Visual Communication.* London: John Calder, 1980.

Weir, Lorraine. "Towards a Feminist Hermeneutics: Joy Macpherson's Welcoming Disaster". *Gynocritics: Feminist Approaches in Canadian and Quebec Women's Writing.* Toronto: ECW Press, 1987.

White, Hayden. *Metahistory: The Historical Imagination in Nineteenth-Century Europe,* Baltimore and London: Johns Hopkins University Press, 1973.

Wilson, Robert. "National Frontiers and International Movement: Postmodernism in Canadian Literature", O.P. Juneja and Chandra Mohan (Eds). *Ambivalence: Studies in Canadian Literature,* 1990.

Wollstonecraft, Mary. *Vindication of the Rights of Women,* rpt. Penguin Classics. London: Penguin Books Ltd., 1985.

Woodcock, George. "The Plots of Life: The Realism of Alice Munro." Queen's Quarterly, 93.2 (June 1986): 235-50.

Woolf, Virginia. *A Room of One's Own.* ed. Jenifer Smith, (Series Editor: Judith Baxter), CUP, Published in South Asia by, Foundation Books, New Delhi: (First South Indian ed., 1998).

York, Lorraine M. *The Others Side of Dailiness: Photography in the Works of Alice Munro, Timothy Findley, Michael Ondaatje, Margaret Laurence.* Toronto: ECW Press, 1988.

———. "The Other Side of Dailiness": The Paradox of Photography in Alice Munro's Fiction, SCL Studies in Canadian Literature, Internet, dt 26/01/2006. <http: www.lib.unb.ca/Texts/ SCL/bin/get.cgi?directory=vol8-l/&filename=york.htm>*Women and Writing,* ed. Michele Barrett. New York: Harcourt Brace Jovanovich, 1980.

Website/Internet Sources

<Amazon.com., Alice Munro (1931-)http:www.kirjasto.sci.fi/munro.htm _dt.30/11/2206>.

<http://www.uwo.ca/english/canadianpoetrv/cpjrn/vol25/davies.htm.>

<http://www.findarticles.com/p/articles/mi_m2455/is nl_v34/ai_20925782/pgl>

<Google;http://www.amazon.com/View-Castle-Rock-unabridged-selections/dp/07339818/ref=bxgy_cc_img_b/105-0032965-3785201>

<The New Yorker< http://en.wikipedia.org/wiki/Alice Munro Dt.02-09-2006>

http://tceplus.com/index.cfm?PgNm=TCE&Params=AlARTA0005522,17-11-2006

<Google;http://www.amazon.com/View-Castle-Rock-unabridged-selections/dp/07339818/ref=bxgy cc img b/105-0032965-3785201/29-11-2006EditorialReviews From Publishers Weekly.> http://www.lib.sfu.ca/womw/authors.html

<http://www.contemporarywriters.com/authors/profile/?p=auth03D29L044112635689/11-1-2006>

<http://www.enotes.com/contemporary-literary-criticism/munro-alice-vol-95/ introduction?prin t=1. 17.12.2006.>

http://www.writersfest.bc.ca/news/f05_alice_munro.html 17-11-2006

<http://www.contemporarywriters.com/authors/profile/?p=auth03D29L044112635689.17/11/2006>

<http://www.vqronline.Org/webexclusive/2006/06/11/awano-interview-munro/An Interview with Alice Munry.dt. 17/12/2006>.

<http://www.serve.com/cpage/LCohen/>

<http://members.aol.com/COHENPoet/>

URL of this page:

<http://www.brocku.ca/english/courses/4F70/postcol.html>

<http://members.aol.com/MunroAlice/>

<http://en.wikipedia.org/wiki/Alice Munro"Date: 22-08-2006>

<http://www.ucalgary.cal/lib.old/specoll/monrobiochtm(1-12) 10/25/200>

<http:// en.wikiquote.org/wiki/Alice-Munro. 12/3/2006.>

<,http://www.randomhouse.com/vintage/read/goodwoman/munro.html>

<http://en.wikipedia.org/wiki/Alice_Munro.Dt.02-09-2006>.

<http://in.search.yahoo.com/search? frushl-in-mail&p=The +House+of Novel %3AThe +of+Fiction-Henry + James dt.3-8-06.>

http://www.bcbookworld.com/terasen/alicemunro.html-14k>

<http:www.lib.unb.ca/Texts/SCL/bin/get.cgi?directory-=vol8_l/&filename= york.htm dt.26/01/2006.>

<Yahoo.com.http://www. English.uindy.edu/reviews/woman.htm>

<http://www.vqronline.org/webexclusive/2006/06/11/awano-interview-munro/>

<http://www.randomhouse.com/vintaige/read/secrets/munro.html21-12-2006>

<http://www.contemporarywriters.com/authors/profile/?p=auth03D29L0 44112635689. -11-2006>